Studies in Theoretical
and Applied Economics
General editor:
B. T. Bayliss

BRITISH ECONOMIC POLICY 1960–1969

C. D. COHEN,
Lecturer in Economics at the University of Sussex

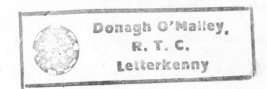
LONDON
BUTTERWORTHS

THE BUTTERWORTH GROUP

ENGLAND

Butterworth & Co (Publishers) Ltd
London: 88 Kingsway, WC2B 6AB

AUSTRALIA

Butterworth & Co (Australia) Ltd
Sydney: 586 Pacific Highway Chatswood, NSW 2067
Melbourne: 343 Little Collins Street, 3000
Brisbane: 240 Queen Street, 4000

CANADA

Butterworth & Co (Canada) Ltd
Toronto: 14 Curity Avenue, 374

NEW ZEALAND

Butterworth & Co (New Zealand) Ltd
Wellington: 26–28 Waring Taylor Street, 1
Auckland: 35 High Street, 1

SOUTH AFRICA

Butterworth & Co (South Africa) (Pty) Ltd
Durban: 152–154 Gale Street

First published in 1971 by
the Butterworth Group

© C. D. Cohen, 1971

ISBN 0 408 70187 0

A / 330.942

Printed in England by Cox & Wyman Ltd,
London, Fakenham and Reading

PREFACE

When work began on this study in 1968 I had at least some forewarning of the complexity of the task which I was attempting. It follows on from a previous seminal study by Christopher Dow, *The Management of the British Economy, 1945–1960* which took some eight years to complete, and was written furthermore under conditions which were in various ways distinctly advantageous. But I have preferred to sacrifice some of the benefits to be derived from more extended investigation of the kinds of economic problems dealt with here to the undoubted gain of relating it more closely in time to the events of the sixties.

My basic aim has been to analyse the development of short-term economic policy in Britain during the sixties—the area of economic policy which is primarily the responsibility of the Treasury. Inevitably, with such a broad study, I have ventured into areas of the subject matter of economics in which I am not a specialist. I can only hope that my treatment of some of these problems is not an affront to specialists, but if studies of this kind are to be available, then there are bound to be trade-offs between specialised knowledge and co-ordinated, comprehensive analysis. The following is not in any way an official history, in the sense of describing what the official view was at any particular point in time. Nor does it draw on any special knowledge or access to official papers which related to my employment as a consultant in the Economic Section of the Treasury in the years 1966–1969. On the other hand, participation in the process of policy making does provide one with unique advantages when it comes to interpreting the official position.

The present study differs in one essential respect from that by Dow. It has excluded a narrative section and the narrative element has been reduced to the minimum necessary to an understanding of economic policy. This for two reasons. Firstly, because the chronological description of events tends to be rather dull and not very rewarding for the reader. Secondly, and perhaps more importantly, because the history of economic policy during the sixties is still relatively fresh in people's minds, and those individuals who want a detailed history of policy have access to this in the *National Institute Economic Review*.

In writing this study I set myself a number of broad objectives, and I believe these have been achieved. There was the relatively simple aim of describing the shifts and changes of policy, and the factors which influenced Government in respect of the action they took, or failed to take. Much more difficult, and infinitely more important, was the objective of assessing quantitatively the adequacy of such policy in its many forms. Unfortunately, economics has not developed sufficiently as a science to permit a completely objective assessment, and to some extent my conclusions are bound to be subjective, although they are, I believe, well founded.

One further objective which was continuously present during the preparation of the study was that of increasing general understanding of economic problems. To this end I have consciously set out to explain, as I understand them, the intellectual foundations of short-term policy. For example, Chapter 3 places the stabilisation problem in its general context, but goes further and discusses the various ways in which tax measures operate on the level of demand and the factors which would influence the decision to use one tax measure rather than another. In the following chapter these techniques are used in assessing the record of fiscal policy between 1960 and 1969. As far as possible I have tried throughout to avoid complicating the argument, but economics is a highly technical discipline, and one result which I believe to be beneficial is the light it throws on the complexity of the problem of managing the economy. If the study achieves little else it will have achieved a great deal if it gets the essential point across that in the formulation of economic policy everyone's views are not equally valid, and that economists do have a special expertise not available to others.

In the preparation of this volume I owe a great debt to Mrs. Betty Seaver of the University of Connecticut for typing a manuscript which at times almost bordered on the indecipherable. And to my wife and family I owe an even greater debt, not least for their encouragement at those times of flagging effort.

C. D. C.

University of Sussex
June 1970

CONTENTS

1

ECONOMIC FORECASTS AND ECONOMIC POLICY

Governments of most of the developed countries have now generally accepted responsibility for the level of economic activity. This entails on their part not only a willingness to use policy instruments of many kinds but also the ability to make reasonably accurate short-term forecasts of economic developments for a period of a year to eighteen months ahead. Increasingly, therefore, Governments have expanded the resources devoted to forecasting and to the collection and analysis of statistical data. For many years now, in Britain, the Treasury has been responsible for the preparation of the official short-term forecasts, the main aim of which has been to provide policy makers with quantified assessments of the national income and balance of payments, on a quarterly basis, as an essential framework within which to formulate budgetary and monetary policy. Few people would argue that economic systems are inherently stable and self-correcting and it follows therefore that Governments must have a view about the future short-term development of the economy if they are to fulfil successfully their stabilisation role. Whether in fact economic policy in Britain has been stabilising or de-stabilising is a matter to which we turn later in the book.

Whereas Governments have accepted the necessity for short-term management of economic systems they are not all equally able to determine policy or to choose the optimum mix of policy instruments. However, they are all faced with the time-lags involved in the exercise of management of demand functions. In the first place there exist clear differences in the speed with which Governments recognise that a problem exists or will exist. This will largely reflect the adequacy of the statistical data available to policy makers and their advisers. There are always bound to be deficiencies in this respect, and one of the most difficult problems facing short-term forecasters is to decide where they are at any moment in relation to short-term developments. Data will almost always be deficient, reflecting perhaps developments in the economy many months earlier. Inevitably, therefore, policy and forecasting errors are made simply as a result of misjudging recent trends or perhaps a failure to note that a turning-point has already been reached. An example of the latter problem is the official pre-Budget investment forecast in 1962 where the forecasters failed to note that private investment had already turned down. Nevertheless, while statistical deficiencies were a major problem for short-term forecasters in Britain during the 1950s, this would appear to be no longer the case.*

The second time-lag occurs in the formulation of policy, and how long this is will depend on a multitude of factors—including institutional ones. Policy response will be more immediate where decisions are centralised and not fragmented between different ministries or authorities. Undoubtedly the administrative innovations of 1964 (the creation of the Department of Economic Affairs) lengthened the policy lags through creative tension (i.e., creating overlapping administrative and policy-making responsibilities). Effective policy will be hindered where the range of stabilisation measures is limited or where other restrictions limit policy formulation, such as extensive discussion in legislatures of any set of proposals. Some countries are clearly able to bring about changes in policy with considerable speed and have in their control a wide range of fiscal and monetary instruments. Others find their capacity for rapid action severely limited and the policy measures available both blunt and slow acting. In these respects the British Government is in a favourable position, exercising overall control of monetary and fiscal policy and with measures available which are both flexible and quick acting.

The third lag is critically important. Given the appreciation of the problem and the choice of the measures, the next most vital factor is the speed with which they are implemented. It is clearly the case that different policy instruments act on different components of demand, but

---

* Mr. Godley: 'I would put it to you that the statistical service we are given has improved absolutely out of all recognition in the last ten years. . . . I would offer the opinion that it is now unlikely that we will make a serious forecasting error through having statistical deficiencies.' Treasury evidence in *Fourth Report of Estimates Committee, Session 1966–1967, on Government Statistical Services*, H.M.S.O. para. 1383 (Dec. 1966).

they also act on demand with different timing. Account will be taken of this factor in the later discussion on fiscal and monetary policy, but for the moment it will simply be stated as one of the criteria to be applied in the choice of policy instruments. A Government which felt that the pressure of demand now was excessive is unlikely to choose as a stabilisation measure a change in death duties or an increase in corporation tax. An increase in employees' national insurance contributions is more likely to have a sizeable and fairly immediate impact on consumer expenditure.

The function of the forecasts, therefore, is to provide a quantitative framework within which to formulate policy. The forecasts are not intended as precise statements of what will happen in the future, and should not be judged as such. Indeed, their role is to isolate the main short-run developments and to provide the basis for policy recommendations. The forecasts are usually constructed on the basis of unchanged policies, i.e., that present policies are maintained. Where it is known to the forecasters that certain policies will cease to operate at a certain time, e.g., they knew during 1966 that the temporary import surcharge was to be removed in November, then this will be taken into account. In some situations forecasts on the basis of unchanged policies would clearly be of little value and the forecasts may explicitly assume certain responses. During 1967 when forecasting a large deficit, the forecasters would almost certainly have taken account of confidence effects on the balance of payments. However, since the function of the forecast is to show quantitatively what are expected to be the main demand developments the implications of this for the level of unemployment and the balance of payments, the forecasts will then become the basis for policy changes. As far as possible the policy changes introduced should take into account the path of developments foreseen in the forecast. That is to say policies will be chosen which have their impact at the right time in the light of the quarterly path drawn by the forecasts.*

The assessment of forecasts becomes, therefore, an extremely difficult task. To simply take the percentage changes forecast by the Treasury, even if these were known, and compare them with outcome is not sufficient. Leaving aside the purely statistical problems for the moment (which measure of outcome does one choose when, for example, there may be any number of measurements of output), there still remains the insuperable problem that the forecasts were intended as a guide to

---

* As in 1966 when the impact of S.E.T. was expected in the autumn and thus fitted nicely a demand forecast which suggested that pressure would emerge at that time of the year.

policy. In so far as this led to policy changes they were necessarily falsified. One cannot say the forecasts were wrong and that policy makers were misled. Indeed, the Estimates Committee on Government Statistical Services clearly felt that this was a proper way to assess the accuracy of Government forecasts in the U.K. They could not directly do so since the forecasts are not published. On the other hand, they felt that a crude comparison of forecasts with out-turn was a justified procedure. The reaction of the Treasury's chief forecaster at the time seems to me the right one—at least in some respects.

> But I do not think that you can present it as the difference between two percentage changes. . . . If we were to try to do it it would be a very real difficulty as to which actual figure you would choose. Furthermore, if you did it, I do not think you would provide the basis for an objective assessment of our work. In other words the real criterion for a forecast, the only criterion in my opinion, is whether or not in retrospect you can say that it did or did not give the general character of the year and more particularly whether or not it did give the basis for the correct advice.*

In such a situation the problem of assessing a forecast becomes very difficult, and any comparison of out-turn with forecast has to be made on the basis of a forecast corrected for the impact of policy changes. This is no simple matter since it entails the quantification of the effects of policy changes—a complicated and imprecise task. On the other hand, in some years the forecasts will have indicated an acceptable set of developments and will not have led to substantive shifts in economic policy. In these cases the forecasts can reasonably be compared with out-turn, conclusions reached on their predictive accuracy and the extent to which the 'no policy change' posture of the authorities, based on the forecasts, was in fact justified. Nevertheless, even in such situations as no policy change, it may still prove difficult to assess the forecasts. It may turn out that the forecasts were right in aggregate but wrong in relation to the components—there may have been compensating errors, as in 1967, due either to faulty estimation of the exogenous variables or to functional relationships which were incorrectly specified. Is the assessment to be based on *changes* or on comparisons of forecast and actual *levels*? Since the official forecasts are expressed in the form of changes *during* the forecast period then how does one assess its conclusions when the evidence available to an outsider is both imprecise and

* Mr. Godley. *Fourth Report of the Estimates Committee, Session 1966–1967, on Government Statistical Services*, H.M.S.O., para. 1381 (Dec. 1966).

relates to year-on-year changes. But to concentrate on year-on-year changes is to concentrate on the crude elements in short-term forecasting, and it is the trend *during* the forecast period which is more important. In the next chapter attempts are made, mainly qualitatively to identify the years in which the official forecasts not only provided a poor guide to policy in terms of year-on-year comparisons but also were misleading as descriptions of trends during the forecast period.

Other purely statistical problems arise in the assessment of the forecasts. There is a continuous process of statistical revision which means that 'post-mortems' on the forecasts carried out at different times will yield different results. The forecasts would obviously have been different if the revised data had been available to the forecasters at the time they made their forecasts, and the problem inevitably also arises of what bases to use in constructing forecast changes. This problem is met in the next chapter by taking the data available to the forecasters when they made their forecast and using these as the base for estimating changes for comparison with out-turn. But even the out-turn is subject to dispute. For example, in Britain the estimates of gross domestic product from expenditure, income and output, follow different patterns in the short-term so that three different estimates of GDP are available. Which one is correct?* There remains ultimately, of course, the question of what precisely one is testing the forecasts against. What has been done in some studies† has been to compare forecasts with so-called 'naive' models, i.e., a comparison of the forecasts with what is basically an extrapolation of trends. But a naive model expressed in these terms is hardly an unambiguous concept, and a comparison of the forecasts with any particular naive model will not yield conclusive results.

In their internal assessments of forecasting procedure, and post-mortems on forecasts, the Treasury was well able to test the validity of their forecasts both in the aggregate and also in respect of particular components. However, outside commentators do not have available the official forecasts (except for the past two years) and must therefore fall back on indirect indications of what was the official view. The Budget speech always contains an assessment of likely short-term developments in the economy on the assumption of no change in policy

---

* The Treasury and National Institute both use a compromise estimate of GDP based on all three measures, but the estimate derived from expenditure has been used here except where specifically noted. The importance of statistical revision to the base of the forecast is demonstrated in the Appendix to Chapter 2, which contains a short assessment of National Institute forecasts.

† See the discussion by C. A. Sims in 'Evaluating Short-Term Macro-Economic Forecasts; the Dutch Performance', *Review of Economics and Statistics*, Harvard University Press (May 1967).

and sometimes quantitative forecasts. Up until 1962 the *Economic Survey* included a few pages on the prospects for the economy, but this was discontinued after the disastrous forecasts of that year. Its substitute, the *Economic Report* contains a factual review of the year in question, but no forecasts for the coming year. However, the *Financial Statement* 1968–1969 marked a sharp departure from recent practice and gave forecasts, at constant prices, of expenditure, imports and gross domestic product. They are provided both in annual and half-yearly terms and include an alternative forecast based on two export projections. It is significant also in that these forecasts take into account the Budget measures and can be more readily assessed, whereas the indications given in earlier Budget statements and Economic Surveys were all pre-Budget assessments and consequently less of a guide to the path of developments expected by the Government after the Budget.* There is still no published forecast of the balance of payments, and Chancellors have always in their pronouncements been particularly obscure about what they expected the out-turn to be.

The reticence of the Treasury has made an assessment of the forecasts very difficult, but within the constraints imposed by lack of data an attempt has been made to assess them in Chapter 2. The assessment is necessarily very crude, and the author is well aware of Mr. Godley's strictures on the procedure pursued here. Nevertheless, the general conclusions drawn on the accuracy of official forecasts seem to be well substantiated and do not depend on the precise numerical data provided here. Some understanding of the form of the official forecasts and the techniques used in their construction is necessary before any assessment, and the rest of this chapter provides a brief account.

SHORT-TERM ECONOMIC FORECASTING IN THE U.K.†

Forecasts are made three times a year covering a period of eighteen

* This step is to be welcomed. Although recent Chancellors have expressed their intention to provide more information on the basis of Government policy, they have generally refused to give information on official forecasts. The arguments never seemed very valid and the U.K. was alone among the major industrial countries in not publishing some kind of official forecast. See *Techniques of Economic Forecasting*, O.E.C.D. Paris 13 and 24–25, (1965).

† An account of the model used by the Treasury was published in *Techniques of Economic Forecasting*, O.E.C.D. Paris ch. 6 (1965). This chapter was previously published in *Economic Trends*, H.M.S.O. (Aug. 1964). A more recent account, giving more data on the equations used in forecasting some of the components of demand, was published as Appendix 7 to the *Fourth Report of the Estimates Committee Session 1966–1967, on Government Statistical Services*, H.M.S.O. (Dec. 1966).

months to two years. As well as these main forecasts intermediate forecasts and assessments are also made as and when necessary. The main forecasts are made on the assumption that current fiscal and credit policies are unchanged and they are timed to fit in with the Budget (usually in April). The autumn appraisal is a preliminary look at the outlook until the end of the next year. In the new year March/April forecasts are prepared covering the whole of the financial year as part of the material for the Budget. In June/July a third set of forecasts is

THE MAIN EXOGENOUS FACTORS AND THE MAIN RELATIONSHIPS TAKEN INTO ACCOUNT IN FORECASTING DOMESTIC DEVELOPMENTS

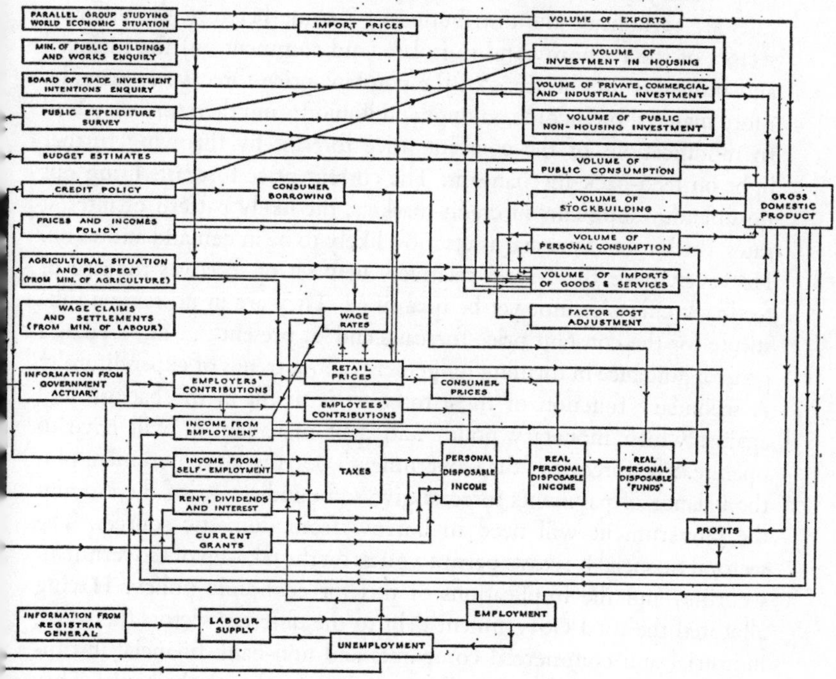

Chart 1.1 (Source: *Economic Trends*, C.S.O. No. 16 Feb. 1967)

prepared taking into account Budget changes and extending further forward the forecast period.

The forecasts are in three parts. Part one consists of a forecast of gross domestic activity built up from the expenditure side. The various components of expenditure are estimated as constant prices, and seasonally adjusted quarterly series are constructed. As part of the process, forecasts of personal income and price developments are made. *Chart 1.1* presents schematically the main factors and relationships taken into account in forecasting developments. The main aim of this part of the forecast is to estimate the level of activity at the end of the forecast period and to chart the path from the base date to the terminal quarter. In general, forecasts are not expressed in a year-on-year form, but in terms of change in a recent quarter to a quarter near the end of the forecast period. The reason for this presentation is self-evident. A forecast presented as a year-to-year change could totally fail to identify changes of trend *during* that period and could mislead policy.

The second part of the forecast is a fairly recent innovation. These are the current price forecasts* made at the same time as the forecasts of output and expenditure at constant prices. The purposes of these forecasts are to indicate the distribution of income between the different sectors of the economy and to isolate (and comment on) the financial and monetary implications of the constant price forecast. It provides more material on income, savings and liquidity and therefore may lead to modifications of the constant price forecast by throwing further light on feed-back mechanisms. The current price forecasts bring out possible developments in credit markets, the likely pattern of interest rates, the kind of financial assets most likely to be in demand and so on. However, since these are a relatively new set of forecasts the size of feedback effects cannot yet be quantified. They are in no sense a substitute for the constant price forecasts and 'at present . . . are used as a general guidance in forming judgements about trends of expenditure'.† A secondary function of these forecasts is to fill in the background against which monetary policy and debt management will have to operate. The forecast of the Government's borrowing requirement plus the balance of payments forecast give some indication of the amount the Government will need to borrow from domestic sources. The sectoral financial forecasts permit a guess on the take-up of Government securities and the implications of this for economic policy. Having allocated the total Government debt to the different sectors (personal, industrial and commercial companies and non-bank financial institutions) the amount left over will have to be placed with the banks. This, plus forecasts of private sector and Local Authorities' borrowing from the banks, leads to a forecast of the increase in bank deposits and the money supply.

The writers conclude that‡ 'this type of financial forecasting is still very much in its infancy, and that it is subject to great inaccuracies of measurement. But it does offer a very considerable potential—both as

---

* Described by L. S. Berman and F. Cassell in 'Short Term Forecasts of Income, Expenditure and Saving' *Economic Trends*, H.M.S.O. (Feb. 1968).

† *Economic Trends*, H.M.S.O., xiv (Feb. 1968).

‡ *Economic Trends*, H.M.S.O., xv (Feb. 1968).

a further check on the consistency of the underlying economic forecasts and as a means of throwing light on the probable context in which monetary policy will operate. It is hoped that this potential can be tapped increasingly as the basic statistics are further improved and, perhaps more important, as more experience is gained in their use.' The promise, therefore, of these particular forecasts lies mainly in the future. For the present their function appears to be mainly to isolate the problem of meeting the Government's borrowing needs and as indicating areas of the constant price forecasts where financial factors may have been incorrectly assessed.

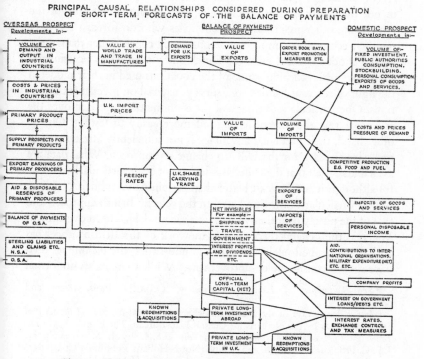

PRINCIPAL CAUSAL RELATIONSHIPS CONSIDERED DURING PREPARATION OF SHORT-TERM FORECASTS OF THE BALANCE OF PAYMENTS

Chart 1.2 (Source: *Economic Trends*, C.S.O., No. 16, Feb. 1967)

The third part of the forecast, and made concurrently with the other parts of the forecast, is of the balance of payments. Forecasts of imports and exports (goods and services) are combined with estimates of property income, transfer payments and long-term capital flows to reach an assessment of how the 'basic' balance of the U.K. is likely to develop. *Chart 1.2* illustrates the principal causal relationships considered in the preparation of the short-term forecasts of the balance of payments.

Such, then, is a brief description of the forecasts. What can be said about the *techniques* used in their preparation? We now have available general descriptions of the U.K. model, and some evidence of the relationships used by the forecasters in deriving estimates of demand, the relationship of output and employment, the forecast of prices and so on. One particular difference between the British practice and that in other countries has often received comment.* This is the fact that the U.K. model is 'eclectic', i.e., the estimations are made on the basis of successive approximation. The alternative approach is a short-term econometric model in the form of that used by the Netherlands or the recent Brookings Quarterly Model of the U.S.A.† The U.K. is unique in not using any econometric model, but, except in the case of the Dutch, the other main industrial countries who do forecast seriously use their econometric models as a consistency check rather than as the central model. Indeed, even the Dutch allow themselves occasionally the luxury of 'disturbing' some of the equations used in their model in the light of relevant factors, e.g., survey material on investment intentions. One particular advantage of the econometric approach over the eclectic is that the former lends itself more easily to testing. On the other hand, their particular advantage is not sufficiently attractive as to make it necessary for the U.K. to change its approach. What data are available suggest that the Dutch model has not been particularly successful although it has forecast better than certain naïve models.‡

This particular distinction between the eclectic British approach and that of the purely quantitative econometric model has been overdrawn. Whereas the general theoretical framework of the British model has basically remained unaltered since the mid-fifties, the techniques used have shown considerable improvement.§ While there exists no formal

* See *Techniques of Economic Forecasting*, O.E.C.D. Paris, 18–20 and 26 (1965).

† For a description of the Dutch model see *Scope and Methods of the Central Planning Bureau* by the Netherlands Central Plan Bureau, The Hague, 1956. *The Brookings Quarterly Econometric Model of the U.S.A.* by J. S. Duesenberry, J. F. G. Fromm, L. R. Klein, and E. Kuh (North-Holland Publishing Co., 1965).

‡ See C. A. Sims, *Review of Economics and Statistics*, Harvard University Press 238–270 (May 1967). Sir Alec Cairncross commented thus on the Dutch model in his evidence to the Estimates Committee, page 86, 'I hope we do things more precisely in some ways than the Dutch, because they are using annual data and we use quarterly data. That makes it perhaps a little chancy but I would be very hesitant to arrive at a prediction of the movement of demand in 1966 or 1967 on the basis of annual data, however much it was reduced to systematic equations. I would want something more recent.' This seems an apposite and valid criticism of those countries which do not have quarterly national income statistics and do not forecast on a quarterly basis.

§ *Fourth Report of the Estimates Committee, Session 1966–1967, on Government Statistical Services*, H.M.S.O., para. 19 (Dec. 1966).

econometric model, econometric techniques are used extensively in the preparation of the forecasts. For example, in the forecasting of imports, in determining the relationship of output and employment, in the forecast of wages and in the estimate of personal consumption. This use of structural relationships has become an important part of the forecasting process, although their use has by no means been taken far enough. There remain many areas of short-term forecasting where econometric techniques could be applied, but where this is either not done so at the present or is inadequately done.*

Charts 1.1 and *1.2* have indicated the general causal relationships used in the British short-term forecasting model. The general procedure of the model is to consider certain variables (exports, private and public fixed investment, public consumption, and wage rates) as exogenously determined. Their values are estimated directly on the basis of an assessment of world demand for U.K. exports, or on the basis of survey data (public and private investment) or on data available on forthcoming/recent wage negotiations (although in the case of both wages and exports functional relationships are also employed.† At the next stage estimates of functional relationships, between output and employment, wage rates and prices, real disposable income and consumption, etc., are used to bring out the implications for total demand and output of the exogenous components of demand. The process is therefore one of successive approximation in which an internally consistent model is constructed, consistent with relationships derived from the past although these are modified in the light of certain factors, e.g., forecasts of wages would be adjusted to take account of incomes policy. As a forecasting procedure it has quite a lot to commend it, but, as we shall see in the next chapter, it has not always produced satisfactory results.

* The Treasury recognises this deficiency in its procedures; see 'Econometric Research for Short-Term Forecasting', *Economic Trends*, H.M.S.O. (Feb. 1967). In 1970 the Treasury announced that there now existed a formal short-term forecasting model. For details of the model see *The Econometric Study of the United Kingdom* edited by K. Hilton and D. F. Heathfield, chapter 17 (Macmillan 1970).

† *Economic Trends*, H.M.S.O. (May 1967), contains a useful assessment of the techniques of forecasting British exports in a note by M. C. Fessey, 'Short-Term Forecasting of U.K. Exports'.

2

ECONOMIC FORECASTS 1960–1969

There have been earlier attempts to assess Government forecasts, the most recent being that of Christopher Dow in his massive examination of policy in the U.K.* During the period he covered there were more data on the official forecasts but much less was known about their techniques, and there were no worthwhile non-official forecasts available as independent estimates. By the end of the fifties the National Institute of Economic and Social Research (N.I.E.S.R.) had begun to publish forecasts but its forecasts were at that stage fairly rudimentary. Since the early sixties the Institute's techniques have developed enormously; its knowledge about the short-run behaviour of the economy is second to none, and it now, and has done for some years, produces articulated forecasts of the domestic economy and the balance of payments. Many of the techniques used by the official forecasters were developed by the Institute, and the personnel of the Institute and Treasury have in effect been interchangeable in recent years. It does not follow from this that any collusion exists between the two organisations, but the general models used by them and some of the more formal relationships are basically the same. This does not mean that at any point in time they are going to produce similar forecasts, since judgement and 'feel' are essential elements in forecasting, but in many areas their views will

---

* J. C. R. Dow, *The Management of the British Economy 1945–1960*, Cambridge University Press ch. 5 (1965). An assessment of the Institute's earliest forecasts was made by Neild and Shirley (*Economic Review*, May 1961). There has since been a general assessment of the Institute's forecasts (*Economic Review*, Nov. 1969), and there has also been a post-mortem on balance of payments forecasts (*Economic Review* May 1970). A short Appendix to this chapter contains a brief assessment of the Institute's forecasts between 1960–1967.

coincide. In what follows, and later in the book, the Institute's forecasts and assessments of the impact of policy changes have been used as a guide to the official attitude, where this is unclear, as well as a source of independent estimates.

ASSESSMENT OF OFFICIAL FORECASTS 1960–1969

The official short-term forecasts of expenditures are reconstructed in *Tables 2.1* and *2.2*. All the estimates are as constant prices since the main intention of the forecasts is to estimate the pressure of demand and thus the degree to which capacity is utilised (using capacity in a sense which includes something more than physical capacity). Several points immediately emerge from the tables. In the first place the forecasters seem to have got the forecast changes of the different components of expenditure right to within a £100 million or so, and have generally managed to forecast the direction of change. Exceptions to this were the forecasts of fixed investment in 1962 (which was expected to rise, year on year, but actually declined), the forecast of a rise in exports in 1967, and the disastrous forecast of consumer expenditure in 1967–1968. Certain expenditure items appear to have been much more badly forecast than others. Exports have clearly been a major source of error with particularly poor forecasts in 1960, 1962 and 1967, although in 1967 events of a non-predictable kind played a large part in the falsification of the forecast. Large errors were made in the forecasts of consumers' expenditure in 1963 (when the full effects of the inflationary budget were much greater than expected) and again in 1968 (the large underestimate in 1967 was due partly to forecast error but also to deliberate stimulation of consumption by the authorities from mid-year). Stockbuilding has continued very difficult to forecast, and there has been a general tendency to underestimate the changes, particularly in 1960 and 1963. There is also considerable evidence that public expenditure, both current and capital, have on occasion turned out to be quite different from what the forecasters had been led to expect. This is surprising given that these expenditures are supposedly under the control of the Government, and is an indication of the difficulties facing the authorities, particularly in respect of the timing of public investment expenditures.

If one turns to the forecasts of Total Final Expenditure, then certain years immediately stand out. Demand rose much faster in 1963 than had been forecast, with personal consumption, stock-building and exports much higher then expected. 1965 was another year when the

Table 2.1

FORECAST AND ACTUAL CHANGES IN EXPENDITURE 1960–1967. £ MILLION AT CONSTANT 1958 PRICES

		Personal Consumption	Public Authorities Current Expenditure	Fixed Investment	Stockbuilding	Exports of Goods and Services	Total Final Expenditure	Minus Imports	GDP at Factor Cost
1960	Forecast	570	170	315	270	430	1 755	295	1 265
	Actual	655	80	365	415	275	1 790	585	1 065
1961	Forecast	460	135	430	−385	50	690	−55	600
	Actual	390	140	390	−120	150	805	−40	805
1962	Forecast	360	120	45	−265	205	465	55	215
	Actual	390	125	−25	−250	85	325	105	650
1963	Forecast	640	160	20	−45	80	855	140	650
	Actual	860	60	80	130	225	1 355	205	950
1964	Forecast	815	150	600	325	300	2 190	590	1 395
	Actual	705	70	785	375	190	2 125	425	1 395
1965	Forecast	470	130	400	−170	220	1 050	40	940
	Actual	340	170	215	−215	260	770	55	730
1966	Forecast	340	140	20	−100	240	640	215	330
	Actual	390	125	90	−140	205	670	100	510
1967	Forecast	160	120	35	5	260	580	265	225
	Actual	400	230	325	−125	−10	820	365	325

Note: Forecasts are based on annual Economic Surveys and Budget Statements, and have been adjusted, where necessary, for tax and credit changes. The base figures used to estimate forecast changes were those given in the relevant Economic Survey (later Economic Report) for the previous year. Actuals are from *Economic Trends*, No. 180 (Oct. 1968).

Table 2.2

FORECAST ERROR 1960-1967 (FORECAST CHANGE COMPARED WITH ACTUAL CHANGE). £ MILLION 1958 PRICES*

	Personal Consumption	Public Authorities Current Expenditure	Fixed Investment	Change in Stocks	Exports of Goods and Services	Total final Expenditure	Minus Imports	GDP at Factor Cost	GDP Error‡ %
1960	−85	+90	−50	−145	+155	−35	−280	+200	+1·0
1961	+70	−5	+40	−120	−100	−115	+15	−205	−1·0
1962	−30	−5	+70	−15	+120	+140	−50	+170	+0·8
1963	−220	+100	−60	−175	−145	−300	−65	−300	−1·4
1964	+110	+80	−185	−55	+110	+60	+65	—	
1965	+130	−40	+185	+45	−40	+280	−15	+210	+0·8
1966	−50	+15	−70	+40	+35	−30	+115	−180	−0·7
1967	−240	−110	−290	+130	+270	−240	−100	−100	−0·3
Mean error 1960-1967	−40	+15	−45	−35	+50	−55	−40	−25	−0·1
Absolute mean error 1960-1967	115	55	120	90	120	175	90	170	0·75
Absolute mean error 1951-1960†	100	75	50	150	75	75	125	150	

* + denotes forecast overestimated outcome.
  − denotes forecast underestimated outcome.

† From J. C. R. Dow, *The Management of the British Economy, 1945-1960*, Cambridge University Press, Table 5·5, 137 (1965). Not strictly comparable with 1960-1967 absolute mean error because of different price assumptions.

‡ Estimated by comparing the forecast increase in GDP in any year with the actual change in GDP in that year, in both cases using actual GDP in the previous year as the base.

forecasters overstated the increase in final expenditure, while in 1967 they again considerably underestimated the increase in demand. 1967 is an interesting year in illustrating the fact of compensating errors within the forecast. The forecast of gross domestic product at factor cost for that year (1967) was reasonably good but the forecasts of personal consumption and fixed investment were too low, and these were balanced by a failure of exports to expand during the year and by a much bigger increase in imports. 1960 is a year in which the forecast of Total Final Expenditure was good, but also one in which the forecast of imports was far too low so that the forecasters produced a forecast which considerably overestimated the growth in GDP.

Before turning to the analysis of certain years it is salutary for economists to look at the two final rows of *Table 2.2*. The final row is taken from Dow,[*] and it suggests that despite the considerable development of quantitative economics, the improvement to statistical data, the development of more refined techniques for forecasting and the expansion of economists in the public sector, that the forecasts are nevertheless no better on average than they were in the period 1951-1960. The final section of this chapter indicates some areas within which there is need for improvement if the forecasts are to be more useful as a quantitative framework for formulating economic policy. As it stands at the moment the above tables throw considerable doubt on the ability of the forecasters to look more than a year ahead and it is clear that in certain years the forecasts have not provided an adequate guide for policy decisions.

Turning next to the balance of payments forecasts in *Table 2.3*. These are necessarily even more uncertain than the expenditure forecasts and must in some years be simply taken as indicators of the magnitudes of the change expected. From the point of view of the forecasters, balance of payments forecasting is a highly uncertain business since, as the Estimates Committee concluded: 'The final figure of the balance of payments required for policy making represents the difference between large aggregates. Estimating the magnitude of these leaves a margin of error which may wholly distort the final figure for the balance of payments. Treasury evidence suggests this will remain a permanent problem in balance of payments forecasting.'[†] Since the state of the external balance has been a continuous problem for the policy makers in the last ten years or so, it seems worthwhile to look in more detail at the balance of payments forecasts than we did at those of expenditure.

[*] J. C. R. Dow, *The Management of the British Economy 1945-1960*, Cambridge University Press, *Table* 5·5 p. 137 (1965).

[†] *Fourth Report of the Estimates Committee, Session 1966-1967, on Government Statistical Services*, H.M.S.O., para. 78, 31 (Dec. 1966).

Table 2.3

FORECAST ANNUAL CHANGES IN BALANCE OF PAYMENTS, 1960–1968

(£ million, year-to-year changes)

		(1) Change in Current Balance	(2) Change in Balance of Long-term Capital	(3) Identified Balance (1 + 2)
1960	Forecast	10	(235)	(250)
	Actual	−408	63	−345
1961	Forecast	190	n.c.	190
	Actual	261	260	521
1962	Forecast	180	−210	−30
	Actual	116	−166	−50
1963	Forecast	25	−25	n.c.
	Actual	−1	−50	−51
1964	Forecast	−360	−100	−460
	Actual	−510	−222	−732
1965	Forecast	310	200	510
	Actual	308	167	475
1966	Forecast	n.c.	110	110
	Actual	106	99	205
1967	Forecast	100	90	190
	Actual	−389	18	−370
1968	Forecast	290	n.c.	290
	Actual	18	−8	10

Forecasting errors (+ = overestimate of forecast value)

1960	+418	(+172)	(+595)
1961	−71	−260	−330
1962	+64	+44	−20
1963	+26	−25	−50
1964	−150	−122	−270
1965	—	+33	+35
1966	+106	+11	−95
1967	+490	+72	+560
1968	+270	−8	+280

Average error

1960–1968	180	80	240

Note: Large errors attach to some of these estimates, and in some years, e.g., 1960, they are intended to give only broad magnitudes. Figures in Column 3 of the above page have been rounded.

Policy response has usually been the result of actual and expected balance of payments developments, and it is perfectly clear from *Table 2.3* that there are certain years, 1960 and 1967 in particular, but also 1964 and 1968, where the forecasts were a poor guide to policy. In other years, for example 1962, the trend of developments during the year on external account was badly out, so that not only were the levels of exports and imports incorrectly forecast but also turning points. As can be observed in the table there has been a persistent bias in the forecasts of the current balance with optimistic estimates in six of the nine years —in some cases excessively so.

The forecasters were clearly quite wrong in their forecast of external developments in 1960. Exports were expected to show 'a further substantial expansion'* in the light of a forecast of world trade which implied a 'further expansion in trade between industrial countries', while primary producers would also fare better than in 1959 due to a rise in the price of raw materials.† Imports were forecast to rise in volume at least as fast as in 1959 (6·5 %) and a slight deterioration in the terms of trade was forecast. The general conclusion was that the 'outflow of capital is likely to lead to a deficit on the combined capital and current account of the balance of payments this year, as in 1959, though the size of the deficit will depend on the extent of the current account surplus which can be earned'.‡ What size of current surplus was being forecast it is difficult to say, but *Table 2.3* implies a figure not very different from 1959. The official forecast was widely out. Instead of a current surplus of £150 million or so, the actual outcome was a sharp deterioration in both the current balance and also on the balance of current and long-term capital (although the balance of monetary movements was not quite so unfavourable because of an exceptionally large balancing item). Exports grew much slower than forecast largely because the forecasters did not anticipate the recession in the United States and Canada in 1960 and the associated slackening in the rate of expansion in Western Europe. Instead of primary product prices rising as forecast, they actually fell. Imports were substantially underforecast, and there was a greater deterioration on invisibles than was forecast.§

There is very little information on the official forecasts for 1961. The forecast given here is very uncertain, as indeed the official forecast seems to have been. The problems of forecasting world trade during 1961 must have been considerable, and the timing of recovery in the United States and Canada difficult to forecast. The other uncertainties in the external account were the likely movement in prices and the effect of the revaluations of the Deutschmark and Dutch guilder on U.K. exports.

---

* *Economic Survey 1960*, H.M.S.O., p. 10.
† *Economic Survey 1960*, H.M.S.O., p. 6.
‡ *Economic Survey 1960*, H.M.S.O., p. 10.
§ See *Economic Survey 1961*, p. 7, for a description of why the export forecast failed to be realised.

Nevertheless, the Budget strategy was based on the assumption that world trade would recover during the year, that there existed pressure on resources and that this pressure had to be reduced so that export growth would not be impeded by a buoyant home market. This was the basic element in the Budget strategy.

What was the outcome in 1961? Forecast and actual changes in the current balance were about the same although there was a much bigger actual improvement in the identified balance than the forecasters had anticipated, largely due to large capital receipts during the year of a special nature. Exports seem to have exhibited rather more growth than expected at the time of the Budget. However, the Budget strategy was based on the assumption that the pressure of demand had to be reduced so as to allow for the growth in exports during the year, whereas exports (goods and services, seasonally adjusted at 1958 prices) were virtually flat through the year, and the fourth quarter level was slightly below that of the first quarter.*

The year 1962 was undoubtedly one of the worst for the forecasters during the period being surveyed, and the downfall of Mr. Selwyn Lloyd was directly related to the policy mistakes made in 1962, themselves the result of erroneous forecasts. It is not obvious that this was the case simply from looking at the year-to-year changes in expenditure (*Table 2.1*) or the balance of payments (*Table 2.3*), and it becomes essential to look at the forecast of developments *during* the year. The import forecast for the year as a whole turned out to be largely correct, with only slight growth (1·3 %) in 1962. Exports (goods and services, constant prices) had been expected to grow by about 4 % in 1962, and the Budget strategy had been based (as in 1961) on the expectation that they would show rapid growth *during* the year. This was made abundantly clear by the Chancellor in his Budget Statement, and again in the review of prospects in the Economic Survey for 1962.† That events were to turn out quite different is admitted by the Treasury in its survey of developments in 1962:‡ 'Early in 1962, it seemed likely that there would be a rise in demand in the course of the year without any substantial stimulus from the Government. The indications were that world trading conditions would provide the opportunity for a

* The actual quarterly path of exports, goods and services seasonally adjusted at 1958 prices was: Q1, £1329 million; Q2, £1311 million; Q3, £1314 million; Q4, £1307 million.

† 'The foremost aim of economic policy in 1962 must be to maintain conditions in which exporters in the U.K. can take advantage of the opportunities open to them to achieve a great expansion in their sales.' *Economic Survey 1962* (Supplement to *Economic Trends*, March 1963), H.M.S.O., p. 8.

‡ *Economic Survey 1962* (Supplement to *Economic Trends*, March), H.M.S.O., p. 3.

considerable increase in our exports. .... The prospects for demand at home were mixed but on the whole the indicators pointed to expansion.'

Evidently the forecasters were thinking in terms of demand being some 4%–5% higher in the last quarter of 1962 compared with the same quarter of the previous year.* The actual increase in Total Final Expenditure over this period was 2·1%, and GDP (at factor cost) was only up 1·4% (both at constant prices). From the Treasury's retrospective account of 1962, it seems the forecasters expected a further rise in demand in the early months of 1963, and this again proved to be mistaken.† The whole emphasis of the forecast was of a rising pressure of demand, falling unemployment and pressure on costs and prices. If home demand developed as forecast, then capacity bottlenecks were thought likely to emerge and these would frustrate exports. Given the priority of improvement in the balance of payments the Budget strategy, based on the forecast, had to be one of restraint.

'Contrary to expectations, activity did not continue to rise in the second half of 1962. One reason was that exports did not rise after the middle of the year. .... A further though less important reason why demand did not rise as expected was a change in investment intentions. ... As a consequence of all these changes in demand production stopped rising after the middle of the year.'‡ As can be seen from *Table 2.1* the main errors were in the forecast of exports and of fixed investment and the other expenditure items were probably right. At the time of the Budget the forecasters failed to note that private investment had already started falling from the level reached at the turn of the year. They forecast the trend of investment during 1962 correctly, but the turning point came earlier. The forecast error of both the level and trend of exports was large. Instead of rapid growth during the year, the second half showed no increase over the first half. Exports actually fell back from their high second quarter level during the rest of the year.§

The current balance had been forecast to improve by between £170–

* The National Institute was in May forecasting a rise in GDP fourth quarter on fourth quarter of 3%—less optimistic than the official forecast, but still too high.

† The increase in GDP (factor cost) at constant prices and seasonally adjusted was 1·8%, and Total Final Expenditure 1·5%, in first quarter 1963 on first quarter 1962. Source; *Economic Trends*, Table A, xvi (Oct. 1967).

‡ *Economic Survey 1962* (Supplement to *Economic Trends*, March 1963) H.M.S.O., p. 4.

§ The path of exports (goods and services seasonally adjusted constant 1958 prices) was Q1, £1312 million; Q2, £1355 million; Q3, £1337 million; Q4, £1344 million; Source: *Economic Trends*, Table A (Oct. 1968).

200 million in 1962, whereas the actual improvement was only just over £100 million. But the miscalculations had their impact not on the balance of payments (a small actual surplus on current and long-term capital transactions) but on internal developments, and in particular the rising trend of unemployment during 1962 culminating in the high figure of the winter of 1963. This unfavourable outcome must be attributed to a considerable extent to poor forecasting and to a Budget strategy based on it. When reflationary measures came during the second half of 1962 they were inadequate in amount and could not prevent unemployment from continuing to increase. One explanation for this is that while the forecasters had revised downwards their estimates by mid-year they still remained too optimistic, and seemed in doubt about the amount of slack in the economy.* The Chancellor, in retrospect, must regret the closing sentences of his Budget statement:

I understand the natural desire to throw off the discipline and restraints of the past year, but that must be a steady process timed to fit in with actual achievement and not wishful thinking. I have great confidence in our capacity to take advantage of our opportunities. It may sound bold to say this, but I believe that events will prove the soundness of our policy and the wisdom of our actions.†

The balance of payments out-turn (current and long-term capital transactions) in 1963 approximated fairly closely to the forecast in the Budget. In his Budget Statement the new Chancellor (Mr. Maudling) forecast a small improvement in the current balance, but, 'The change in the capital side might offset any improvement on current payments.' However, while the outcome was roughly as forecast, it was clearly not due to correct forecasting of either imports or exports. In his Budget the Chancellor thought 'that prospects for world trade as a whole are that it will increase at a much slower pace in 1963 than in recent years. This is bound to be reflected in our exports of goods over the year. Exports of services have been doing rather better lately, and may continue to do well in 1963.'‡ Exports in value actually increased by 7%, a welcome surprise for the Chancellor. Imports seem to have been forecast to rise at a relatively slow rate in 1963 since the Chancellor expected the current balance to improve. Imports did rise more slowly than

* 'A policy of expansion must not be based on the assumption that there is a very large margin of immediate slack.' *National Institute Economic Review*, p. 11 (Aug. 1962).

† *Hansard*, 9 April 1962, col. 994.

‡ *Hansard*, 3 April 1963, col. 469.

exports, but were still in value terms some 6·5 % up on the 1962 level. This was hardly a slow rate of increase.*

What view was taken by the forecasters of the trend in the balance of payments during 1963? The pre-Budget forecast was for an increase in demand equal to potential capacity.† The aim of the Budget was to stimulate demand so as to achieve a 4 % growth rate, and in the initial stages of expansion to take up spare capacity. The Budget stimulus given was large, as we shall see later certainly excessive, and implied a growth in real expenditure during 1963 of 5 %–6 % (fourth quarter 1963 to fourth quarter 1962). This was clearly not a sustainable rate of increase in the long-run and seemed likely at the time of the Budget to eliminate the current surplus by the end of 1963, or earlier.‡ The seasonally adjusted current balance worsened throughout 1963 and was barely in surplus by the fourth quarter. While exports continued to rise quite fast in the second half of the year (4·3 % up on the first half-year), imports rose much faster (by 8 % in the second half compared to the first half). Whereas the seasonally adjusted current surplus was £90 million in the first half of 1963, it had fallen to £25 million in the second half. This kind of development was something the Chancellor had prepared the ground for in his Budget statement, and he had already made various contingency arrangements during 1963. Nevertheless, a situation where the surplus had virtually disappeared by the end of 1963 and the expectation that the big increase in stocks (generating imports) would come in 1964 must have given Mr. Maudling 'food for thought'.

However, the Chancellor's whole strategy since 1963 had been expansion brought about through budgetary action so as to achieve the National Economic Development Council (N.E.D.C.) target growth rate of 4 % per annum. The effect of budgetary stimulus plus extremely fast growth in exports during 1963 (10 %) was for the economy to grow at an annual rate in excess of 5 %. This was considerably faster than the

---

* 'It is, of course, possible that in the early stages of a programme of more vigorous expansion, imports may rise faster than exports. But the pace at which imports are likely to rise with expansion is frequently overestimated because there is usually a lag in the building up of stocks to correspond to higher levels of output.' *Hansard*, 3 April 1963, cols. 470–471.

† 'Our capacity to produce would be rising about as fast as demand.' (*Hansard*, 3 April 1963, col. 472.) At this time the Treasury estimated that productive potential was rising at a little more than 3 % per annum. *Economic Survey 1963*, H.M.S.O., p. 14.

‡ This was the view of the National Institute in its May assessment. It remained complacent about the position in both its August and November issues, although by the end of the year it was forecasting 'a significant, though not dangerous, worsening of the balance of payments'. *National Institute Economic Review*, p. 5. (Nov. 1963).

growth in productive potential. Unemployment fell during 1963 by some 150 000 from the peak levels reached in the winter. Such a pace of expansion could not be maintained, and the forecasts of expenditure made by the National Institute indicated the economy was likely to grow in 1964 almost as fast as in 1963. (They were forecasting in February a fourth quarter figure in 1964 for Final Expenditure which was 5% up on the same period of the previous year.) Such a rate of expansion implied a very low level of unemployment by the end of 1964, and falling further in 1965. The impact of such rapid growth had already been felt by the balance of payments and the current balance was in deficit at the time the 1964 Budget was being prepared.

The Chancellor was faced with a simple problem, and it seems impossible to believe that the official forecasters did not provide clear advice on the necessary action. It was evident that before the end of the year there would be excess pressure of demand and a sharply deteriorating balance of payments. Some action was taken in the Budget to restrain the growth in expenditure, perhaps equal to 0·5% off total demand in 1964, but this was clearly inadequate when expenditure in real terms was rising by some 6% (year on year) and with productive potential increasing by only about 3% per year. By March the unemployment rate was already down to 1·7% and was bound to fall further irrespective of the action taken by the Chancellor in the Budget.*

What was implied by the demand forecast for the balance of payments? The Chancellor was very 'cagey' in his Budget statement about this expected out-turn but he obviously anticipated further deterioration. Indeed the expectations since 1963 had been that expansion would inevitably in the short-run mean a worsening external balance, and that this would be financed rather than adjusted. One must infer the size of the deficit expected from various points in the Budget and elsewhere. The Chancellor thought it very likely that there would be a sharp worsening in the long-term capital account and a further deterioration was foreseen on current account. Import prices presented a problem for the forecasters but these were expected to increase by perhaps 3%–4% in 1964. Putting these estimates together yields a deficit on the balance of current and long-term capital transactions of £500 million. The actual deficit was £744 million (reduced below its 'real' level by a 'bisque' on the North American Loan).

The forecasters were, therefore, out on their forecast of the current account by some £100–150 million, and substantially underestimated the net long-term capital outflow. The actual deterioration in the

* Total final expenditure at constant prices increased by 6·5% in 1964, *Economic Trends*, Table A (Oct. 1968).

identified balance was £779 million, whereas the forecast had been one of a worsening of about £500 million. The forecasters did get the demand forecast about right, and it was perfectly clear from this forecast that by the end of 1964 and in the first half of 1965 that the economy would be operating at a dangerously high pressure of demand, with a consequential quickening of wage increases and a substantial deterioration in the balance of payments. They failed to forecast the actual size of the balance of payments deterioration, but their forecast would appear to have been sufficiently right to form the basis for correct policy action. That policy action was inadequate is a different matter, but it is not unlikely that the coming election exerted some pressure on men's minds.

The new Chancellor (Mr. Callaghan) was not very forthcoming in the April Budget statement about the quantitative size of the expected improvement in the balance of payments during 1965. Nevertheless his objective was perfectly clear. 'The strategy of this Budget is to achieve a state of balance on our combined current and long-term capital account. We have already made considerable progress. I aim to get most of the way towards closing the gap this year and to complete this process in the course of 1966. In doing so I am taking into account the need to reduce and later to abolish the temporary import duty as our progress warrants it.' Since the pre-Budget forecast was of a £350 million deficit on identified current and long-term capital transactions* and since the Budget aimed to reduce demand by some £250 million and act *directly* on invisibles and the capital account, then the post-Budget forecast must have been for a very substantial improvement. *Table 2.3* suggests that the balance of payments forecast, after taking into account the Budget measures, was of an identified deficit on current and long-term capital of about £200–250 million. Government statements about the impact of the temporary import charge (T.I.C.) were still very optimistic at this stage, whereas the actual impact on imports would appear to have been substantially less than forecast.† However, while imports were certainly higher than forecast, this was partly offset by a higher growth in exports (7% increase in 1965 compared with the previous year).‡ The current account improved in the

* The Prime Minister, quoted in the N.I.E.R., May 1965, p. 18.

† The Government estimated the annual saving on imports at £200 million when it was introduced in October 1964. By the time of the November 1964 Budget this had been raised to £300 million. The actual effect has subsequently been estimated to have been only £100–£150 million in 1965. (See Chapter 8.)

‡ In the Budget speech Mr. Callaghan spoke of export prospects in these terms: 'The opportunities exist for a substantial growth in exports. An increase of more than 5% in value is a considerable challenge, but it is within our reach.' Actual performance in 1965 was better than this.

second half of the year, and even moved into a small surplus in the fourth quarter. On the other hand, this improvement was not matched on capital account, and there was a large net outflow of long-term capital in the second half. The path through the year was certainly not the smooth transition to surplus suggested by the Chancellor, and so both the T.I.C. and the capital measures were much weaker than forecast. In spite of the new capital controls, introduced in the Budget, the net outflow in 1965 was above the average for the previous decade.

By the Budget of 1966 the Chancellor's time horizon in relation to a surplus in the balance of payments had been further extended. No longer was it a question of balance in 1966* but one of reaching 'balance by the end of this year'. 'The underlying trend is what matters' and it is our 'aim progressively to eliminate (the deficit) and move into surplus.'† Even this objective was out of reach without further direct action on the capital account (the introduction of 'voluntary' controls on investment in developed countries of the overseas sterling area and further cuts in government expenditure overseas). These measures were expected to save up to £100 million in a full year on the capital account. The main deflationary effect of the Budget was delayed until the autumn, when S.E.T. was to come into force, and it was always possible that the further postponement into the future of external balance might lead to further difficulties for sterling. The seamen's strike provided a setback and led to a sterling crisis. The July measures were the result.

The balance of payments did improve substantially in the second half of the year; but all the improvement cannot be put down to the effect of the reduction in home demand.‡ Stocks of surcharged goods were run down in October and November, in anticipation of the surcharge's removal, and only part of this run-down was made good in December. By the end of 1966 the balance of payments on current and long-term transactions was back in surplus, but precariously so, although for the year as a whole a substantial improvement had been achieved on external account. A bigger improvement had taken place than had been expected in April, but in the meantime the July measures had slowed the growth of the economy to an annual rate of less than 1·5 %. The improvement had been achieved at a high cost in terms of growth and through a trade-off of imports against employment. Nevertheless, the current balance, adjusted for the effect of the T.I.C., was in precarious

---

* Budget forecast in 1965.
† Budget Statement 1966.
‡ The seasonally adjusted current balance was, Q1, −£38 million; Q2, −£62 million; Q3, −£11 million; Q4, +£175 million.

surplus in the second half of the year, although its removal was bound to lead to a higher level of imports in 1967.

The year 1967 was disastrous for the British economy. The Chancellor in his Budget speech announced his intention of being more forthcoming about the official short-term forecasts so that the forecasts in *Tables 2.1* and *2.3* were more certain in their origin. The forecasts of expenditure were in aggregate reasonably close to actual changes, but this was due to compensating errors within the forecast. A source of major error was the forecast of exports, which were expected to rise in volume (goods and services) by 3 %–4 % between the second halves of 1967 and 1966 (exports of goods were forecast to increase by 6 % in 1967 compared to 1966). Actual exports in the second half of 1967 were some 7 % *less* in volume (goods and services) compared with the second half of 1966,* while the exports of goods (value) were 1·7 % less in 1967 than in 1966. The failure to forecast exports correctly was due to two developments. In the first place world trade slowed down much more than the forecasters had anticipated (they had expected world trade to expand at a slower rate during 1967).† The second reason was the dock strike which is estimated by the National Institute to have accounted for a loss equal to at least 1·5 % of the 1966 level.‡ Imports rose faster than forecast, partly because some components of demand increased at an unexpectedly fast rate and partly due to the Middle East crisis.

The forecast in the 1967 Budget had been quite explicit. 'Taking everything together, the overall balance of payments should improve again substantially between 1966 and 1967. We should move from last year's deficit of £189 million to a surplus in 1967 as a whole, with an even bigger one in 1968.' The outcome was quite different. Instead of an improvement of more than £190 million in 1968 in the identified balance there was a further deterioration of £370 million leaving the current and long-term capital account in heavy deficit (£417 million). The expected (Budget speech) improvement in capital account and net invisibles did not occur, although the main error of the forecast was in relation to the visible balance. The path through 1967 was not one of movement towards a 'substantial surplus' in 1968 as forecast by the Chancellor. Rather the path was one of almost continuous deterioration in the identified balance, from a large surplus in the fourth quarter

* The path followed by exports (goods and services at 1958 prices, seasonally adjusted) was second half 1966 £3178 million, first half 1967 £3242 million, second half 1967 £2974 million.

† World trade in manufactures rose by 7·4 % in 1967 compared with 1966, but was flat or slightly falling during the year (*National Institute Economic Review*, Appendix, table 23, Aug. 1968).

‡ *National Institute Economic Review*, p. 5 (Feb. 1968).

of 1966 to a deficit in the fourth quarter of 1967 of almost £350 million.*

The implications for domestic output and employment of the fall in exports during the year were considerable, although a faster rise in personal consumption and fixed investment than had been forecast produced an *overall* forecast which was reasonably good in year-on-year terms. However, the actual movement of GDP during the year was quite different from that forecast in the Budget.† Nevertheless, the main consequences of the short-term forecast lay on external account which developed quite differently from that forecast by the Treasury. By the middle of the year the Chancellor clearly faced a dilemma: if exports did not pick up the external account would worsen appreciably. The failure of exports to grow had adversely affected employment, and with unemployment rates already high by normal standards, some reflation was necessary.‡ Reflation came in June and August, with hire-purchase relaxations, but these were bound inevitably to make the problems on external account more severe. It is clear, in retrospect, that many of the difficulties later in the year, together with the large reserve losses, could have been avoided by a change in the exchange rate at an earlier point in time. Certainly part of the blame for the inadequacies of economic policy in 1967 must lie with the short-term forecasters whose prognostications proved a poor basis for policy action. The Chancellor was certainly misled by them into major policy errors, as is witnessed by the final statement of his last Budget speech.§

The Financial Statement 1968–1969 gave official forecasts of expenditure, imports and GDP, all at constant prices. These forecasts, together with provisional estimates of out-turn are given in *Table 2.4*. The growth in GDP was some 0·5 % higher than forecast, but there were much larger errors in some of the components. The largest, and most

* The quarterly path of the balance of current and long-term transactions, seasonally adjusted was: 1966: Q4 +£157 million; 1967: Q1 +£51 million, Q2 −£105 million, Q3 −£23 million, Q4 −£340 million.

† The Budget speech forecast a rise in total output in volume of slightly less than 3 % end 1966 to end 1967. GDP, at factor cost, 1958 prices and seasonally adjusted, showed virtually no rise during 1967.

‡ The situation was similar to that faced by Selwyn Lloyd in 1962. But in one respect it was quite different in that the Chancellor in 1962 had repaid the outstanding debts to the I.M.F. and reflation could start from a 'clean-slate'. Whereas at the time of the Budget in April 1967 the U.K. owed very substantial sums to the I.M.F. Additionally there could be no further trade-off of full-employment against external surplus, since this had already been attempted in July 1966—and signally failed.

§ 'I sum up the prospects for 1967 in three short sentences. We are back on course. The ship is picking up speed. The economy is moving. Every seaman knows the command at such a moment, "Steady as she goes."' *Hansard*, 11 April 1967, col. 1010.

Table 2.4

1968 FORECAST AND OUTCOME

CHANGES: SECOND HALF 1967 TO SECOND HALF 1968

	Forecast		Estimated Outcome	
	£ million at 1958 prices	%	£ million at 1958 prices	%
Consumers' expenditure	−190	−1·9	120	1·2
Public authorities consumption	70	3·0	−10	−0·4
Fixed investment	170	5·7	60	1·9
Exports of goods and services	390	13·1	550	18·5
Stockbuilding	40		140	
Total final expenditure	480	2·6	860	4·6
Imports of goods and services	20	0·6	270	7·9
Adjustment to factor cost	−20	−1·1	50	2·7
GDP at factor cost	480	3·6	540	4·0

Alternative forecast on high export assumption:				
Exports of goods and services	440	14·8		
GDP at factor cost	530	4·0		

Source: *Financial Statement and Budget Report 1968–1969*, H.M.S.O., Table 1 (April 1969).
Note: All figures in *Table 2.4* are based on the 'compromise' estimates of GDP, i.e., they are a compromise between the estimates available of GDP derived from expenditure, income and output data, which differ in their movement.

important error, was that of personal consumption, which rose by 1·2% as opposed to a forecast decline of 1·9%. Other sizeable errors were made in forecasting exports and imports, which proved too low, with the error larger in relation to imports. Foreign trade developments post-devaluation are analysed in greater detail in Chapter 8, but it is clear that the relatively poor performance of exports during the forecast period reflected errors with regard to the timing of the devaluation effects—the forecasters were operating in unknown territory and were simply guessing. Imports rose very sharply in the early months of 1968, but thereafter flattened out but still left the rise in import volume very high. Once again, there were errors in the timing of devaluation effects, but otherwise the excessive level of import volumes reflected the unexpectedly high level and fast growth in domestic demand. Errors were also made in the forecasts of stockbuilding and public authorities consumption, but in these cases the error lay in part with faulty base figures. No precise forecast was given of the balance of payments, but it is self-evident that the out-turn in 1968 was much less favourable than expected. The reasons for this were a much weaker balance of trade in volume terms, together with much smaller receipts of interest, profits and dividends than had been expected. Also export prices rose rather less than expected and import prices rather more. It appears, reading between the lines of Finstat 1968–1969, as if an *improvement* in the balance of payments (identified balance) of about £300 million was expected between 1967–1968, whereas the actual improvement was a mere £10 million. Altogether not a particularly good set of forecasts.

CONCLUSIONS

The previous section has been severely critical of recent official short-term forecasts. They have in certain years clearly misled policy makers and this, in the end, is the only criterion by which to judge them. Several questions immediately arise. Firstly, is the British performance in this respect much worse than that of other countries? Any answer to this must be inconclusive, but there does not appear to be any evidence to suggest that other countries are much more successful. Some countries do not even present forecasts in a quarterly form so that their forecasts are more crude and less adequate as a base for policy decisions. One possible criticism of the British procedure is that while there are internal assessments of the economic situation between main forecasts, these remain 'ad hoc' and incomplete. The U.S., in particular, has a more continuous programme of re-assessment, which permits a closer watch being kept on the developing economic situation so that policy action can be more immediate.* One suggestion, therefore, for improving the quality of economic policy in the U.K. is for a regular and continuous assessment of economic developments plus review of the forecasts. Ministers need to be reminded continuously of divergencies from the short-term forecasts.

The second, more fundamental, criticism is that forecasting can never

---

* A. W. Phillips in his inaugural lecture at the London School of Economics in 1962 showed that corrective action, to be successful in stabilising the economic system, had to be based on recently observed rates of change in economic activity (as well as on the level), and that this action had to have a large immediate impact on demand ('a quarter of it occurs within three or four months of the occurrence of the error it is designed to correct'). 'Employment, Inflation and Growth', *Economica*, p. 8 (Feb. 1962).

be successful and that we should give up the attempt. This view has been expressed by Professor Phillips, who would have policy based not on forecasts but on 'observations of the economy and its changes'.* But this line of argument and its conclusion is not very convincing. While the forecasts have in certain years led to policy errors, they have not generally done so. Other countries have had similar experiences, but they have reacted not by giving up the attempt to forecast, but by trying to understand why the forecasts went wrong and thereby to improve their understanding of the short-term behaviour of their economic systems. Basing policy on certain leading indicators does not seem a valid alternative to a set of quantified short-term forecasts, inadequate as these may have turned out to be on occasion. If this proposition is accepted, then it leads on to a discussion of the ways in which the British short-term forecasts should be improved.

One way of achieving some improvement is through their publication. Economic policy has been conducted in a highly secretive manner, and this has undoubtedly contributed to policy errors. Greater informed public discussion of the basis of Government economic policy is essential if Ministers are to follow the 'right' policies. It is difficult for anyone to judge the adequacy of the Budget proposals unless the framework upon which it was constructed is made generally available. The publication of the official short-term forecasts in the Financial Statement in April 1968 is a welcome departure from the former secrecy of the Treasury in this respect. It is likely to improve both public discussion of policy, and also to bring the forecasts within the realm of critical assessment. This can only be beneficial.

There are many other more specific proposals which would improve the quality of the forecasts. The forecasters clearly require a continuous flow of statistical data which is not subject to major revisions and which is nevertheless available quickly. This is vitally important if the forecasters are to get their starting points right. At the present time the forecasters when preparing the critical pre-Budget forecast have quarterly national income data only for the third quarter of the previous year, which is clearly unsatisfactory. Compared with some countries (particularly the U.S.A.) the speed with which quarterly national accounts data (and also that of the balance of payments) is made available is inadequate, and the first estimates are then subject to extensive revision. An important element, therefore, in improving the forecasts lies in the devotion of more resources to the collection of the main expenditure series required by the forecasters, and, in particular, improvement in the speed with which they are made available.

* *Economica*, p. 7 (Feb. 1962).

A more general criticism of the forecasts is that at the present time they are cast in an expenditure framework with the assumption that output will be called forth to meet the demands placed on the economy. This in itself may be an oversimplification and the forecasters clearly know relatively little about the output responses of firms in different sectors of the economy, or their response to price developments, changes in liquidity, etc. It may be the case that the constant price forecast is an inadequate model for analysing reactions within the economic system which are themselves based on current price developments. At the present time (see Chapter 1) the current price forecasts are simply a translation of the constant price forecasts into current prices. This is an unsatisfactory procedure, since the whole forecast will be different once financial and monetary variables are explicitly introduced. It is evident that part of the mistakes in recent economic policy can only be explained in terms of the relative neglect of monetary and financial factors. It follows, therefore, that more attention should be given to current-price forecasting, and that this should not be a 'mirror-image'. It should be developed separately, but alongside, the constant price forecast and are thus given a greater weight. This is not simply a matter of devoting more resources to forecasting (it is partly this), but also a change in approach. A concern for output responses (and lags); and a greater weight given to current price forecasts in the formation of economic policy.

Far too little is known about the determinants of many of the components which are being forecast. What is required is a great deal of research, either within the Treasury or within universities (but financed directly by the government). This means an expansion of the numbers of economists and statisticians engaged on short-term forecasting as compared to the small number presently engaged full-time in this activity. There are a number of areas which urgently need investigation. Personal consumption is one of these. It accounts for about 75 % of GDP (at factor cost) and relatively small errors in the forecast of this can cause large errors in the forecast of total final expenditure. A number of critical steps are necessary in deriving the forecast of personal expenditure and at any of these steps errors can be made, and are made. Various guideline equations are used in forecasting wage rates, although more reliance is placed on Ministry of Labour data on recent and impending wage awards, while the methods of forecasting profits, property income paid to persons and income from self-employment are still rather crude.* The forecast of personal income needs then to have

* *Fourth Report of the Estimates Committee, Session 1966–1967, on Government Statistical Services*, H.M.S.O., Appendix 7, para. 16 (Dec. 1966).

direct taxes deducted (it is not known by the Treasury how the Inland Revenue does this) and then personal disposable income is deflated to get it at constant prices. The next stage is a forecast of the savings ratio (the marginal propensity to save has been very unstable in recent years and this is very imperfectly understood by the authorities).* At this stage also, an attempt is made to forecast hire-purchase debt although, 'no satisfactory equation has yet been specified for explaining or predicting changes in hire-purchase debt' and 'the assumptions made [about the amount of durable goods bought on credit] do not rest upon any very systematic evidence.'† As for advances from the banking sector, 'a judgement of the prospect is made'. These practices do not inspire much confidence in the result.

Quite clearly much more research is necessary into the determinants of consumption behaviour. There are too many areas (some of them important for policy action, e.g., hire-purchase controls) about which too little is known. There is implicit in the above procedure a great deal of guesswork and too little knowledge. Errors in the forecast of consumption have occasionally been large (e.g., in 1963 and 1967) and in the first quarter of 1968 the Treasury was caught quite unprepared by the strong expansion of personal consumption. There is no direct evidence on consumer attitudes or intentions (developed on a wide scale in the U.S.A. and generally considered of value in forecasting aggregate consumption)‡ and little is known about the determinants of hire-purchase debt take-up. One huge and glaring deficiency relates to savings behaviour, and it appears the Treasury knows very little about the factors affecting short-run savings decisions.

Exports have been a major source of error, not only in the U.K. but also in other countries. Not much improvement can be expected in this area, although a great deal more fundamental research is required into the factors determining export prospects in the short-run, into such matters as export pricing policies of firms, and perhaps in the development of a world trade model. There have been substantial forecast errors caused by poor forecasts of stockbuilding, since changes in the rate of stockbuilding can be very large. The Treasury model, from which the forecast of stocks is derived, involves a belief in the tendency for stocks to be maintained in a 'normal' long-run relationship taking into account cyclical factors. Once again more fundamental research is needed into stock/output relationships in the short-run, plus experi-

* *Techniques of Economic Forecasting*, O.E.C.D. Paris, p. 139 (1965).

† *Fourth Report of the Estimates Committee, Session 1966–1967, on Government Statistical Services*, H.M.S.O., Appendix 7, paras. 19, 21 and 22 (Dec. 1966).

‡ See E. Mueller, 'Ten Years of Consumer Attitude Surveys; Their Forecasting Record', *Journal of the American Statistical Association*, **LVIII** (1962).

mentation with more complex models. Fixed investment is based largely on survey data of business intentions, and this should be a reasonably reliable method given experience in adjusting the survey data. However, this is only a useful predictor for a relatively short period ahead (when in any case much of the investment is already planned or in process of implementation and is relatively unresponsive to short-run developments in the economy). On the other hand there exists no model for explaining longer-term investment behaviour and little empirical evidence on the determinants of investment, e.g., the investment response to interest rate movements, the effect of liquidity changes or changing profit levels and so on.* Survey data have only very short-run value and do not give much guidance about investment behaviour in the longer term. Public investment, although nominally under the control of the authorities, has also been badly forecast (the tendency has been to overestimate the level during the forecast period), and here again more analysis and research is required, particularly into the timing of investment and lags in this sector.

One function of the forecasts of output is to provide a base for estimating employment and unemployment during the forecast period.† There is evidence, both in the N.I.E.R. and also in the Economic Reports for 1966 and 1967‡ that there have been fundamental changes in this forecasting relationship. These may have been permanent (an increase in the trend rate of growth in productivity associated with rationalisation of industry etc.) or may be temporary (an over-rapid shakeout of labour in the period after the July measures of 1966 which may result in an excessive take-up of labour once output begins expanding again). On the other hand since the relationship is based on past data, the devaluation and other measures may have changed the pattern of output and thus the response of employment/unemployment to output changes. If this is so, then the previous forecasting relationships may be of little guidance and so further research is needed into these developments in order to develop new formulae. In any case, there is plenty of evidence that during 1966 and 1967 there were periods

---

* Some research has been done into such matters by the Bank of England. See J. P. Burman, 'Capital Utilisation and the Determination of Fixed Investment', a paper delivered to the Conference on Econometric Models of the U.K., South-ampton, April 1969.

† The precise formula and its derivation, is described in 'Productive Potential and the Demand for Labour', *Economic Trends* (Aug. 1968).

‡ The Treasury have been using a relationship initially developed by the National Institute. The National Institute in a number of *Reviews* has commented on the change in the relationship (*N.I. Economic Review*, Nov. 1967, p. 13; Feb. 1968, p. 6; and Aug. 1968, p. 10 plus footnote). The Treasury comments are made in the *Economic Report for 1966*, p. 23, and in the *Economic Report for 1967*, p. 23.

when the relationship (and therefore the unemployment forecasts) went seriously astray. Some of the lags in the adjustment of employment to output proved quite different from what could have been expected on the basis of previous experience, and the relationship has signally failed to forecast adequately cyclical variations in employment and output.

APPENDIX: ASSESSMENT OF NATIONAL INSTITUTE FORECASTS

Appendix: Table 1

DEVIATIONS OF MAY FORECASTS FROM ACTUAL OUT-TURNS. FOURTH QUARTER TO FOURTH QUARTER CHANGES, £ MILLION, 1958 PRICES SEASONALLY ADJUSTED AND PERCENTAGES*

	1960 1961	1961 1962	1962 1963	1963 1964	1964 1965	1965 1966	1966 1967
GDP	−27	+89	−126	−23	+107	+113	+102
	−0·3	+1·6	−2·0	−0·5	+1·8	+1·8	+1·6
Consumers'	+4	−54	−85	−53	+55	+94	−182
expenditure	+0·2	−1·3	−1·9	−1·0	+1·2	+1·8	−3·7
Public authorities	−17	−6	+63	+15	−16	+2	−20
consumption	−1·5	−0·5	+6·4	+1·4	−1·6	+0·2	−1·8
Fixed	+18	+29	−63	−47	+47	+11	−90
investment	+1·8	+2·6	−5·6	−3·6	+3·4	+0·8	−6·4
Exports	+15	+61	−40	−16	−41	−21	+245
	+0·8	+5·1	−2·9	−1·1	−2·8	−1·3	+1·5
Total final	+20	+30	−125	−101	+45	+86	−47
expenditure	+0·3	+0·4	−1·6	−1·2	+0·5	+1·0	−0·5
Stockbuilding	+41	+35	−84	+62	+60	+149	+35
Total final							
expenditure	+61	+65	−209	−39	+105	+235	−12
plus stocks	+1·1	+1·2	−2·6	−1·6	+1·3	+2·6	−0·1
Less imports	+73	−15	−29	+14	−28	+100	−74
	+5·2	−1·0	−2·1	+1·0	−1·8	+5·9	−0·4
Less factor	+15	−6	−54	−30	+26	+22	−40
cost	+2·0	−0·8	−7·5	−3·4	+2·8	+2·5	−4·8

* + = forecast overestimated outcome.   − = forecast underestimated outcome.
   I am grateful to Mr. D. Kennett for preparing the tables

TABLES I AND 2.

The figures in *Table 1* are from the May (post-Budget) forecasts of the National Institute Review for the years 1960–1967. *Table 2* contains various statistics relevant to the assessment of the deviations of the forecasts from actuals. It is clear from column 1 of *Table 2* (Mean Error) that the Institute has consistently undervalued consumers' expenditure and fixed investment while the other categories were generally overvalued. However, mean error is a crude and not very valuable test and

Appendix: Table 2

STATISTICS RELEVANT TO DEVIATIONS OF MAY
FORECASTS FROM ACTUAL OUTTURN

	(1) Mean	(2) Absolute Mean	(3) Variance	(4) t-score
GDP	+33·6	83·8	8 832	0·95
Consumers' expenditure	−33	76·7	8 585	0·94
Public authorities expenditure	+4·4	20·0	863	1·26
Gross fixed investment	−13·6	43·6	3042	0·65
Exports	+29	63	10 193	0·76
Total final expenditure	−13·1	65	—	—
Stocks	+53·4	77·4	5 325	1·93
Total final expenditure plus stocks	+40·3	114·6	—	—
Imports	6·0	52·3	3 217	0·33
Factor cost	9·6	27·6		

can be misleading in so far as large errors can be self-compensating and thus give a false impression of accuracy. An example is imports, where the forecast errors are distributed fairly evenly about zero giving an impression of precision because of the low mean. However, if we take the absolute mean (column 2) it is evident that imports were rather badly forecast while other components of expenditure improve their position, e.g., stocks. The figures on variance (column 3) indicate that some components were widely scattered round the mean (consumers' expenditure and exports particularly), while others were more closely grouped round the mean, e.g., public consumption. A t-test for bias in the forecasts yielded no significant t-scores indicating that no important bias was present.

TABLE 3.

It is clear from *Table 3* that in general the Institute made few mistakes in predicting direction of change; only in four years were any mistakes made and there were only six errors out of 49 predictions. This is quite creditable until it is recognised that, neglecting stocks, every forecast during these years (except fixed investment 1966/1967) was positive and

Appendix: Table 3

ERRORS OF OVERESTIMATION AND UNDERESTIMATION AND OF DIRECTION OF CHANGE
IN THE MAY FORECASTS 1961–1967

Forecasted Component	Number of Years Forecast Exceeded Actual	Number of Years Actual Exceeded Forecast	Number of DCs Correctly Forecast	Number of DCs Incorrectly Forecast
GDP	3	4	7	0
Consumers' expenditure	3	4	6	1
Public authorities expenditure	3	4	7	0
Gross fixed investment	4	3	5	2
Exports	3	4	6	1
Total final expenditure	4	3	7	0
Stocks	6	1	6	1
Total final expenditure plus stocks	4	3	6	1
Imports	4	3	5	2
Factor cost adjustment	3	4	6	1

that the vast majority of actual outcomes were as well, the only negative occasions being those in which a direction of change error was made. In the case of stocks, where only one mistake of direction was made, the record was impressive given that this category switched frequently from positive to negative. The main turning-point error was in 1966, but the Institute can be exonerated in that its May forecast was followed by the July measures.

Institute forecasts of the balance of payments have been as unsatisfactory as those of the Treasury. The average error in the forecast between 1959–1969 was £225 million, and in four years the error averaged £450 million. Between 1963–1969 the average error at £250 million 'was virtually as big as the variation themselves and about as large as the errors which would have resulted if the forecast each year had been "no change"'.*

* 'Errors in the N.I. Forecasts of the Balance of Payments', *Review*, No. 52, p. 35 (May 1970).

3

ECONOMIC INSTABILITY AND
THE ROLE OF FISCAL POLICY

The aim in this, and in the following two chapters, is to analyse the main developments in British fiscal policy during the sixties. Certain areas of the subject have been deliberately ignored, for example, matters relating to the structure of taxation or to the size of automatic stabilisers, mainly because there exist several recent investigations of such matters.* Use is made, nevertheless, of the conclusions of such research where it is relevant to our main objective. Throughout the following chapters the discussion is focused, almost entirely, on the purely short-term aspects of fiscal policy, although one aim of this chapter is to place these developments in a broader context. Developments in public expenditure, again where relevant to short-term stabilisation policy, are discussed in Chapter 5.

ECONOMIC POLICY AIMS

For all Governments in post-war Britain the single most important policy aim has been the maintenance of a high and stable level of employment. This particular aim was, of course, enshrined in the famous

---

* See Bent Hansen, *Fiscal Policy in Seven Countries, 1955–1965*: O.E.C.D., H.M.S.O. (March 1969); R. A. and P. B. Musgrave, 'Fiscal Policy', in *Britain's Economic Prospects*, Allen and Unwin (1968) and *Fiscal Policy for a Balanced Economy*, O.E.C.D.: H.M.S.O. (Dec. 1968). A valuable econometric study is that of E. T. Balopoulos, *Fiscal Policy Models of the British Economy*, North-Holland Publishing Co. (1967).

White Paper of 1944 on Employment Policy where it was assumed that the achievement of this policy goal, in the light of experience during the thirties, would be difficult and yet ought to be the main criterion for judging the adequacy of economic policy. Governments have come to believe that any failure to achieve this aim will lead to political suicide, and has thus led Cabinet discussion on economic policy to concentrate almost exclusively on the 'trade-offs' between employment and other policy aims. It is instructive that only in two years since 1957 has the annual rate of unemployment exceeded 2%, in 1962 and in 1967, and in both cases the Chancellors responsible (Mr. Selwyn Lloyd in 1962 and Mr. Callaghan in 1967) were removed from the Treasury.* Simply in terms of employment aims, excluding regional problems, Governments have been extraordinarily successful—beyond the wildest dreams of the authors of the 1944 White Paper or the authors of the Beveridge Report.

Various conclusions follow from the primacy of the employment aim. Firstly, the most critical economic indicator for most ministers is the unemployment rate, and they are generally unwilling to follow policies for even a relatively short period which will raise unemployment above 2%-2·5%, partly because of the explicit recognition of the resource costs entailed in keeping labour idle (and with it physical capacity), but also because of its regional incidence. Secondly, the key role of the unemployment rate leads inevitably to avoidable lags in policy making; unemployment lags behind output changes so that policy response to changes in the unemployment rate may be in the right direction but entail recognition lags and therefore be wrong in their timing. Thirdly, the expectation that no Government could seriously contemplate any substantial rise in unemployment for any length of time has had significant effects on the behaviour of employers. They have correctly anticipated that reflationary measures would relatively quickly follow any package of restrictions and have behaved accordingly. This has had certain advantages; firms have been able to plan investment on the assumption that no Government could afford to allow demand to rise by less than productive potential except for very short periods. This has undoubtedly had favourable effects on business expectations, and must have contributed to the greater stability of post-war private investment (and thus of employment). Furthermore, firms faced by policy-induced slowdowns in the economy, have reacted by not releasing labour on any substantial scale. This has been entirely rational on their part since, expecting reflation within a rela-

* The years 1968 and 1969 are exceptions in that unemployment exceeded 2% and the Chancellor maintained his position, but only until the Election of 1970.

tively short period, they wished to hold on to their labour (especially skilled craftsmen) so as to avoid labour shortages once demand began to expand.*

Finally, while a high level of employment has been welcomed by all, it has also led to a recognition that this entails certain costs. In particular, that a fully-employed economy will suffer from wage and price pressures which may have undesirable effects on the country's balance of payments. The relationships between the rate of change of wages (or prices) and the level (or rate of change) of unemployment have increasingly become the focus of economic policy and in recent years have been a powerful factor in leading to a (slight) redefinition of the full-employment target. A high and stable level of employment remains the primary policy goal, but not quite so high, and there has been an acceptance within the present Government that a shift to a slightly higher unemployment rate, an average rate nearer to 2·5 %, has distinct advantages from the viewpoint of wage/price stability.

But this redefinition of the full employment target does not imply that price stability as an end in itself has suddenly been given much greater weight in the formulation of policy. No Chancellor—with one exception—has ever set price stability as his primary aim. This is not to suggest that price developments have not been watched very closely, but instead to emphasise that prices have been considered important because of their relationship to a deteriorating external balance, and that action taken to improve the balance of payments has usually succeeded in slowing down the rate of price increase. The only occasion when prices were given primacy in economic policy was during the brief Chancellorship of Mr. Thorneycroft in 1957–1958 when the authorities became convinced that an unemployment rate of about 3 % was essential to achieve price stability. However, the disappearance of Mr. Thorneycroft in January 1958, together with rising unemployment, soon led to a reversal of this policy. Otherwise the main attack on prices has come through prices and income policies of various types, beginning with the wage freeze of 1948–1950, the price plateau of 1958, the pay pause of 1961, the guiding light of 1962–1964 and the statutory policy from 1965 to 1969. How effective these policies were in restraining inflation and in achieving other policy aims (such as raising the rate of productivity growth) is discussed in Chapter 9.

From about the mid-fifties economic growth began to receive

* After July 1966 a change in attitude of employers is observable. It was finally accepted by the Government that draconian deflation was necessary in order to protect the exchange rate, and this led to a redefinition of demand prospects by employers so that a large, and untypical, shake-out of labour took place.

increasing attention from the Government and this was made an explicit aim in the 1956 White Paper on the Economic Implications of Full Employment where it was stated that 'the Government is pledged to foster conditions in which the nation can, if it so wills, realise its full potentialities for growth in terms of production and living standards'.* This new emphasis on growth reflected an obvious desire to raise the rate at which the standard of living increased but partly also reflected a growing awareness of the relatively poor growth performance of Britain compared to other countries. Government policies were introduced favourable to raising the growth rate, and led in 1962 to the establishment of the National Economic Development Council. Subsequently various growth targets were adopted for the economy; initially 4% in the first N.E.D.C. plan, 4·25% in the National Plan of 1965, but with no firm commitment to any particular rate in the Green Paper of 1968.† At one point in 1963–1964 the Government was convinced that raising the rate of growth would assist in solving the persistent balance of payments problem through raising the rate of productivity growth and thus increasing the competitiveness of the economy. Mr. Maudling's policies during 1963–1964 were clearly a failure, although a more detailed analysis of these is reserved for Chapter 8. Obviously the authorities have failed to achieve their growth objectives, although the average rate of growth has been slightly higher during the sixties than during the fifties. Nevertheless, the rate of growth has remained low in relation to other countries, and there have been years when the economy has expanded at a rate significantly below the growth in productive potential. Governments, while strongly holding beliefs about the desirability of a higher and steadier growth in output have, nevertheless, had to sacrifice these aims to the overriding need of correcting external payments deficits. To this, the main constraint on the achievement of policy aims in recent years, we now turn.

It is only possible to fully understand the development of economic

---

* *Economic Implications of Full Employment*, H.M.S.O., Cmd. 9725, p. 25.

† Both the N.E.D.C. plan and the National Plan set growth targets which were significantly higher than recent growth performance, and above productive potential (estimated at slightly higher than 3% in the early sixties). The Department of Economic Affairs' Green Paper, 'The Task Ahead—Economic Assessment to 1972', published in 1969 is neither a plan nor a forecast but an 'initial assessment of economic prospects'. In the basic case GDP growth 1969–1972 was taken as 3·25%, slightly more than the estimated growth in productive potential (put at 2·9% on average during 1969–1972), but variants of the basic case are also described. It represents a substantial change in the Government's estimate of the possibilities for a rapid transformation of the economy and for a substantially increased rate of growth.

policy, and the failures of demand management, if the critical role of the balance of payments is recognised. There were no less than six major sterling crises between 1955 and 1967—in 1955–1956, 1957, 1960–1961, 1964–1965, 1966 and 1967. The external problem has, therefore, both long-term and short-term aspects. Full analysis of its causes is delayed to a later chapter and at this stage of the argument perhaps a few general points will suffice. In the first place the authorities have possessed, at least since Radcliffe, a general aim in relation to the balance of payments. The Treasury in evidence to the Committee, in November 1957, spoke of the need to achieve 'a surplus on our current external trade of £300–350 million' and by April 1959 the Treasury expressed the view 'that resources should be found for a surplus or current account averaging about £450 million a year in the early 1960s'.* Such an aim has never been fulfilled, and the largest surpluses on current account during the sixties have both been equal to slightly more than £100 million in 1962 and 1963, both years when unemployment was relatively high.† Secondly, the foreign exchange reserves have always during the post-war period been inadequate by almost any criteria, for a country running a reserve currency. While the authorities have not (at least publicly) declared what the minimum level of the reserves is below which they will not be permitted to fall, it can be assumed that this was finally reached in November 1967. Hitherto the surpluses on current account (when they infrequently occurred) were not sufficiently large to meet rising Government expenditure abroad (on military and aid account) to continue to finance the export of long-term capital and to build up the reserves. Attempts to reflate domestic demand, because of rising unemployment, have usually been excessive (particularly in 1959 and 1963) and have inevitably led to current account deficits. While it might have been possible for a time to finance these deficits (plus the export of long-term capital) either by running down the reserves or through borrowing, the pressure on the reserves finally became unmanageable because of speculative attacks on the sterling rate. To protect the exchange rate, stability of which remained a constant aim of policy until November 1967, the authorities were forced to relinquish the other policy aims of economic growth and full employment. Generally, corrective action took the form of domestic deflation, but as we shall see later, other more adventuresome techniques have also been used. The result of this process has been a

---

* Lord Radcliffe *Report of the Committee on the Workings of the Monetary System*, H.M.S.O., Cmnd. 827, para. 62 (1959).

† The largest current account surplus was in 1969 (£416 million) but was in part the result of the continued restrictions on trade and payments, together with a high level of unemployment.

pattern of domestic demand development which has been characterised as 'stop-go'.

Such then are some of the essential points relevant to an understanding of balance of payments developments. But it leaves unexplained a number of curious questions. None of the above adequately explains the determination by the authorities to hold on to an unrealistic value for the exchange rate when it was obvious to many commentators by the early sixties that sterling was overvalued. When the devaluation finally came, as it was inevitable it would, it came as a result of a massive attack on the reserves by speculators (compounded by a deficit in the balance of payments) and was not in any way a planned movement to a new realistic parity. Secondly, there remains the critical short-run problem of why, when the authorities did reflate demand, they generally did so to an excessive extent so that balance of payments difficulties became inevitable. To the first question an answer is attempted in Chapter 7, and to the second a tentative explanation is advanced in the next chapter.

THE EVOLUTION OF BUDGETARY DOCTRINE

Economists began to analyse the essential conditions for successful contra-cyclical policy during the 1930s in the face of, and, partly at least because of, persistent and severe economic problems in all of the industrial countries. Led by Keynes they developed analytical tools which permitted the formulation of general principles in respect of fiscal and monetary policy which, if followed by governments, were expected to diminish the amplitude of economic fluctuations—to diminish but not to eliminate, since fluctuations were considered, at least by some economists, to be part and parcel of the functioning of the economic system.* Since the results of their labours were expressed in purely general terms it has been the task of stabilisation authorities in the post-war period to develop and extend these general rules in order to equip themselves with the specific tools and techniques essential to the achievement of their objectives.

Governments were capable of understanding, and in time of accepting, that where a deficiency of aggregate demand occurred the correct policy response was to vary taxes and Government expenditure,

* For example, in the accelerator/multiplier models developed during the thirties by Samuelson ('Interactions between the Multiplier Analysis and the Principle of Acceleration', *Review of Economics and Statistics*, **21**, 75–78, Harvard University Press (May 1939), and, more recently, the numerous capital-stock adjustment models (see R. C. O. Matthews, *The Trade Cycle*, C.U.P. 1959).

together with appropriate changes in monetary policy, in order to remove the deficiency. At this stage of the cycle Governments should deliberately destabilise the budget by cutting taxes and/or increasing Government expenditures. Indeed factors would already be at work in this direction through the reduction in tax receipts as income declined and through the increase in welfare and unemployment expenditures. The expectation was, however, that such automatic stabilisers would not prove strong enough and that discretionary changes in policy would also be required.* Opposite policies would be needed during periods of excess demand where again automatic fiscal effects would assist in the restraint of private expenditure growth but would be insufficient in themselves to restrain inflationary forces. Subsequently these general principles were expanded to include also the concepts of 'fiscal drag' or full employment budget where the problem was seen as a tendency for automatic increases in tax revenue, generated in a growing economy over time, to exert a deflationary influence on the economy. This concept developed mainly in the U.S.A., has not had much relevance to British post-war problems, and at least one examination of British fiscal policy has found no evidence of fiscal drag.†

Such then are the broad principles thought of as appropriate for successful stabilisation policy. But important developments as they are they, nevertheless, contain serious inadequacies. Different instruments of policy have quite different effects on demand, not merely in the broad sense of fiscal measures versus monetary instruments, but in terms of the quantitative impact of alternative fiscal measures on demand (including multiplier and accelerator effects), and the time lags associated with different policy instruments. It has long been recognised that a change in Government expenditure which is exactly matched by a change on the revenue side, leaving the budget surplus or deficit unchanged, does not necessarily have neutral effects on demand (the balanced budget multiplier), and that in general expenditure changes by government have a bigger multiplier effect on income than an equivalent change in taxes. But governments, particularly where they face a fine-tuning problem and not a massive deficiency of demand, need to know more than this. The post-war period has seen, therefore, a gradual improvement in their techniques of analysis by the stabilisation

---

* Dow concluded that the post-war British tax system was not an important 'built-in disinflator', *Management of the British Economy*, p. 191. This deficiency of the tax system has been emphasised particularly by Hansen, *Policy in Fiscal Seven Countries 1955–1965*, pp. 439–443 and *Fiscal Policy for a Balanced Economy*, pp. 67–68 O.E.C.D. (Dec. 1969).

† R. A. Musgrave in *Britain's Economic Prospects*, Brookings Institute: Allen and Unwin, 29 (1968).

authorities which allows the relative merits of different policies to be more effectively assessed. Why certain categories of government expenditure entail bigger effects on demand than others, or how to analyse and compare the impact of changes in indirect as against direct taxes, and what precisely is the timing of such measures in their impact on demand. The fourth part of this chapter reviews some of the developments in official techniques, and these are subsequently used in the following chapter in the analysis of stabilisation policy during the sixties.

It is these factors, among others, which influence Governments in the choice of policy instruments. Governments are never, of course, entirely free to choose between different policies on the basis of purely economic criteria; they are bound to be constrained by social, political, economic and administrative considerations. For example, increases in the flat-rate employees National Insurance contribution is undoubtedly an effective device for restraining private expenditure, but would also be regressive and therefore conflict with other strongly-held tax principles. In practice, because of administrative difficulties, changes in income tax, whether in rates or reliefs and allowances, can only be made once a year at the time of the Budget and no one any longer seriously believes that the problems of control over the economy's development can be fully taken care of with an annual Budget. Indeed, given the imperfect nature of short-term forecasting, it would be very foolish to hold any such view.

Governments have gradually accepted the need for mid-term adjustments in policy and there is certainly less political approbation attached to the introduction of supplementary measures in an autumn Budget or to changes in policy at any other time considered essential. However, while it should be noted that Governments have accepted the need for more frequent interference in the management of the economy they have retained a predilection to wait too long before taking policy action. This is natural enough since Chancellors of the Exchequer are political animals concerned, at least in part, with their long-term survival within the Government. But the delays in taking appropriate policy action have other explanations, particularly in the lagged response of employment to output and the lag between changes in the external reserves and the underlying balance of payments. The unemployment rate and the level of the reserves have been the critical indicators for all Governments during the fifties and sixties, and since they have responded to unfavourable movements in these they have inevitably responded with a lag to the underlying changes—a continuing and serious deficiency in the making of economic policy.

Nevertheless, Governments have attempted to improve the policy instruments at their disposal and to make their response more flexible, but even some of the fiscal innovations of recent years have serious disadvantages associated with them. For example, one of the most praised innovations of the sixties was the introduction by Selwyn Lloyd in 1961 of the 'regulator', i.e., the power to adjust by up to 10%, up or down, all indirect taxes at any time thought necessary. The effect is instantaneous and the impact of the regulator on demand is substantial when used to the full extent. (See *The Analysis of Tax Changes* below.) On the other hand, while highly regarded by some eminent economists,★ the regulator has serious drawbacks and has not been used frequently since its introduction. Because indirect taxes are highly concentrated on a narrow range of goods the use of the regulator leads inevitably to severe disruption of trade in a small number of industries, with unfortunate effects on the forward planning of investment and often with geographically localised effects on employment (in this respect it has effects similar to hire-purchase controls). A movement to a broader based system of indirect taxation would obviate some of these deficiencies, and in the process would improve the stabilising role of the tax system. But the regulator has a further serious disadvantage (shared with variation in S.E.T.) in that it has its effect on demand through changes in prices—primarily prices of goods bought by consumers. It does, therefore, when moved in an upward direction, give an undesirable twist to the price level, which inevitably leads to pressure for general increases in wages.

Changes in corporate taxation have numerous disadvantages when used for stabilisation purposes. Most important, perhaps, is the fact that they have their impact on demand with an extended time-lag, because of the lag of collections behind liabilities. Given the nature of post-war fluctuations a time-lag of this length is so serious as to eliminate change in corporate taxation as a stabilisation weapon. This criticism is not, of course, true in respect of fiscal devices aimed at changing private investment such as investment allowances or initial allowances which have (not always successfully) been used for contra-cyclical purposes. However, if such grants/allowances are to succeed in their main purpose (the raising of the level of private investment in the long-term) then their changing availability is only to be condemned.†

★ One of the few things the *O.E.C.D. 1968* study found to praise, and recommend to other countries, was the regulator (p. 68).

† For the results of a number of surveys into the impact of initial and investment allowances see D. C. Corner and Alan Williams, 'The Sensitivity of Businesses to Initial and Investment Allowances', *Economica*, **XXXII** 32–47 (1965). In their own survey they found that 20% of firms responded to the allowances,

While much emphasis was placed in early writings on contra-cyclical variation in public expenditure, this device has in fact been used very sparingly, for reasons which are examined more closely in Chapter 5. In general the main lines of public expenditure developments, both in total and in terms of its distribution between different uses, are already settled by the turn of the year so that when decisions have to be taken at the time of the Budget (in the light of the short-term economic forecast) changes are more easily made on the revenue side than on the expenditure side (with transfers and subsidies thought of as reverse direct and indirect taxes respectively). Furthermore, the adjustments in taxation have generally had their impact (at least their direct effect) on consumer expenditure, because this has continued to be the most easily controlled component of demand, as well as accounting for almost two-thirds of total domestic expenditure. Changes in corporate taxation have substantial disadvantages when used for stabilisation purposes, while variation in public expenditure programmes is believed by the authorities to be costly in terms of interruption of programmes which are believed to be nationally desirable. None of these considerations applies to changes in consumers' expenditure brought about by fiscal (and monetary) policy.

In the event, therefore, while Governments have many measures available to them in pursuit of their main policy aims, there remain serious disadvantages in the use of many of these. Indeed, as well as these technical restraints on policy, there remain other, broader, forces at work—including purely political factors. The success of Governments in post-war elections has not been uncorrelated with election-year Budgetary policy, and it is evident that a good part of the explanation of Government fiscal performance in some years (1955, 1959, 1964) is due to this consideration. But even in other years political factors may have exercised powerful influences on policy. For example, in 1958 the new Chancellor (Mr. Heathcote Amory) went to great lengths to stress that no change was contemplated in the anti-inflationary policies of his predecessor, although it was clear from early 1958 that reflation was necessary. The result was that reflationary measures were not taken until the autumn and in the Budget of 1959—action when it came was both too late and too strong. Similarly, in 1962 the policies of Selwyn Lloyd went sadly wrong, and led to his downfall, but given the position

---

although it varied among firms according to size and rate of growth. For a more recent econometric analysis, which found considerable sensitivity of investment to allowances and investment grants, see R. Agarwala and G. C. Goodson, 'The Analysis of the Effects of Investment Incentives on Investment Behaviour in the British Economy', *Economica*, **XXXVI** (Nov. 1969).

he had taken could not be easily reversed so that once again reflationary action came too late and when it did come, mainly in the Budget of 1963, it was excessive by any standards. In a very broad way the denigration of stop-go policies during the sixties if anything made Governments even more cautious, and although it was based on perfectly reasonable premises, it led to a reduction in the flexibility of policy, a trend which was entirely unwelcome.

SOURCES OF ECONOMIC INSTABILITY

Basic to much of the discussion of the theoretical role of fiscal policy during the 1930s, and after, was the assumption that the main unstable components of demand were within the private sector. Both public current and capital expenditure were believed to be determined primarily by longer-term social and economic forces and there was thus little reason to expect that variation in the rate of growth of these expenditures would constitute a major cause of instability. Although perverse reactions by Government, e.g., cuts in public expenditure to achieve stability of the budget in the face of falling revenues, could exacerbate a worsening situation. In the event Governments in post-war Britain have not reacted in this way, although as we shall see in a later chapter, public investment has not behaved in a way which was particularly desirable from the viewpoint of contra-cyclical policy.

Nevertheless, not all forms of private expenditure were considered to be inherently unstable, and its largest component (personal consumption) was believed to be fairly stable. Indeed, a stable long-run relationship between income and consumption was one of the basic postulates of the General Theory and while subsequent research has confirmed the long-term stability of the consumption function it has also demonstrated its short-term instability. (See *Chart 3.1.*) However, clearly a good deal of this short-term instability is itself directly due to the use of economic policy weapons, changes in indirect tax rates and the use of hire-purchase and credit controls, which have their main impact on personal consumption. They do not, however, have an even incidence in their impact and effect primarily expenditure on durables. Non-durable consumption has grown in a much more stable way. Nevertheless, not all of the fluctuation in durable-goods expenditure has been caused by changes in economic policy, and other non-policy variables have operated which in themselves would have caused fluctuations—particularly durable replacement cycles.

The main sources of instability were identified as private investment demand and export demand. The former was believed to be unstable because of widely held beliefs about the theory of investment which identified factors leading to investment fluctuations; the dependence of investment on the rate of change of income (the accelerator), Schumpeterian bunching of innovative activity, echoes and shocks and the basic volatility of entrepreneurial expectations. The latter, because of lessons drawn from the pre-war experience—and in particular the role

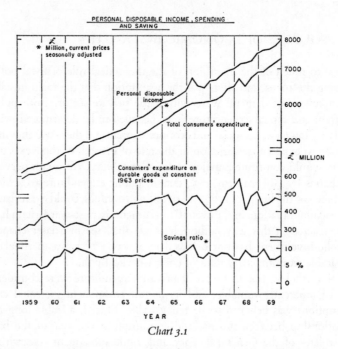

Chart 3.1

of declining export demand in the onset of the 1929 downturn. What part have these two main components played in the fluctuations in economic activity in recent years, and to what extent have they faced the authorities with especially difficult problems?

As can be seen from *Table 3.1* and *Chart 3.2* there have been three cycles in output (GDP) since 1958. Upswings occurred 1958Q3–1960-Q3 and 1962Q3–1964Q4 and during these periods output growth was at an annual rate of about 5%. In both the downswings, 1960Q3–1962Q3 and 1964Q4–1967Q3, GDP growth fell to 2%. Between 1967Q3 and 1969Q3 the economy was 'scheduled' for an upswing, but in fact expanded at a rate rather below the average for the previous decade (2·7% compared with 3·2%): 1967Q3–1969Q3 differs from the previous two cycles in a number of other respects. In both the earlier

Table 3.1

CONTRIBUTION OF PRIVATE INVESTMENT AND EXPORTS TO CHANGES IN GROSS NATIONAL PRODUCT AT CONSTANT 1958 PRICES

Year	(1) % Change in GNP at Factor Cost	(2) Contribution of Change in Private Non-residential Fixed Investment to % of Change in GNP	(3) Contribution of Change in Exports (Goods and Services) to % of Change in GNP	(4) Cols. (2 + 3)
1958	0	0·1	−0·4	−0·3
1959	3·3	0·4	0·6	1·0
1960	4·7	1·1	1·2	2·3
1961	3·8	1·0	0·7	1·7
1962	1·2	−0·3	0·4	0·1
1963	3·5	0	0·9	0·9
1964	5·7	1·3	0·7	2·0
1965	3·3	0·5	1·0	1·5
1966	1·7	−0·1	0·8	0·8
1967	1·8	−0·1	−0·02	−0·1
1968	3·3	0·3	2·5	2·8

Sources: *National Income and Expenditure 1968* (H.M.S.O.), *Monthly Digest of Statistics, March 1969* (H.M.S.O.).

upswings both private fixed investment and consumer durables expenditure played leading roles in the expansion of activity, whereas between 1967Q3–1969Q3 durable expenditure fell, even though output was rising, and private investment expenditure increased at a slower than average rate. Exports, on the other hand, grew very strongly while public investment fell sharply. Not only did the upswing of

GROSS DOMESTIC PRODUCT AND COMPONENTS OF FINAL EXPENDITURE

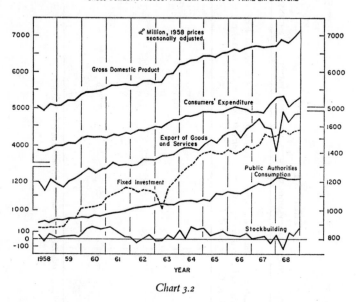

Chart 3.2

1967Q3–1969Q3 differ with respect to the components of expenditure but it also varied with respect to employment trends.

The trend in private fixed investment (excluding dwellings) is dominated by three distinct cycles which were, from peak to peak, first quarter 1957 to third quarter 1961; a second cycle from third quarter 1961 to first quarter 1966; and a third cycle beginning in the first quarter of 1966, which is incomplete. The average length of the investment cycle, as with GDP, is about four to five years, but both cycles have different turning-points and there is clear evidence that investment tends to follow changes in demand rather than to lead. The lag of investment behind demand is not asymmetrical, and is longer on the upswing (perhaps two quarters) than it is on the downswing of the cycle. One expects this kind of lag where some form of accelerator is functioning since, during the early stages of the cycle, firms will be able to meet rising sales from existing capacity. On the other hand, any slowing down in demand will lead to faster adjustment of investment expenditures, particularly since such slowdowns during the sixties have been caused primarily by Government restrictions which had a quick impact on sales and therefore on business expectations.

It is important to note also that the range of fluctuations of private investment, as a share of the change in GNP, has not been large during the last 10 years; from -0.3% of GNP in 1962 to $+1.3\%$ of GNP in 1964, and with an average range equal to 0.6% (neglecting sign). Clearly a private investment cycle has existed, with peaks in 1961/1962 and 1964/1965 although it is evident that as well as a lagged accelerator other, autonomous, forces have also been operating. This is true, for example, of investment in the steel industry, which reached a peak in 1961–1962—a peak where the 1961 level was more than double that of 1959—but was followed by a sequence of years in which investment remained below that of 1959. Again, investment in the motor industry has not been closely related to demand developments, and the big upsurge in investment during 1961–1963 ante-dated the boom in car sales of 1963/1964. In conclusion, it can be said that there may have been a pure investment cycle in which purely cyclical influences were at work, although clearly some of the fluctuation in investment has been caused by Government policy. In so far as the investment cycle continues to exist it presents the authorities with a stabilisation problem.

What of the other main potential source of instability, that of export demand? Fluctuations in export demand, primarily exogenously determined in the short-run, raise quite different problems for the authorities. Not only do such fluctuations have consequences for domestic employment (through the foreign trade multiplier) but they may have much more serious implications for the reserves. Demand fluctuations resulting from changes in overseas demand are much more difficult to foresee (given the very imperfect forecasting ability of the authorities in relation to exports) but is otherwise no more difficult conceptually to offset than other forms of expenditure. However, declines in export demand which lead to a worsening of the current account of the balance of payments, especially where this is already in deficit or only a small surplus, together with inadequate reserves, face the authorities with a very difficult choice. Reflation of domestic demand to offset the fall in overseas demand, will lead to further deterioration in the balance of payments through a rise in imports. This was exactly the dilemma facing the Government in 1967; falling export demand leading to rising unemployment from early on in the year faced the Chancellor with the unenviable choice of letting the unemployment continue to rise or reflating and taking a risk with the reserves (compounded with the fairly certain threat of speculative attacks). The result we all know. But the pattern of export development has not typically been so unfavourable as in 1967. Only in one other year (1958) in the last 15 years or so has there been an actual fall in the export of goods and services at constant prices. Further, the annual range of variation has been relatively slight (see *Table 3.1*) apart, that is, from 1968 and 1969, and in five of the years since 1960 has lain within the range of £150 million to £260 million. These annual comparisons no doubt hide more substantial fluctuations which are only apparent in the quarterly data, and it needs to be borne in mind that trends over a few months have been sufficient to severely weaken the foreign exchange position. For example, exports of goods and services, 1958 prices, fell hardly at all between 1967 and 1966 on an annual comparison, but were 14% *below* their fourth quarter 1966 level in the final quarter of 1967. Nevertheless, the annual fluctuations in exports have not been great (certainly nothing like the inter-war experience) and have not been a major source of instability. Some part of the cyclical downturn in GDP in 1961–1962 was due to autonomous developments in export markets (developments not foreseen by the authorities) and the same can be said of the recession during 1966–1967, although clearly the July measures of 1966 were intended to bring economic growth down to an annual rate of about 1.5%, but had superimposed on their effects a severe, unexpected, decline in export demand.

The following points need to be made at this stage. Some form of cycle has continued to operate during the fifties and the sixties, but it is a cycle significantly different from its pre-war relation. Not only is the amplitude of the cycle (in terms of output and unemployment) much reduced but it is also much shorter. A cycle with a peak to peak length of four to five years poses severe problems for the stabilisation authorities. In particular, it implies that measures which are taken in one phase of the cycle may be entirely inappropriate by the time they begin to have their impact on the economy; reflationary measures which operate with a time lag of only eighteen months or so may add substantially to reflationary forces already operating. It follows, therefore, that in the choice of policy weapons a definite understanding of the time-lags involved in their operation, including multiplier and accelerator effects, becomes of critical importance. It cannot be said that these considerations have had a sufficient weight in the formulation of economic policy in Britain during the post-war period. Inadequacies in this respect, plus the imperfect nature of economic forecasting, together with a natural preference on the part of Chancellors to wait and see, are to a large extent the explanation of the poor performance of economic policy during the sixties (as also during the fifties). We turn, in the next section, to a discussion of the lags involved in the operation of the main tax measures used by Governments in pursuit of their stabilisation aims.

THE ANALYSIS OF TAX CHANGES

The authorities have, for reasons which were noted earlier, relied primarily on tax changes as the main means of controlling the level of demand. This has led, within the Treasury, to the development of techniques for estimating the short-term effects (eighteen months to two years) of changes in taxation on the main national income components. The results of this research have been published in the *National Institute Economic Review** and an understanding of their techniques and an acquaintance with the results, are essential for any assessment of fiscal policy during the sixties.

It was found conceptually valuable to distinguish two main classes of tax effects—direct and indirect. In the first category would fall a reduction in income tax which led to a rise in disposable income and thus to an increase in personal consumption (although not necessarily proportional). The initial rise in consumption would raise output in the consumer goods industries and lead to the usual multiplier and accelerator effects. These would consist of a rise in incomes, due to the rise in output, and to further increases in spending, which again raises output. The higher level of output would lead to an increase in private fixed investment, as firms adjusted their actual stock of capital to a new higher desired level, and to an increase in the rate of stockbuilding. These effects are classified as indirect.

In what follows several examples are given of the direct effects of three different important tax measures; a change in income tax rates, a change in National Insurance benefits and contributions, and a change in the indirect tax regulator. The aim of the analysis is to isolate the ways in which such tax measures have their effect, having regard particularly to the timing of the change, any consequences for the distribution of income, the final effects on Government revenue, and, in the case of indirect taxes, the factors which determine the speed and size of consequential adjustment in prices. Only when the direct effects of each

---

* W. A. B. Hopkin and W. A. H. Godley, 'An Analysis of Tax Changes', *National Institute Economic Review*, No. 32 (May 1965); and J. R. Shepherd and M. J. Surrey, 'The Short-term Effects of Tax Changes', *Review*, No. 46 (Nov. 1968). The whole of this section draws very heavily on these two important articles.

measure have been separately estimated is it then possible to quantify the multiplier/accelerator effects. Since these indirect effects depend on general economic relationships (the propensity to consume, the investment function, the stocks/output equation, etc.) then it is a relatively simple matter, once these general relationships have been specified in a formal model, to calculate from any set of direct effects what will be the indirect (and therefore the total) effects on demand and output. The model can also be used to estimate the implications for the balance of trade and for the level of employment. Nor is its use confined to the analysis of tax measures alone; the model will also yield quarterly estimates of indirect effects for any set of direct effects whether they had their origin in tax measures or in other ways, e.g., as a result of change in hire-purchase regulations, an autonomous change in export demand or through variation in public expenditure programmes. The model is, therefore, very versatile and is used in the analysis of fiscal policy in the next chapter.

THE DIRECT EFFECT OF TAX CHANGES

A fairly accurate estimate can be made by the Inland Revenue of how a change in direct taxation will affect different income groups and what the timing of tax payments will be. The timing question is important since taxes are frequently paid well before the Exchequer actually receives them—in the case of PAYE payments there is an average delay of up to two months from the time tax is deducted and the time it is paid to the Exchequer. A change, therefore, in the standard rate of income tax (which would for administrative reasons only be made in the Budget) would mean altering PAYE codings. This takes time and there would thus be little change in tax payments in the first quarter of operation of the new rate, although this would be followed by compensating repayments in the next quarter. Having once allocated the effects of the tax between different income groups (wages and salaries, and other personal incomes) a consumption function has to be applied to each income group separately so as to take account of differing marginal propensities to save. This procedure yields the direct effects of the tax change (it entails assuming that the import content and indirect tax adjustment for each category of consumption is similar to that of consumption in total).

Obviously changes in direct taxes, which have the same effect on Government revenue, will have quite different demand effects. They will be larger for a change in reduced rates of income tax, or a reduction in personal allowances, than they would be for a change in the standard rate of income tax. This follows from the fact that the main beneficiaries of a reduction in the standard rate of income tax are the higher income groups. Their marginal propensity to save is undoubtedly higher than for other income groups (probably approaching 20%) and therefore the impact on consumer spending would be dampened. Similarly, a rise in the standard rate would have a smaller impact, and would be delayed, as the higher income groups drew on savings in order to maintain expenditure (the 'ratchet-effect' of Duesenberry). Shepherd and Surrey estimated that the revenue loss of a reduction in the standard rate of income tax by 6d. and in the two reduced rates by 3d. in the pound, on the assumption that the change occurred in April 1968, would be £215 million. But the *direct* real demand effects (GDP at factor cost) are significantly less than the revenue effects and are equal to £92 million in the first year and £116 million in the second year. The example also produces an odd quarterly path, because of the timing of PAYE payments, although some anticipatory expenditure in the first quarter after the change is included. It's worth noting that some 80% of the direct effects comes through in the first year of operation of the new rate, although this is equivalent to only two-thirds of the *total* effect on demand (direct effects plus multiplier/accelerator effects.)*

Some part of a reduction in the standard rate of income tax, in the period prior to the introduction of corporation tax (in the Budget of 1965), would have been received by companies. This measure would probably have led, with a lag, to both higher dividend distributions and to higher fixed investment. The time lags would have been very long (especially for fixed investment) and dividend distributions would only build up into something substantial in the second year after such a change. Furthermore, any rise in dividend distributions would have had a damped effect on demand since they are received primarily by income groups with high marginal propensities to save (estimated by Shepherd and Surrey at almost 30%).

The 1965 reform in corporate taxation was aimed primarily (at least in its domestic effects) at providing companies with a greater incentive to retain a large proportion of their profits in the belief that this would raise the level of investment.† The rate was set at 40%, in order to maintain the yield unchanged, and this appears to have been sufficient

* J. R. Shepherd and M. J. Surrey, *National Institute Economic Review*, Table 2, p. 39 (Nov. 1968).

† 'It gives a strong incentive to all companies to plough-back more of their profits for expansion' (Budget Statement, *Hansard*, 6 April 1965, col. 255). For a perceptive analysis of the change see, 'The 1965 Reforms in the British Tax System', *Moorgate and Wall St.* (Autumn 1965). For a more recent analysis see *Britain's Economic Prospects*, Brookings Institute: Allen and Unwin, pp. 55-63 (1968).

to achieve the objective of reducing the tax burden on retained profits while raising the tax on distributions. The reform also altered the timing of tax payments, which now became payable nine months after the end of the accounting period instead of with a twenty-one months lag as under the old system. Nevertheless, Professor Sayers has been led to comment that 'the lags in payment will remain substantial and potentially destabilising'.* Only two changes in the corporate rate have occurred since its introduction and included an increase to 42·5 % in November 1967 as part of the post-devaluation package. The new rate became effective in fiscal year 1967–1968, and the decision to raise the rate was clearly determined by incomes policy considerations rather than to meet the needs of demand management.† The authorities are well aware of the disadvantages of changes in the level of corporate taxation as a fine-tuning measure, and this particular change probably had only minor effects on demand. (It may have had some impact on consumer expenditure, through higher prices, and may also have raised companies' resistance to wage claims; but in the post-devaluation environment both these effects were understandably weak.)

While substantial lags remain in the collection of corporate taxes there are no such lags in the effect on personal incomes of a change in employees' National Insurance contributions. But this does not hold for a change in employers' payments which is usually simultaneous with a change in employees' contributions. Indeed, the analysis of the impact of employers' contributions on demand is closer to the analysis of a change in indirect than of direct taxation. An increase in National Insurance contributions by employers will be treated as a rise in wage costs to be shifted forward into final prices. (In certain circumstances it might be shifted backwards on to labour, through a slower rise in wages than might otherwise have occurred.) There will, however, be a time-lag between a change in wage costs and a change in retail prices so that most of the price effect probably does not come through until the second or third quarters after a change in contributions. Further, probably only about half of the effect of any change in employers' contributions will work through into consumer prices and the other half will

* R. S. Sayers, 'The Timing of Tax Payments by Companies', *The Three Banks Review* (Sept. 1967), pp. 26–27. Further progress, according to Sayers, is required in reducing the collection lag.

† The devaluation was expected to lead to some redistribution of income in favour of profits and the authorities, concerned to maintain the competitive advantage provided by the devaluation, had both to impress the unions that they were tackling this problem while still holding that 'an increase in profits—particularly from the somewhat depressed level at which they have been running in the past eighteen months—is in many ways desirable' (Budget Statement, *Hansard*, 19 March 1968, col. 297).

have only a slight effect in reducing demand. This is because neither Government nor purchasers of investment goods will be likely to change their expenditure much on account of a small rise in prices.

This has important implications for assessing the demand effects of an increase in National Insurance contributions on the one hand and increases in benefits on the other. Because contributions are raised by the same amount as benefits does not lead to neutral effects on demand. Increased benefits will generate spending immediately. But higher employers' contributions will have a delayed effect on raising prices and half the eventual price increase (that on goods not entering personal consumption) will have only limited effects in holding back demand. The coefficients suggested by Hopkin and Godley are that spending will be raised by 90% of the rise in benefits (this is probably too low) reduced by 85% of the rise in employees' contributions, and further reduced by an amount rising to 80% of half the rise in employers' contributions. In their example an increase in benefits of £300 million (at 1965 first quarter prices), exactly offset by employees' contributions of £175 million and by employers' of £125 million, will substantially increase real demand, building up (with multiplier and accelerator effects) to £185 million a year at factor cost.*

Turning finally to the demand effects of direct taxes on wealth, such as death duties, these can essentially be analysed in the same way as income tax adjustments. Estimates can be made of how much additional revenue will be brought in and how this will be shared out between different sized estates. With a tax of this kind the revenue effect may be substantial, while the impact on consumers' demand will undoubtedly be slight. One recent example of a tax change in this category is the tax announced by the Chancellor in the 1968 Budget. This was a special charge on investment income, which fell only on the highest ranges of income, and for one year only. The full year effect on the Revenue was approximately £100 million, although the savings offset was expected to be as high as 75%.†

The analysis of indirect tax effects is much more complex. This follows from the fact that indirect taxes are not levied on the person whose spending is likely to be affected. There are two main problems.

* Hopkin and Godley, *National Institute Economic Review*, Table 9, p. 42 (May 1965).

† In the words of the Chancellor, 'There can be little doubt that, with fortunes producing really large investment incomes, expenditure is determined much more by possession of capital than by the size of net-income. . . . I hope and believe that this special charge will lead to some reduction in consumption' (Budget Statement, *Hansard*, 19 March 1968, col. 300). The National Institute estimated the consumption effects in the four quarters from April 1968 at a fall of only £14 million (*Review*, May 1968, Table 1, p. 5).

E

Firstly, how much of the tax will work its way through into prices, and how quickly. Secondly, by how much will real demand be affected by any change in prices. Of the goods subject to the main indirect taxes (see *Table 3.2*) about 80% are bought by consumers, 18% are intermediate goods bought by business, and about 1% is purchased by

Table 3.2

DISTRIBUTION OF MAIN INDIRECT TAXES IN 1968
(£ million)

	Private	Business	Government	Total
Drink	750	25	—	775
Tobacco	1 080	—	—	1 080
Hydrocarbon oils	635	410	35	1 080
Purchase tax	850	75	45	970
	3 315	510	80	3 905
%	(85)	(13)	(2)	100

Source: *National Income and Expenditure 1969*, Tables 26 and 38, H.M.S.O. There exists no official breakdown of the distribution of taxes between sectors, and the above distribution is based on estimates made by the author.

Government. According to Hopkin and Godley, a full application of the regulator, i.e., all these tax rates reduced by 10%, will show itself immediately in lower prices for about 90% of the goods bought by consumers, and almost all the rest will work through during the following twelve months. For the business sector a less complete and less immediate effect is to be expected. The tax changes on intermediate purchases will work through more slowly, and perhaps only about a half will come through on consumer goods (equal to the ratio of personal consumption to Total Final Expenditure). Of the rest there will be some consequent fall in investment goods' prices and some fall in the prices of goods and services bought by Government, but neither investment demand nor Government demand is likely to be price elastic.

Within the consumer field the effect of the price fall on demand will depend on the price elasticity of demand for the good. It will also vary, in its effect on demand for real resources, according to the extent to which the good is already taxed. This is especially important for goods such as tobacco and drink which are heavily taxed. For example, a tax reduction of 10% on tobacco and drink would not lead to a rise in real incomes equal to 10% of expenditure on the two goods, and to an equivalent increase in demand for output and imports. The rise in demand for real resources will be less than this, because the increase in demand will be disproportionately concentrated on drink and tobacco themselves which bear very high rates of tax. A relatively high proportion of the increase in demand will, therefore, be siphoned off, and only a relatively small proportion of demand will generate domestic output and imports. The effect, therefore, of applying the regulator to the full extent (in 1965) would have been to raise expenditure at market prices by £244 million per annum, but by only £164 million at constant factor cost, and with the full direct effect coming through with a considerable time-lag (due to the fact that the change in the tax on intermediate purchases will not raise final prices immediately).*

INDIRECT EFFECTS OF TAX CHANGES

The secondary multiplier/accelerator effects are a substantial part of the effects of tax changes on output and occur with entirely different timing. For example, a change in the standard rate of income tax in 1968 by 6d. in the £ and of 3d. in the reduced rates, has been estimated by Shepherd and Surrey as leading to an increase in GDP at factor cost of £208 million a year (second year effects), of which the direct effects are equal to only 56%. Of the total (indirect plus direct effects) only 66% comes through in the first year, compared with 80% for direct effects.

It is probably preferable, in dealing with the analysis of indirect effects, to distinguish the multiplier from the accelerator. The multiplier is the process whereby any increase in output generates additional consumer demand, and this can be thought of as occurring in four conceptually separate stages: (a) a change in employment, (b) a change in the average level of earnings, (c) changes in profits and thus in non-wage personal incomes, and (d) the consequent change in personal consumption.

It is well known, and there has now been considerable research into, the lags in the adjustment of employment to changes in output. In the short-term the adjustment of employment is less than proportional to the change in output and employment takes longer to adjust fully to a rapid rise in output (as in 1959–1960 or 1963–1964) than to a moderate rise or fall. It is necessary, therefore, in estimating the output effects on employment to adjust the model to take account of the rate at which

* Hopkin and Godley, *National Institute Economic Review*, May 1965, Table 8, p. 42. Only some 60% of the direct effect comes through in the four quarters following the change in the regulator, and the time-lag when secondary effects are included is even longer (a 40% rise in total demand, at factor cost, in the first year). Changes in indirect taxation will affect savings as well as spending. By how much will depend on the precise goods on which taxes have been reduced; if luxury goods then a large part of the price effect will go into increased savings. If they are articles of mass consumption, e.g., beer or tobacco, then the savings effect will be much smaller.

output is expanding. Changes in output, as well as leading to adjustment of employment, also give rise to changes in average hours worked and, perhaps, to modification of piecework earnings. Regression analysis, undertaken within the Treasury, suggests that a 1 % change in output results in about 0·33 % change in the average level of wages and salary earnings. This, plus an estimate of the effect of output changes on employment, yields an estimate of the effect on income of any change in output.

However, the change in GDP will also have some effect on non-employment incomes, i.e., profit incomes. Some of the change in profit incomes will be retained by companies and public corporations and not be distributed. Nevertheless, on the basis of past experience it is possible to estimate what proportion of profit incomes will be allocated to dividends and also how self-employment income will react to changes in output. This process provides estimates of the income effects of the change in output, which then have to be adjusted to take account of income tax payments. To the resulting series on personal disposable income a consumption function is applied so as to get figures of personal expenditure on the assumption that changes in wage incomes have a faster and bigger effect on consumption expenditures (the marginal propensity to consume out of wage income is estimated at 90 %, while the propensity is put as low as 73 % for profit incomes, in both cases at the end of a year).

A combination of the above relationships allows the complete multiplier effects to be estimated. This is done in *Table 3.3*. It shows the estimated effect on consumption of a sustained stimulus to gross domestic product of £100 million a quarter as a result of tax changes. These build up to £42 million a quarter by the fifth quarter after the change, and in the first year amount to £125 million.

In addition to the multiplier there are also accelerator effects and these need to be included in the complete model of indirect effects. The accelerator is a familiar economic concept which has had considerable fascination for economists because of its relative simplicity as an explanation of investment* and in its usual form is expressed as a relationship, not necessarily rigid, between the rate of change of output and expenditure on assets—including expenditure on fixed assets and on stocks. Any rise in investment causes further increases in output, incomes and expenditure through the familiar income multiplier.

There is considerable evidence that the most important factor determining the rate of stockbuilding is change in the level of output, or

* This and other theories of investment are given more detailed analysis in Chapter 7 in the section on *The Determinants of Investment*.

Table 3.3

MULTIPLIER EFFECTS ASSOCIATED WITH A SUSTAINED INCREASE OF £100 MILLION A
QUARTER IN GROSS DOMESTIC PRODUCT
(£ million)

	I	II	III	IV	V	VI
Personal income from employment						
Via employment	14	23	26	27	28	29
Via average earnings	20	20	20	20	20	20
Total	34	43	46	47	48	49
Other personal income	15	17	19	21	23	25
Total personal income	49	60	65	68	71	74
Less tax	−16	−19	−21	−22	−23	−24
Personal disposable income	33	41	44	46	48	50
Personal consumption	20	30	36	39	42	42

Source: *National Institute Economic Reveiw*, No. 46, p. 39 (Nov. 1968).

more precisely, the gap between the actual level of stocks and the level required for a normal relationship between stocks and output. Any sharp rise in demand, perhaps associated with a reduction in taxation which has not been fully anticipated by firms, leads initially to a reduction in inventories so that output levels have to be adjusted to meet both higher current sales and also to restore the normal stocks/output ratio. However, for fixed investment a formal, unvarying, accelerator relationship is less satisfactory, although in a broad sense investment is related to changes in the rate of growth of output. Furthermore, the full adjustment of investment to output probably takes several years and the Treasury model, which incorporates a simple accelerator model, can be criticised in its formulation of the investment function. A number of other equations are included in the model including one expressing a relationship between exports and the domestic pressure of demand, although no significant effects on GDP are expected from any adverse effects on exports of increases in domestic demand pressure. Other equations permit the imports associated with the *indirect* expenditure changes to be estimated, and for these expenditures to be expressed at factor cost.★

It is immediately apparent, from *Table 3.3* and from the example

★ The full model for estimating indirect effects is set out as an Appendix to the article by Shepherd and Lurney in the *National Institute Economic Review* (Nov. 1968), page 41.

given on page 55, how significant are these indirect multiplier/accelerator effects in relation to the total effect on output, and failure to take full account of these can lead to serious policy error. The full magnitude of the GDP multiplier is more easily seen in the following Chart which represents the effects of a reduction in both the standard rate of income tax and of the reduced rates of tax.

Appendix: Chart 1

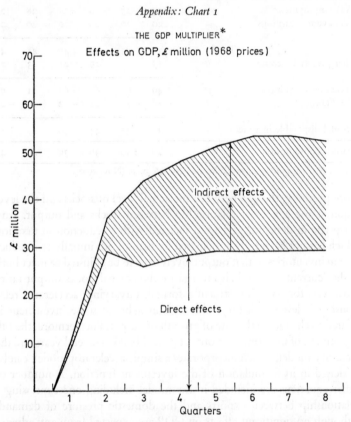

THE GDP MULTIPLIER*

Effects on GDP, £ million (1968 prices)

* Direct and indirect effects of hypothetical reductions of 6d in the standard and 3d in the reduced rates of income tax, financial year 1968/69. Source: *National Institute Economic Review*, Table 2, p. 39 (Nov. 1968).

The scale of the indirect effects (multiplier only) can be illustrated by the income tax changes introduced in the 1970 (April) Budget. The Chancellor (Mr. Jenkins) raised personal income tax allowances and abolished the reduced rates of tax. For 1970–1971 the tax changes were estimated to reduce revenue by £147 million, and for a full year by

£185 million. These tax changes, together with easier monetary policy, were intended to provide a certain amount of stimulus for the economy (to raise the rate of growth in output between the first half of 1970 and the first half of 1971 to 3·5%, compared with an increase of 3% without the measures). Once again timing is important; the reflationary effects of the income tax measures did not begin to operate until the second half of 1970 when they appear to have added about 0·33% to real GDP growth. The full year tax changes were equivalent to a rise in real personal disposable income (1963 prices) of about £130 million. Assuming a marginal propensity to consume of 0·9 (at the end of the year) leads to a first round increase in expenditure of about £115 million. With a multiplier of 1·41 the total increase in consumers expenditure (excluding accelerator effects) is approximately £160 million. The indirect effects, in this example, are equal to about a third of the total (direct plus indirect) effects.

4

THE STABILISATION RECORD OF
FISCAL POLICY, 1960–1969

To be able to judge whether budgetary policy has been stabilising or de-stabilising during the sixties one needs to know what the alternative position would have been in the absence of policy changes. This we do not know, and while we do have recorded data on the economy which indicate that growth has been far from smooth—periods of rapid growth followed by periods of stagnation—this in itself is not proof of the failure of contra-cyclical policy. Such cycles of economic activity, perhaps even more intense, might have occurred even in the absence of stabilisation policy.

Discretionary tax changes between 1959–1969 are summarised in *Table 4.1*, where yields on a full-year liabilities basis are estimated (collections, of course, lag behind liabilities). Reductions in taxes occurred in five of the eleven years, with the cuts in 1959 and 1963 exceptionally large, equal to 1·4% and 1·7% of GDP respectively. The very substantial increases in taxation in 1965 and 1968 stand out in the table, and most of the years when taxes were increased on any scale were ones of balance of payments difficulties. One striking trend during these years was the increasing reliance, particularly since 1965, on taxes falling on expenditure. These increased from 14·9% of GNP at factor cost in 1958 to 19% in 1968.

One way of measuring the fiscal impact of the public sector is through weighting various categories of expenditure and different types of receipts so as to take account of their real effect on output. Such a calculation is necessary in order to derive the multiplicand of the

Table 4.1

DISCRETIONARY CHANGES IN CENTRAL GOVERNMENT TAXES, UNITED KINGDOM, 1959–1969*

(£ million and %)

Year	(1) Taxes on personal income and capital	(2) Taxes on company profit	(3) Taxes on expenditure	(4) Total taxes	(5) Total taxes as % of GDP
1959	−122	−63	−112	−297	−1·4
1960	−56	31	−10	−36	−0·2
1961	−79	71	70	62	0·3
1962	−28	18	31	21	0·1
1963	−223	−184	−36	−443	−1·7
1964	−60	−51	95	−16	−0·1
1965	66	69	341	475	1·6
1966	—	—	293	293	0·9
1967	−4	—	−10	−14	−0·04
1968	233	98	592	923	2·6
1969	−9	105	249	345	0·9

Sources: Musgrave, *Brookings Study*, Tables 1–5, 1959–1966; and *Financial Statements* (H.M.S.O.) for recent years.

* Full-year tax changes calculated from annual budgets plus supplementary budget for 1964.

Table 4.2

THE WEIGHTED BUDGET DEFICIT

(£ million)

	Current Prices					1968/1969 prices
	1964/1965	1965/1966	1966/1967	1967/1968	1968/1969	1969/1970
1. Weighted expenditures*	9 367	10 419	11 436	12 794	13 695	14 217
2. Weighted receipts†	6 045	6 910	7 588	8 286	9 378	10 156
3. Weighted budget deficit	3 322	3 509	3 848	4 508	4 317	4 061
4. Change in weighted expenditures		1 052	1 017	1 358	901	522
5. Change in weighted receipts		865	678	698	1 110	778
6. Change in weighted budget deficit‡		+187	+339	+660	−209	−256
7. Weighted discretionary tax receipts	81	220	167	9	288	134
8. Other tax receipts (weighted)	5 964	6 609	7 120	7 809	8 613	9 257
9. GDP	29 488	31 352	33 102	34 794	36 535	37 631
Ratios						
10. Row 3 as % of GDP	11·3	11·2	11·6	13·0	11·8	10·8
11. Row 6 as % of GDP		+0·6	+1·0	+1·9	−0·6	−0·7
12. Row 6 as % of GDP (including multiplier effects)		+0·8	+1·4	+2·7	−0·8	−1·0

Source: *National Institute Economic Review*, No. 51, Tables 7 and 8 of ch. 3 (Feb. 1970).

* Weights are applied to estimate the domestic output content of expenditures (i.e., net of import and savings leakages) as follows: public authorities' current expenditure on goods and services, 95%; public authorities' fixed capital formation, 85%; current grants, 81%; subsidies, 76%; debt interest, 44%. (Expenditures and receipts of public corporations excluded.)

† Weights applied to receipts allow for savings offsets of 10% overall for taxes, 15% for local authority income (rent, dividends and net interest), and 40% for central government net dividends and interest.

‡ + denotes increase in weighted budget deficit.

Musgrave 'leverage' concept.* *Table 4.2* presents estimates, made by the National Institute, of the public sector's weighted budget deficit for the financial years 1964/1965 to 1969/1970 and includes estimates of weighted discretionary tax receipts. A number of important conclusions can be drawn from these estimates.

Firstly, throughout these years the public sector had a weighted budget deficit that was very substantial, with an annual range of 10·8 % to 13·0 % of GDP. Secondly, as is clear from a comparison of rows 4 and 5 of the table, increases in weighted tax receipts were swamped in the years 1964/1965 to 1967/1968 by increases in weighted expenditure. As a result the public sector, measured by the change in the weighted budget deficit, imparted substantial expansionary effects between 1964/1965 and 1967/1968 which, including multiplier effects, ranged from 0·8 % to 2·7 % of GDP. Thirdly, the financial year 1968/1969 marks a decisive break and amounts to a reversal of the previous expansionary impact of the public sector. This was continued in 1969/1970, and this turn-round in the position of the public sector was in both years associated with large increases in discretionary taxation. Finally, discretionary changes in taxation in the five years prior to 1969/1970 accounted for some 10 % of the total tax 'drag' on output.

Table 4.3 gives estimates, made by Mr. M. J. Surrey of the National

Table 4.3

RATES OF GROWTH OF GDP, % PER ANNUM

Period	Length (years)	Recorded	No measures
1955–1958/1959*	3·5	0·8	0·7
1958/1959*–1960	1·75	5·6	4·8
1960–1962/1963†	2·5	1·9	2·5
1962/1963†–1965/1966‡	3	4·2	4·3
1965/1966‡–1967§	1·5	1·5	2·5

* 1958Q2–1959Q1.   † 1962Q3–1963Q2.   ‡ 1965Q3–1966Q2.   § 1967Q4.

Institute and using the techniques outlined in *The Analysis of Tax Changes* in the previous chapter, of the full effects of discretionary tax

* The 'leverage' concept is defined as L = K (w₁E − w₂R) where K equals the multiplier, E and R are actual Government expenditures and receipts, and w_1 and w_2 are relevant weights (see footnote to *Table 4.2*). In deriving the estimates of the multiplier effects of the change in the weighted budget deficit a K of 1·41 has been assumed. See R. A. Musgrave and P. B. Musgrave, 'Fiscal Policy', in *Britain's Economic Prospects* (Brookings Institute: Allen and Unwin, 1968) for a discussion of the leverage concept, and for the derivation of the multiplier see M. C. Kennedy, 'How Well Does the National Institute Forecast?' *National Institute Economic Review*, 50 (Nov. 1969), Appendix 1.

changes on personal expenditure during the sixties compared with a 'no measures' case.* This is, as noted above, a doubtful practice since we cannot know what would have happened if the Government had followed a neutral policy or had not acted at all. Such an outcome is, of course, an illusion and Governments cannot pursue purely neutral policies no matter how defined. For example, there can be no certainty that the economy would have expanded in a satisfactory way in 1963 if the Budget had not cut tax rates—although the balance of the evidence suggests it would have done so. Again, Government influences private investment not only through Budgetary measures but also through the commitment to full employment, and this in itself limits the response of private investment to particular measures.

Nevertheless, in spite of the deficiencies of the procedure followed here, *Table 4.3* does throw up some interesting observations about the stabilising impact of Budgetary policy. In the first place discretionary tax changes operated in a weak anticyclical manner in 1962/1963–1965/ 1966 and were significantly pro-cyclical in 1958/1959–1960, 1960–1962/ 1963 and 1966–1967. With the caveat noted above about the alternative position it is clear that in general budgetary policy over the period as a whole has been destabilising, in the sense that growth would have proceeded more smoothly in the absence of discretionary tax changes. A conclusion which confirms the results of earlier studies of British fiscal policy over this period.† However, the caveat is an important one, and we return to it in the final section of this chapter after a more detailed analysis of budgetary policy during the sixties.

* These estimates exclude the effects of changes in corporate taxation, hire-purchase controls and of public expenditure variation. This is not perhaps so unreasonable in that corporate taxation has not been primarily used as a short-term stabilisation measure, neither has public expenditure, although hire-purchase controls have been important in this respect. On the other hand, hire-purchase controls have generally been used in sympathy with tax changes and while of importance (see Chapter 7) probably don't change the picture all that significantly.

† See Musgrave in *Britain's Economic Prospects*, Brookings Institute: Allen and Unwin (1968), pp. 42–44, and Bent Hansen, *Fiscal Policy in Seven Countries, 1955–1965*, O.E.C.D. (1969), pp. 443–447. Dow concluded 'that variations of fiscal policy were in fact not stabilising, but rather themselves one of the main causes of instability; and that demand would have remained much more nearly in balance with supply if fiscal policy had, throughout the period [1950–1960], been less actively interventionist'. He held out the hope that 'some of the lessons of these mistakes have since been learnt', but developments during the sixties prove this to have been premature.

1958–1962

That the reflation of 1959 April was excessive has been noted by many commentators, and, while it cannot be proved, it seems very probable that even without the measures demand would have grown at a rate in excess of 4% between 1958/1959 and 1960. Trends at work in the economy argued, if not for deflationary measures, at least for prudence in the implementation of economic policy. In particular the position on external account remained weak, since the 1958 surplus was due not to any shift in import or export propensities but to a fall in world commodity prices. By the last quarter of 1959 real GDP was more than 6% above its level a year earlier, while the capacity/output index even before the close of 1959 suggests that pressure in labour markets was excessive.

As we have already seen the official forecasts for 1960 were reasonably accurate in their estimate of domestic demand developments, although wrong in their assessment of external trends, and this led the Chancellor to conclude 'that the prospective increase in demand . . . is likely at least fully to absorb, and might even involve a danger of outrunning, the increase in production which can be expected'.* Nevertheless, the Budget was virtually a 'no-change' one and the task of slowing down the economy was left to monetary measures of which hire-purchase restrictions were the most important. At the same time public expenditure continued to rise rapidly so that the fiscal leverage of the public sector was equal to 2·3 % of GDP in 1960.† The result was an increase in the pressure of domestic demand and a massive deterioration in the balance of payments. In retrospect it is clear that the stance of budgetary policy during 1960 was inappropriate, that increases in discretionary taxation should have come before July 1961, and that far too much weight was thrown on monetary weapons.

Domestic demand pressures continued to increase during the early months of 1961 and the balance of payments remained in deficit. However, the new Chancellor (Mr. Selwyn Lloyd) while recognising the dangers of cost/price inflation together with an unsatisfactory balance of payments position introduced a budget which was only mildly deflationary. The motor vehicle licence and the tax on hydrocarbon oils were raised together with an increase of 2·5 % in the company profits tax. The only other tax change of note was the raising of the

---

* Budget Statement, *Hansard*, 4 April 1960, col. 45.

† Musgrave in *Britain's Economic Prospects*, Brookings Institute: Allen and Unwin, Table 1.6 (1968).

surtax level, but both this change and the increase in company profits tax probably had negligible effects on demand in 1961, although there may have been some effect on company investment in the year following. The Budget did relatively little, therefore, to restrain the expansion of the economy, the pressure in labour markets remained excessive with personal disposable incomes continuing to rise at a very rapid rate (in the quarter following the budget at an annual rate of 9 %) and with the foreign exchange reserves continuously falling.

The failure to take realistic tax measures in the Budget, and with public expenditures rising at a rapid rate, clearly contributed to the sterling crisis of July and to the mini-budget of that month. The measures taken then, which included the full use of the regulator, produced a general slackening of demand from the third quarter which deepened in intensity during 1962 reaching its bottom in the early months of 1963. Overall the effects of the tax measures in the April and July budgets may have been to reduce the rate of increase in GDP by some 0·75 % per annum, with some part at least of the deflationary effects of the taxes occurring during 1962 when the economy was no longer suffering from an excess pressure of demand. Clearly the strategy of the April Budget, to make room for export growth, was not successful, and indeed it made very little room available, since rising Government expenditures continued to swamp the tax increases taken then. Once again the timing of the fiscal measures was poor and corrective action came about solely as a response to the sterling crisis.

The budgetary strategy of 1962 was seriously misled as a result of the poor economic forecast on which it was based (see pages 19–21). This led the Chancellor to believe that 'the increase in home demand over the next twelve months looks like being substantial. Since it is so necessary to keep the way clear for the growth of exports, this must be carefully watched. By the end of 1962—and there is no good our trying to avoid this possibility—the cumulative effect of all the factors I have mentioned could result in too great a call on our resources if we do not keep the balance right.'* In the event, therefore, in spite of the fact that unemployment in February was some 85 000 higher than it had been a year earlier and was still rising, the Chancellor made no attempt to reflate the economy through discretionary tax changes (the tax adjustments were minor and had little effect on demand). This failure to reflate in April 1962 proved critical and is difficult, with the advantage of hindsight, to understand. It must have been perfectly obvious to the Chancellor and his advisors that if they were to prevent unemployment from rising to undesirable levels that reflationary action had to be

* Budget Statement of Mr. Selwyn Lloyd, *Hansard*, 9 April 1962, col. 965.

taken early. This follows from the lags in the impact on demand of fiscal measures which are, as was suggested in *The Analysis of Tax Changes*, fairly long, together with the lag in the adjustment of equilibrium employment to rising output. By the middle of 1962 the case for stimulating demand was very strong, but all the authorities did was to relax various monetary measures and to promise the accelerated repayment of post-war credits. So that reflation finally came in the Budget of 1963.*

It is evident, therefore, that both the upswing of 1958/1960 and the downswing of 1960/1962 can be attributed largely to the effects of Government policy. If the 1959 Budget had not happened there would probably have been no need at all to deflate in the following three or four years. In a very real sense Government policy during this period can be classified as destabilising. Export demand was certainly not as buoyant as in some earlier years, but was in no way as depressing a factor as in 1958. While the drop in private investment was a more significant factor during the recession, this itself was almost certainly in part the result of the restrictive monetary and fiscal policies introduced by the Government from 1960, particularly the tightening of hire-purchase controls. Restrictionary fiscal policy measures were not taken early enough to restrain the boom of 1959, and ought to have been introduced in the 1960 Budget which was, as noted above, virtually a no-change one. Similarly, reflation ought to have been the main aim of the April 1962 Budget, but once again fiscal policy took the wrong stance. The inevitable result for the economy was a miserable growth performance, entailing an unnecessary waste of resources during the whole period of the recession. Between the first quarter of 1961 and the first quarter of 1963 seasonally adjusted real GDP rose by only 1·25%, while unemployment reached a peak of 3·29% in the first quarter of 1963. Only partial indicators of policy failure, but sufficient in themselves to indicate the orders of magnitude involved.

1963–1966

At the time of the preparation of the Budget in 1963 the authorities were well aware that the economy had already begun to expand and

---

* From May the National Institute had been pressing for some reflation, although it recognised that the problem remained of how to set the economy on a steady growth path without threatening external stability in a situation where the exchange rate was considered sacrosanct. What it did warn specifically against was 'a spurt of demand like that given in 1958–1959, which was heavily concentrated on durables. . . .' (*National Institute Economic Review*, Aug. 1962, p. 12). What a pity Mr. Maudling did not heed this warning.

that even with a no-change Budget demand could reasonably be expected to grow in line with productive potential. The upswing in demand had already begun in the third quarter of 1962 and in the fourth quarter personal expenditure on durable goods rose by 13 % in real terms (seasonally adjusted) compared with the previous quarter. Most of this increase in expenditure was concentrated on motor vehicles which rose by no less than 32 % and can be attributed directly to the purchase tax reductions introduced in November, although part of the recovery must have been due to the wearing-off of the hire-purchase controls. It was also fully anticipated that a boost to personal consumption would take place from the second quarter of 1963 as a result of the rise in National Insurance benefits. Other factors were also at work to bring about a revival of growth; private fixed investment reached the bottom of its cycle about the turn of the year and some recovery was foreseen by the Treasury, while a large programme of public investment had been deliberately set in train and had simply been delayed by the severe winter of 1963. Furthermore, export demand had begun to expand, at an annual rate of some 9 % in the first quarter of 1963.

The point which the foregoing is intended to emphasise is that Mr. Maudling had, broadly speaking, correctly interpreted the trends at work in the economy but still concluded in his 1963 Budget 'that tax concessions in the current year of the order of about £250 million are required to stimulate the economy if we are to realise our target of vigorous expansion without inflation.'* In the pursuit of this aim the Chancellor introduced measures aimed at increasing private investment and personal consumption. An improvement in investment allowances had already been announced by the Chancellor in November, and these were expected by the authorities to lead to a substantial rise in investment towards the end of 1963 and in later years. This turned out to be the case, with the recovery in private investment coming in the final quarter of 1963 but with the large expansion of capacity taking place in 1964 and with investment remaining at a high level until the first quarter of 1966.

However, most of the tax concessions in the Budget were concentrated on individuals and involved changes in allowances and in the reduced rates of tax. As the Chancellor observed: 'While, in most cases, the benefits in absolute terms will be highest at the highest levels of income, which is both inevitable and just with any reduction in direct taxation, proportionately the benefits that I propose will be greatest in the lower ranges of income.'† Of the tax remissions 42 %

* Budget Statement, *Hansard*, 3 April 1963, col. 472.
† Budget Statement, *Hansard*, 3 April 1963, col. 493.

were expected to accrue to those earning less than £1000 a year. The Chancellor deliberately chose to introduce changes in direct taxation which would have the biggest impact on demand because of the high marginal propensity to consume of the recipients, and where the direct demand effects could be expected to come through relatively quickly.

The aim of the tax concessions was twofold. Firstly, to put the economy on the 4 % growth path recommended by the N.E.D.C.; and, secondly, to contribute to the long-term solution of the balance of payments. The tax concessions in the Budget were very substantial, particularly so in the light of the demand trends already at work in the economy. Clearly a large part of the full effects of the personal tax reductions came through during 1963 and added to the factors (higher National Insurance benefits, reductions in purchase tax and the easing of bank liquidity) raising consumers' expenditure. As a result of the recovery of private investment, the sharp pick-up in public investment and growth in exports, the economy rapidly expanded. By the fourth quarter of 1963 GDP in real terms was already almost 8 % above its level a year earlier, and demand was rising dangerously fast. (It increased at an annual rate of 16 % between the third and final quarters of 1963.) As measured by the Capacity/Output index an excess pressure of demand was already present by the fourth quarter. A rate of expansion of this order, with only part of the effects of the Budgetary measures coming through and on top of autonomous growth forces already present, was clearly excessive by any standards and led inevitably to a deteriorating internal and external situation.

These developments were not lost on the Chancellor when he presented his Budget for 1964 and his Budget strategy was based on the assumption that 'our current rate of expansion is one that cannot continue indefinitely without leading to the familiar difficulties internally and externally. . . . The best judgement I can make is that if taxation is increased in this Budget by the equivalent of £100 million . . . I should be doing enough to steady the economy without going so far as to give a definite check to expansion.'* It is strange in retrospect (as it was at the time to the National Institute) that the Chancellor while holding out prospects for a vigorous growth in demand, should have thought that tax increases of this order, to be achieved through a 10 % rise in the duties on tobacco and alcohol, should have been enough. Both private and public investment was booming; public current expenditure was rising rapidly, and a substantial part of the effect on demand of the 1963 Budget was still to come through. By the final quarter of 1963 the pressure in labour markets had become excessive, and given the lags

* Budget Statement, *Hansard*, 14 April 1964, cols. 268–269.

F

in the employment/output relationship, would tighten further during 1964 even if strong Budgetary policy had been the order of the day.

What had the Chancellor achieved? The economy had expanded very fast indeed during 1963, but at an unsustainable rate. To a large extent this was due to economic policy, and the Budget of 1963 had added excessively to the demand trends already present in the economy through direct tax reductions and through public expenditure expansion. Largely because 1964 was an election year the Chancellor, in spite of broadly accurate economic forecasts (see pages 23–24), did relatively little to dampen the boom. Monetary policy was rendered relatively ineffective by the need to finance a sharply rising negative net borrowing requirement, while little could be quickly done to restrain the boom in private and public investment without substantial costs. At the same time the Chancellor had reduced the effectiveness of the regulator by raising duties on tobacco and alcohol in the Budget, which made it difficult to raise these taxes again. In effect, he had compromised the use of the regulator and its full use on the remaining indirect taxes would have raised only £100 million. At the same time the failure to reduce the pressure of demand by Budgetary action necessarily entailed a reduction in the effectiveness of the new policies, aimed at providing the balance of payments with direct assistance, which were being investigated within the Treasury during 1964 in preparation for the massive external deficit forecast for the year. As the National Institute so correctly observed in May: 'The country is now committed to running risks for the sake of quick expansion, with only a modest range of ready instruments in reserve for the short-run regulation of demand. The risk taken in this year's Budget is the risk of having to take uncomfortably severe action at some future date, and of having to endure another period of comparative stagnation in order to ease the pressure of demand.'* How right they were.

Unfortunately the new Socialist Government in October was hardly any more realistic in its assessment of the economic situation than Mr. Maudling had been. While accepting that the balance of payments called for new direct policies—the Temporary Import Charge (T.I.C.) and the Export Rebate—they nevertheless found that 'there is no undue pressure on resources calling for action. Moreover, the Government reject any policy based on a return to stop-go economics.† They were not permitted the luxury of these views for long, and the pressures of

---

* *National Institute Economic Review*, p. 15 (May 1964).

† *The Economic Situation*, para. 7, p. 2 (Statement by H.M. Government, 26 Oct. 1964).

the external situation soon led, on the 11th of November, to what appeared, at first sight, a more realistic set of measures.

The November Budget included an increase in the duty on petrol effective immediately; an increase in the standard rate of income tax effective April 1965; a new corporation tax to come into operation in April 1965 and increases in National Insurance benefits and contributions effective end of March 1965. The way in which these measures have their impact on demand was discussed in the previous chapter, and the National Institute using these techniques estimated in November 1964 that the direct plus multiplier effects of the *total* package (i.e., including the T.I.C.), would be to *add* to the pressure of domestic demand and lead to a faster rate of increase in consumer prices in 1965. Excluding the T.I.C. the package was neither significantly inflationary nor deflationary in its impact on demand.

During the early months of 1965 it became clear to the authorities that the November measures were not producing any substantial degree of deflation. Incomes were rising rapidly; 'other personal income' in the first quarter was £100 million higher than in the previous quarter, mainly because of higher dividend payments. Personal consumption continued to rise, although at a slower rate than at the end of 1964, while unemployment fell further to the extremely low level of 1·3 %. The pressure of domestic demand remained very high, and this led Mr. Callaghan to the conclusion that the Budget must reduce the level of demand.* Substantial increases in taxation were imposed amounting to £164 million in 1965/1966, of which the main changes, apart from the introduction of corporation tax, were increases in indirect taxes plus higher motor vehicle licence fees. Shortly after the Budget the restraint on credit was re-inforced by a call for Special Deposits together with requests on bank lending to the private sector.

The indirect tax changes in the Budget perhaps reduced consumers' expenditure by about £60 million a quarter at 1958 prices. However, their impact was substantially less than this when adjustment to factor cost is made: i.e., the tax increases on drink and tobacco raised the CPI by slightly more than 1 % and consequently reduced consumers' expenditure by about £200 million a year. But a good deal of the drop in consumers' expenditure was on drink and tobacco itself, so that the reduction in demand for real resources, at 1958 factor cost, was much less than this, at about £160 million a year (£40 million a quarter). In effect, therefore, the tax increases in the Budget perhaps only reduced

---

* 'Taking the early months of next year as my reference, I have concluded that we must act so as to reduce home demand in that period by £250 million at an annual rate.' Budget Statement, *Hansard*, 6 April 1965, col. 287.

consumers' expenditure at constant prices and at factor cost by about £100 million in 1965. Since the effect of the November 1964 package was to raise the level of demand by some £25 million the *net* impact on demand of both the November and April Budgets was to reduce expenditure at factor cost by only some £60–£70 million in 1965.

This is quite different from the results one would expect from consideration of tax data alone, and suggests an impact on demand of quite a different order of magnitude from the conclusions reached by Musgrave and Hansen.* In total the two Budgets of November and April had only a mildly deflationary effect on the economy. The increase in GDP at 1958 prices, seasonally adjusted, slowed down in the first quarter of 1965, although a good deal of this was due to a sharp reduction in the rate of stock accumulation directly associated with the impact of the T.I.C. on imports. In the quarter following the Budget in April GDP fell slightly but subsequently recovered and was increasing at an annual rate of 4% in the final quarter of 1965. Real personal consumption, falling after the Budget, recovered sharply during the second half of the year, as did real personal disposable income. During the whole of 1965 the labour market remained very strained, and the capacity/output index continued to measure an excessive pressure of domestic demand. This situation persisted in spite of a further set of measures in July.†

Nevertheless, the Government's measures together with autonomous forces at work in the economy, were sufficient to limit the year-on-year growth in real GDP to 3% in 1965 and to produce a substantial improvement in the balance of payments. In spite of their apparent harshness the Budgets of November 1964 and April 1965 were only mildly deflationary and the rise in personal incomes (almost 9% in 1965) and in prices continued at an excessive rate. It became perfectly clear once the Budget proposals had been made that a balance of payments surplus would not materialise before 1966 and this delay together with a continuance of inflation, led to a sterling crisis in November. Budgetary policy during 1964/1965 can, therefore, be justly criticised for being too mild although the strategy adopted by the Government undoubtedly made sense given their precarious political position. Their determination to avoid stop-go policies made much less sense and they failed to appreciate the strength of external forces and the unwillingness of

* Hansen seems to have misinterpreted the deflationary impact of policy during 1964–1965 (see *Fiscal Policy in Seven Countries 1955–1965* p. 432) as also did the *Brookings Study* (Tables 1–5 and 1–8).

† These included a tightening of hire-purchase controls, deferments of public investment and further foreign exchange controls.

holders of sterling to accept a more gradual achievement of external surplus than that originally held out by the Government.

The rise in output had by the first quarter of 1966 been slow for about a year and real GDP was only some 2 % above the level of the same quarter in 1965. Nevertheless, in spite of this slow growth in output the level of unemployment had continued to fall, an outcome which rather surprised the authorities. More importantly, perhaps, the balance of payments by the first quarter ceased to improve and this was undoubtedly partly due to the substantial rise in consumers' expenditure (in part anticipatory but also reflecting the 21 % rise in 'other personal income' during the quarter). Hire-purchase controls were tightened during February and further direct and indirect measures to strengthen the balance of payments were introduced in the Budget. Since the official forecasts pointed to a recovery of domestic demand towards the end of the year the Chancellor chose a fiscal instrument—S.E.T.—which would have its deflationary impact in the autumn. This is not the place to discuss this controversial tax measure, with its multitude of aims, but it is worth noting that it has its effects on demand in a way similar to a change in indirect taxes and can be analysed in the same way. While the Chancellor in his Budget Statement gave no estimate of the demand impact of S.E.T. it seems likely that he expected price increases of something less than 1 %. At the time of the 20 July measures the Prime Minister estimated the demand effects at £300 million—presumably full year at current prices—which seems to have been based on the assumption that S.E.T. would be fully passed on in rising prices.*

However, the strategy of the May Budget, a more gradual return to external surplus than had been earlier forecast by the Government in an attempt to avoid the necessity of further harsh deflationary measures on an economy which had already flattened out, could only be successful if foreign confidence was willing to accept this time-table. But the setback of the seamen's strike (15 May–1 July) severely affected overseas confidence and led to continuous speculation against sterling during June and July. The May Budget was overtaken by events; monetary policy was tightened in mid-July and on 20 July a harsh package of deflationary measures was introduced by the Prime Minister. Hire-purchase was tightened further; the regulator was used to the full 10 %; postal charges were raised and a one-year surcharge on surtax incomes

---

* Reddaway has subsequently demonstrated that in the distributive trades nothing was recovered from consumers to compensate for S.E.T. between 1966–1969. Profit margins were reduced and the rest of the tax was offset by greater efficiency. See W. B. Reddaway, *Effects of the Selective Employment Tax, First Report*, H.M.S.O. (1970). The Treasury estimated in 1970 that one-third of S.E.T. was passed on in higher prices.

of 10% was imposed for 1965/1966. Cuts in public expenditure were imposed; a freeze on prices and incomes for six months introduced and further direct measures to assist the balance of payments were taken. These measures were expected to reduce demand in a full year by £500 million and were in addition to the £300 million deflationary impact of the May Budget.

On the assumption that a substantial part of S.E.T. effects on demand came through in 1966 (perhaps £80 million off real GDP growth) and that the fiscal measures in the July package (the regulator plus public expenditure deferments) reduced demand by a further £100 million, then the fiscal effects amounted to about three-quarters of 1% of real GDP in 1966. If all the other measures are included (hire-purchase restrictions and the tightening of monetary policy), then the total effect is probably in excess of 1% of real GDP in 1966, which built up into an even larger effect during 1967 (perhaps of the order of 1·5% of real GDP). They were sufficient to shift the economy on to a 1·5% growth path.

The severe deflation came, therefore, not during 1965 but in 1966— and it was due primarily to the July package with the quick, substantial impact of the regulator. Once again the imperatives of the external situation had forced the Government into a policy of deflation as a possible solution to the balance of payments problem. In terms of their effects on demand the measures were exceptionally successful. Real GDP in the six quarters to the end of 1967 rose by only 2·2%— an annual rate of increase of only 1·5%. Unemployment reacted sharply to the July measures, as a shake-out of labour occurred, so that between July and January the unemployment rate increased from 1·3% to 1·94%, and continued to rise until the autumn of 1967. However, while it seemed at the turn of the year as if the domestic deflation had succeeded finally in producing an external surplus, developments during 1967 were to prove how fragile was the balance of payments position.

But the costs of the policies followed during 1964–1966 were substantial; between the end of 1964 and the end of 1966 real GDP increased by only 1·9% at an annual rate and amounted to a prolonged and drawn-out movement to a lower pressure of demand. In retrospect, it is evident that the reflation of April 1963 was excessive. The long drawn out deflation of 1964/1967 might not have been necessary, balance of payments considerations apart, but for this policy error. But the fundamental question remains of why the Government, having engineered substantial slack in the economy during 1966 and early 1967, waited to be forced into devaluation rather than choosing the optimal moment.

1967–1969

The main problem facing the Chancellor as he drew up his 1967 Budget, or so it appeared at the time, was how to prevent the rise in unemployment from continuing into 1968, which seemed inevitable on the basis of unchanged policies. The experience of 1962 was a salutary reminder of the delays in reflating demand, although in other respects the position in 1967 was quite different. In particular the country was saddled with very large external debt—accumulated in 1964–1966—which placed a severe constraint on any reflationary moves. Failure to achieve a balance of payments surplus could only bring disastrous consequences, and little more could be expected by way of further deflation since the 'trade-off' of full employment for external surplus had already taken place as a result of the July measures.

The Government decided to play it safe; apart from an easing of monetary policy no significant reflationary measures were taken during the first five months of 1967. The Budget contained no significant tax proposals and amounted to 'no change'. Instead the reflation came about primarily through the relaxation of hire-purchase restrictions in June and August, which provided a large stimulus to personal consumption in the third and fourth quarters, plus other measures (including the regional employment premium, increases in family allowances, and increases in certain social security payments). The total effect of all these reflationary measures was perhaps less than half of 1 % of GDP during 1967, with the fiscal measures relatively unimportant. What was opened up by these reflationary measures was the probability of a consumer-led expansion in 1968—a repetition of the 1959 and 1963 pattern only in this case taken from a base of external deficit rather than of precarious surplus.

The measures achieved at least some of their objectives since the seasonally adjusted unemployment rate levelled-out in August/ September at about 2·4 %, but although the rise in unemployment had been checked, the prospects on external account had considerably weakened. From early in 1967 exports fell so that from May onwards sterling came under continuous pressure, which led finally to devaluation together with accompanying measures on the 18 November. This final act represented a clear defeat for the Government's economic strategy since achieving office in 1964, and even apart from the proximate causes of the crisis it had long been inevitable that direct measures —including devaluation—would be necessary. What was difficult to understand about policy during 1967 was why it took so long to accept the necessity for a change of parity.

In retrospect, and even to certain commentators at the time, the measures accompanying devaluation looked inadequate. The cuts of £200 million in Government expenditure were cuts from a sharply-rising trend and the reductions in demand flowing from the increases in taxation were not, because of their distribution, very great, although their nominal value amounted to £300 million. These taxes were the export rebate, corporation tax and S.E.T. Changes in the first two probably had little effect on demand and all three together perhaps only reduced personal consumption by 0·5–0·75%.

The total package was plainly inadequate and even before the Public Expenditure cuts announced on 16 January it was clear that the Budget would need to be extremely restrictive (a view encouraged by the Government). Rising prices, following on from the devaluation, were widely expected, together with expectations of higher purchase taxes in the Budget, so it is not surprising that a consumer boom took place in the first quarter of 1968. Between the last quarter of 1967 and the first quarter of 1968 real consumers' expenditure increased by no less than 3·2%, the savings ratio fell, and this boom was itself superimposed on a substantial recovery of personal consumption during the second half of 1967. Inevitably, therefore, the import figures began to rise.

The Budget of 19 March (brought forward because of the consumption boom) was on the whole well received and thought adequate. As a result of the increases in taxation it was generally thought that consumers' expenditure would be cut on the 'first round' by some £400 million. If multiplier and accelerator effects are included, then the Budget was expected to reduce the growth in output (at factor cost) by perhaps 1·5% to 2% (some £500–£550 million at 1958 prices). This was easily the most severe Budget in the post-war period, with estimated full-year revenue effects of £923 million. In retrospect the main criticism of the Budget is not one of the scale of action but rather one of timing, and it is evident that simply in terms of its effect on overseas confidence more stringent fiscal measures in December 1967 (including changes in personal tax rates and/or the regulator) would have been more appropriate. Tax changes would probably also have done something to forestall the consumer boom, although it is a matter of dispute as to whether the out-turn for 1968 would in fact have been significantly different.★

★ The argument used by the Government for postponing further deflation was set out in the *Economic Report for 1967*, and amounted to a belief that an early release of resources would not be taken up by the balance of payments, given the time-lags, so that deflation could reasonably be delayed.

By the middle of the second half of 1968 it was clear that the post-devaluation strategy had gone seriously astray. Consumers' expenditure recovered sharply in the third and fourth quarters, following a fall after the Budget, and instead of falling in 1968 as forecast by the Treasury actually increased in real terms. Early in November hire-purchase restrictions were imposed and later in the same month the regulator was used to the full 10 %, together with the introduction of the Import Deposit Scheme and a further tightening of bank lending. Altogether these measures were expected to reduce consumers' expenditure in 1969 (first half) by about 1 %.* These measures were related to an uncertain international monetary situation but also to a failure of imports to respond to the devaluation as well as to the persistently high level of personal consumption.

By the end of 1968 the essential elements of a successful demand policy to support devaluation had fallen into place. In particular, fiscal and monetary measures had been taken on a scale sufficient to permit the relatively easy transfer of resources into the balance of payments so as to achieve the balance of payments target of £500 million. Further-more, for the first time in many years, fiscal measures and monetary measures were working in the same direction instead of in frustrating opposition. While it is easy to be critical of fiscal policy during the post-devaluation phase, it has, nevertheless, to be remembered that policy was dealing with difficult and intractable problems—not easily foreseen —and that, timing problems apart, it had by the end of 1968 begun to grapple with the critical economic problems facing Britain.

Following from the November measures there occurred a substantial decline in demand compared with the final quarter of 1968 (by 3 % of real GDP, expenditure method). But taking the fourth quarter of 1968 and the first quarter of 1969 together and comparing it with the previous half-year there was still an increase in demand of 2·5 %. This outcome led the Chancellor to conclude that 'I must therefore limit the growth in home demand so that there is room for a substantial and continuing balance of payments surplus to develop'.† Once again substantial tax changes were introduced (equivalent to £345 million in a full year), while public expenditure growth was severely controlled. The result was to make the Central Government a large net-repayer of debt in fiscal 1969/1970. Among the tax measures was an increase in corporation tax of 2·5 %, which probably had but slight effect on company expendi-ture during 1969. Other measures included changes in income tax concessions, increases in S.E.T. rates, in purchase tax and in the petrol

---

* See *National Institute Economic Review*, p. 85 (Feb. 1969).
† Budget Statement, *Hansard*, 15 April 1969, col. 1002.

tax. The Budget also foreshadowed increases in pensions and in social security benefits together with higher contributions. Most of these measures operate on demand with a fairly extended time-lag and thus the full effect probably did not come through until 1970. This is particularly true of the change in corporation tax, the rise in S.E.T. rates and the impact on prices of the higher employers' National Insurance rates. Altogether the Budget probably reduced the growth in real output between the fourth quarter of 1968 and the fourth quarter of 1969 by about one-third of 1 % compared with what it would otherwise have been.

By the end of 1969 the fiscal strategy, allied with tight control of the money supply, had succeeded in shifting sufficient resources into the balance of payments to achieve a surplus on the balance of payments of £500 million at an annual rate. For the first time in many years the Government had found a strategy whereby growth could occur and yet be consistent with external surplus. But the path had been long and strewn with policy failures.

CONCLUSIONS

Most of the conclusions have been drawn as the argument proceeded and the aim in these paragraphs is simply to identify the most important of these. First among these in importance is the conclusion that, in spite of the frequency with which tax rates have been adjusted, and the relative ease of doing so, fiscal policy during the sixties has continued to be destabilising. It has not merely been imperfectly stabilising but has actually increased the instability of the economic system. While the Treasury has developed techniques for assessing the accelerator and multiplier effects of taxation changes, it would appear, from the evidence, that they have continued, particularly in 1959 and 1963, to underestimate the full impact on demand of expansionary budgets. Both these years stand out as ones of excessive reflation, and the recessions which followed, again engineered by economic policy, might not have happened but for miscalculations in the assessment of the impact of tax measures. It is to be hoped that the lessons of these years have been fully learnt, and there are signs that this is, in fact, the case.

The relatively frequent use of the regulator in recent years has much to commend it. As a flexible fiscal device it is very valuable, but it does have undesirable side effects through its impact on the general price level, and is excessively concentrated on a narrow range of expenditure. This latter deficiency is characteristic of indirect taxes as a whole and leads, therefore, to a reduction in their effectiveness as automatic stabilisers. Similarly, corporate taxes, because of lags in their collection, are not closely correlated with GNP changes, and much needs to be done to reduce this critical lag. On the whole, automatic stabilisers have worked unsatisfactorily during the sixties and have not, in any case, been particularly important. Indeed, the problem facing the authorities has not primarily been one of instability *per se* and the weakness of automatic stabilisers has not been critical. Nevertheless, a movement to a broader-based system of indirect taxes would have undoubted advantages, and not simply from the point of view of stabilisation objectives.

One point which has not been laboured so far relates to the desirability of budget deficits. No one seriously believes that budget deficits are necessarily bad, but one implication of budget deficits has perhaps received too little attention. In any particular year the faster the increase in the Government's borrowing requirement the greater the likelihood that it will have to borrow from the banking system, with consequent effects on the money supply and on the liquidity of the system. Undoubtedly, during the sixties this critical link between budget deficits and the consequences for monetary policy at a later stage was sadly neglected. In other words, there is a cost in attempting to sustain a particular pressure of demand in the economy through running a budget deficit; a cost which shows itself in increased difficulty in managing the economy at a later date. This is not inevitable, but in the conditions of the sixties proved in fact to be the case. The increased liquidity of the private sector enabled them to finance expenditure, even in the face of restrictive monetary policy, at a rate in excess of the available resources. This particular problem is looked at in more detail in Chapter 6, but it remains an unsolved problem. It is one thing to criticise Governments during the sixties for failing to take enough notice of the link between the borrowing requirement and domestic liquidity, but quite another to say precisely how far Government should go in the trade-off between the level of economic activity now against a lower level of liquidity at a later date. Economists do not have any foolproof answer—if any kind of answer at all—to such a question.

5

DEVELOPMENTS IN PUBLIC EXPENDITURE

For a number of reasons the Treasury has not sought, to any significant extent, to use public expenditure for contra-cyclical purposes. In their forecasting, Treasury economists take public current and capital programmes as autonomously determined and few of them believe that variation of public investment programmes has much to commend it as a short-term stabilisation weapon. Nevertheless, during both the 1950s and 1960s public investment has been cut-back on occasion, usually when an impact effect on foreign confidence has been sought. Public sector expenditures are, of course, very substantial in Britain and are perfectly large enough to be used for contra-cyclical purposes should this be desired. Central Government current expenditure alone is equal to about one-third of GNP (1967 current prices) with current expenditure on goods and services amounting to 13 % of GNP. On the other hand, public investment accounts for only about 10 % of GNP so that variations in it would have to be so large as to be obviously undesirable if they were to be big enough to offset other fluctuations in demand.

The general attitude of the authorities has much to commend it since the post-war problem in Britain has not been one of massive deficiency of demand but rather a fine-tuning problem requiring adjustments in the level of demand which can more easily, with more certainty and more quickly, be achieved through other fiscal and monetary measures. Given the nature of the short-term stabilisation problem and continuous difficulties on external account, the authorities have generally chosen not to use public current and capital programmes for fine-tuning purposes in the belief that to do so would entail undesirable social and economic costs. They have, with other Governments, been criticised for this approach in an influential O.E.C.D. report where it is held that public expenditure is more flexible than is commonly assumed and that 'it may well be just as disadvantageous, in terms of economic efficiency, to concentrate the entire adjustment on the private sector—or in any particular part of the private sector—as it is to concentrate it on the public sector'.*

However, this criticism, while no doubt valid in relation to other countries, misses the real essence of the British problem. Restrictive policies have usually been introduced to meet a seriously deteriorating external position, often accompanied by speculative attacks on sterling, so that policy weapons have been used which affect demand quickly and are known both within the Government and outside it to operate effectively. This latter fact is important; both within the U.K. and abroad there exists general scepticism about Government ability to control the growth in public expenditure. Given this attitude, it would be foolhardy on the part of a Government faced by an external crisis to rely heavily on public expenditure cuts as a means of restoring the situation. Furthermore, unless the expenditure cuts fell essentially on those types of public expenditure with a large foreign exchange cost (military expenditure abroad and overseas aid particularly), the change in public expenditure to achieve any given reduction in the level of imports would have to be much larger than the change in private expenditure. This follows from the low import propensity of general government expenditure.† Where cuts have been made in public expenditure, for purely balance of payments reasons, they have fallen on defence expenditure abroad (as in July 1966 and December 1967) and on overseas aid, although there are very long time-lags between the decision to cut these expenditures and any substantial foreign exchange savings.

---

* *Fiscal Policy for a Balanced Economy*, O.E.C.D., Paris, 108 (Dec. 1968).

† The import content of each of the major categories of final expenditure in 1963 showed limited variation between 15% and 23% except for public authorities current expenditure, which had an import content of only 9% (reflecting the high proportion of employees' factor services in the inputs). No import propensity exists for public investment by itself. Source: 'Expanded Provisional Input-Output Tables for 1963', *Economic Trends*, No. 178, Table 7 (Aug. 1968).

CONTROL OF PUBLIC EXPENDITURE

Seen from the point of view of the authorities the main problem with regard to public expenditure has been its very fast growth during the 1960s, as can be seen from *Table 5.1*. Certain categories of civil expenditure (especially education, roads and social security benefits) were already rising fast during the late 1950s, but this growth was masked to some extent by changes elsewhere (particularly the stability—falling in real terms—of defence expenditure). The public sector has increased its average share of GNP from 26% during 1955–1959 to more than 31% in 1968, with most of this change in share concentrated in the period since 1964.* This rapid expansion has posed extremely difficult problems for the authorities, not least with regard to its financing. The problem is looked at more closely, in the context of monetary policy, in a later chapter, but undoubtedly the authorities' ability to influence economic developments during the last five or six years has been severely weakened because of the need to finance a rapidly rising expenditure programme. Indeed, many of the decisions taken with regard to public expenditure in the post-devaluation period would inevitably have been required, and it was only the severity of the crisis which finally forced the Government to face the facts.

A comparison of *Tables 5.1* and *4.1* is rewarding and brings out the extent to which increases in public expenditure have exceeded, usually by a large amount, annual changes in discretionary taxation. If one followed the practice of some commentators (particularly Hansen) and thought of expenditure changes as discretionary then it would follow that these have been the decisive factor in relation to discretionary action as a whole. This observation holds true not only for the public sector as a whole but also for the Central Government alone. However, for reasons which are given below, it is unrealistic to view expenditure changes as being discretionary, and the whole rationale of economic policy is the assumption that tax changes will adjust the level of demand after taking account of public expenditure changes.

The planning and control of public expenditure first emerged as a serious matter during the 1950s as the scale of the public sector increased and the fact that there existed no complete picture of public expenditure developments. In particular, public expenditure decisions could no

---

* There is no single way of measuring the size of the public sector, and the estimates given here relate to public sector current expenditure on goods and services plus gross fixed investment as a proportion of GNP at factor cost (all at current prices). Average share was 26·5% in 1960–1964 and 30% during 1965–1968.

Table 5.1

ANNUAL CHANGES IN EXPENDITURE OF THE PUBLIC SECTOR UNITED KINGDOM, 1959–1969

(£ million and %)

Year	Current Goods and services	Capital Goods and Services		Transfers to Public*	Total	Total as % of GDP
		Central and local	Corporations			
1959	251	−3	41	163	452	2·1
1960	247	19	10	251	527	2·3
1961	334	83	137	357	911	3·8
1962	331	115	21	208	675	2·7
1963	264	77	58	228	627	2·3
1964	328	292	208	175	1 003	3·5
1965	524	96	99	520	1 239	4·0
1966	529	197	198	332	1 256	3·9
1967	674	303	248	768	1 993	5·8
1968	456	207	−82	749	1 330	3·7
1969	413	42	−189	306	761	2·0

Source: *National Income and Expenditure*, H.M.S.O. (1969 and 1970)
* Subsidies, grants to personal sector, net transfers abroad, and debt interest.

longer be fitted into a short-term planning horizon since many forms of expenditure require only small outlays at the start and only later build up into bigger sums, so that by the time substantial demands begin to be made on the Budget, policy is too far advanced to be reversed, and the bill has to be met through increased taxation or borrowing. It became imperative, therefore, for decisions on public expenditure to be taken against some future perspective, independently of whether such decisions were taken for short-term stabilisation purposes or for other reasons. At the same time the role of the Budget had changed and had come 'to be recognised as primarily concerned with adjusting the short-term situation in the economy as a whole so as to bring supply and demand into balance in the year in question; but since the planning of public expenditure could only sensibly be done over a longer period, the question was posed of how to gear the management of public expenditure to the management of the economy, while providing sufficient stability for public expenditure to be planned and run efficiently'.*

Attempts were made to solve this problem. Time horizons were extended in relation to defence expenditure, initially of five years (in 1958) and subsequently of ten years. Forward school building programmes have been developed, extending over several years and all public investment programmes have been brought together, judged against a five-year assessment of the economy, and the investment programmes published in the form of a White Paper. Finally, these public investment surveys were absorbed into the more comprehensive public expenditure surveys recommended by the Plowden Committee in 1961.† These annual surveys of public expenditure have been presented to Ministers on the lines recommended by Plowden and provide data on expenditure of the public sector analysed by functional and economic category so as to be compatible with the national income accounts. Each survey looked five years ahead, each following survey rolled the figures forward one year and each survey was viewed against a five-year economic survey for the whole economy. A more recent development (1969) has been the publication of an annual White Paper on the prospect for public expenditure as a whole, and is in a form which emphasises the public sector's claims on resources. Claims on resources

---

* *Public Expenditure: A New Presentation*, H.M.S.O., Cmnd 4017, 17 (April 1969).

† The main conclusion of Plowden was, 'Decisions involving substantial future expenditure should always be taken in the light of surveys of public expenditure as a whole, over a period of years, and in relation to prospective resources. Public expenditure decisions . . . should never be taken without consideration of (a) what the country can afford over a period of years having regard to prospective resources and (b) the relative importance of one kind of expenditure against another.' *The Control of Public Expenditure*, H.M.S.O., Cmnd 1432 para. 7 (1961).

were inadequately specified in earlier public expenditure presentations, and this failure undoubtedly contributed to the policy errors of the sixties.

Such, then, is the planning framework for public expenditure decisions. Basic to this procedure of planning and control is the presumption that the activities of the public sector require advance planning, and that this is particularly true of public investment, which is often a highly complex process, with a long gestation period, and where interruption of any major kind can lead to substantial waste and cost. This is true of both increases and decreases of the programme since increases can lead to higher costs through inadequate planning. In general, readjustments cannot be spread evenly through public expenditure programmes—at any particular point of time only a small part of total expenditure relates to operations in their early stages—and the more advanced the stage the more painful and costly any change becomes. Contractual and other commitments also limit flexibility. The result is that real scope for changes in public expenditure as a whole up or down, without substantial cost through disruption of programmes, is believed by the authorities to relate to year three of the planning horizon.* This being so, for public expenditure as a whole, it follows that where changes have been needed in the programme for short-term economic policy reasons, these have been concentrated on that part of the programme which, although it has been planned, has not been started.†

A further point which requires emphasis is that different categories of public expenditure have different short-term effects on demand. For certain types of expenditure only small adjustments to gross expenditure have to be made to estimate the effect on demand, e.g., in the cases of the employment of public servants or purchases of materials, one needs only to deduct indirect taxes paid on civil servants (S.E.T.) and import duties. The impact on demand of transfer payments is much more varied because of differential tax and savings adjustments, although allowance can be made for these in assessing the demand for resources consequent on any marginal change in such payments. Such

---

* *Public Expenditure: A New Presentation*, H.M.S.O., Cmnd 4017, para. 27 (April 1969).

† The Treasury has held this view consistently through the 1960s and this is undoubtedly partly due to the strictures of Plowden, who commented most unfavourably on the variation of public expenditure as a short-term weapon. For an alternative view see *Fiscal Policy for a Balanced Economy*, O.E.C.D., pp. 106–110 (Dec. 1968), where it is suggested that more flexibility exists than is commonly supposed in relation to both current and capital expenditures. What the O.E.C.D. fails to sufficiently take note of is that where effects are wanted quickly the variation in public expenditure is unlikely to produce them, and it is quick effects which have typically been needed in Britain during the 1960s.

G

transfers include investment grants, social security benefits, subsidies and debt interest. For example, an increase in grants and subsidies to industry probably has its main effect on company liquidity and works through in later years to higher levels of expenditure. Debt interest payments will generate income and surtax payments, and some rise in savings, while the rest will be spent on goods and services of which about one-fifth of the additional expenditure flows back to the Government through increased indirect taxes. Only about a half of the increase in debt interest payments will be reflected in a rise in the demand for resources. Similar considerations apply to family allowances and other grants to persons. As for other social security benefits, the impact will depend on the precise nature of the change. A general rise in contributory benefits will be considerably offset by the associated rise in contributions, and while some contributory benefits are tax-free, others are subject to tax. In all cases, about one-fifth comes back to the authorities through purchase tax, excise duties, S.E.T., local rates and other taxes on expenditure.*

This, then, is the general view of the Treasury about the possibilities open to the authorities in using public expenditure as a contra-cyclical measure. But it may be countered that whereas Central Government expenditure is not easily varied, that this may not hold true for Local Authorities. These organisations are responsible for a very substantial volume of expenditure (if one simply takes those categories of expenditure which enter into final demand, i.e., current expenditure on goods and services plus gross fixed investment, then Local Authorities' expenditure was equal to 12 % of GNP in 1967 compared with 14 % for Central Government). In terms of capital expenditure Local Authorities are almost as important as manufacturing industry and undertake more than one-fifth of gross capital formation in the economy. Local Authority current expenditure on goods and services has been, in the post-war period, about equally financed from rates and by grants from the Central Government. Such grants, including general grants, have constituted an important source of Government control over the development of Local Authority expenditure in the longer term, but it cannot be used to bring about immediate changes in Local Authority current expenditure. Local Authorities can always, if necessary, fall back on rate finance to maintain expenditure even though they are generally unwilling to do so on account of the lack of buoyancy of rate revenue and the unpopularity of this tax with electors. From the point of view of managing the economy, this system of financing Local Authority

* See: *Public Expenditure: A New Presentation*, H.M.S.O., Cmnd 4017, 24–25 (April 1969).

current expenditure has, therefore, serious disadvantages, and cannot be used to any great extent for short-term economic management purposes.

What, then, of the possibility of varying Local Authority capital expenditure as a stabilisation measure? This is financed mainly from loans and before a project can be financed by a loan, a 'loan sanction' is required from the appropriate central government department (there may also be more detailed control of certain categories of expenditure). Unfortunately, for the stabilisation authorities, loan sanctions are a very imprecise form of control because of the time-lag between the loan sanction and related expenditure—a lag which it is difficult to predict.

In spite of such difficulties, and because of their importance as spenders, Local Authorities have often been included when the economic situation required cuts in public expenditure, e.g., in July 1965 and July 1966. There are powerful and good reasons for not behaving in this way, but, nevertheless, circumstances have often forced the Government to do so. The precise form of the cuts, when they have been imposed, has taken account of the extent of Central Government control, so that while cuts in loan sanctions in general are impracticable (and, therefore, not favoured), other cuts can be forecast with much greater certainty. This is particularly true of housing approvals, which can be more easily adjusted, and operate relatively quickly and with a fair amount of success. In general, however, it cannot be said that Local Authority expenditure, either current or capital, is easily controlled for short-term management purposes or that it is desirable to do so. Much of their expenditure is vital to the functioning of society, and can only be scaled down at the cost of a worsening of the quality of life. Given the essential nature of much of Local Authority expenditure (most of it imposed by Central Government), it is to be expected that the Central Government should be reluctant to vary local programmes for reasons of conjunctural policy. This basic reluctance is further strengthened by the present system of controls which provides the Central Government with little power to alter quickly the level of local expenditure with any certainty that cuts will be effective.

PUBLIC INVESTMENT OBJECTIVES

The above considerations have not been lost on Governments, but they have still, both in the 1950s and 1960s, attempted to vary public investment in order (typically) to reduce the pressure of demand. However, cuts have been imposed somewhat less frequently during the sixties than in the fifties, although economic problems during recent years were both more continuous and more difficult to handle. Governments have, undoubtedly, chosen to use other policy measures in preference to public investment cuts. This was partly the result of criticism levelled at this practice, on account of the costs entailed through interruption of long-term programmes during the fifties; it was partly due also to a gradual realisation that sizeable and quick results on demand were not to be expected, and, finally, a recognition that such a policy was contrary to the objective of raising the gross investment ratio in order to achieve a higher rate of economic growth. This latter objective began to figure in Government aims around the turn of the sixties, and all Governments in recent years have deliberately chosen stabilisation measures which, as far as possible, did not adversely affect the level of investment. In other words, the authorities have preferred to use measures affecting consumers' expenditure, and have tried to insulate investment expenditures, both public and private, within limits, from the necessities of short-term policy. In some respects the authorities have been successful, and the gross investment ratio has been raised significantly compared with the 1950s (from an average level of 17·2% in 1955–1960 to 19·6% during the sixties). Any success is bound to be partial, since measures reducing consumer expenditure inevitably affect adversely private investment expectations.

While this view has much to commend it, it cannot be said that the level of public investment has always been appropriate to the short-term economic situation as it developed in the sixties. The authorities have not set out to use public investment as a flexible contra-cyclical weapon, and perhaps it is unfair to judge them by this criterion. Indeed, as noted earlier, the problem has been one of fine-tuning rather than one of cyclical instability. Nevertheless, as can be seen in *Table 5.2* in 1962 and 1963 private investment (exclusive of dwellings) fell in both years, while public investment showed only a slight rise. Undoubtedly, a further increase in public investment at this time would have been desirable in terms of employment and growth objectives, while the balance of payments had ceased to impose a constraint on reflation from late 1961. The disastrous economic forecast of 1962 must be held primarily to blame for this failure to expand public investment. On the other hand, the massive expansion of public investment in 1964, deliberately set in train as the Government's contribution to the achievement of the N.E.D.C. 4% growth target, was imposed on an economy simultaneously facing a strong cyclical upswing of private investment (see *Chart 5.1*). It is clear, with hindsight, that a much smaller public investment programme in 1964 would have better served short-term

Table 5.2

GROSS DOMESTIC FIXED CAPITAL FORMATION AT CONSTANT 1958 PRICES

(£ million)

Year	(1) Public Authorities	(2) Public Corporations	(3) Public Sector (1 + 2)	(4) Change in (3)	(5) Private Sector Investment	(6) Change in (5)	(7) Dwellings Private	Public
1959	562	761	1 323	+104	1 771	+84	400	274
1960	580	785	1 365	+42	2 009	+238	484	274
1961	601	880	1 481	+116	2 230	+221	527	286
1962	626	884	1 510	+29	2 151	−79	515	324
1963	628	953	1 581	+71	2 144	−7	512	345
1964	719	1 077	1 796	+215	2 483	339	625	462
1965	734	1 135	1 869	+73	2 604	121	616	491
1966	781	1 226	2 007	+138	2 600	−4	553	530
1967	901	1 372	2 273	+266	2 585	−15	580	611
1968	980	1 318	2 298	25	2 680	95	600	665

Source: *Economic Trends*, H.M.S.O. (Oct. 1968), *Monthly Bulletin of Statistics*.
Note: Columns 1–6 exclude investment in dwellings.

objectives. The huge expansion of public programmes directly contributed to the excess pressure of demand in the economy in 1964/1965 and to the massive deterioration in the balance of payments in 1964 (a substantial part of the rise in imports during 1964 was in the form of investment goods, partly at least induced by the high pressure of demand on the domestic capital goods industries). In 1966 and 1967 the increase in public investment was appropriate, at least in the sense that it more than offset declines in private investment. This was, if the Chancellor is to be believed, deliberate Government policy.* The expansion in 1967, while desirable from the viewpoint of employment and output stabilisation (given that the demand forecast for 1967 proved too high and reflationary policies proved necessary from mid-year) was nevertheless a contributory factor to the deterioration of the balance of payments during 1967.

The occasions on which the authorities have cut public investment have all been associated, in the sixties, with balance of payments crises. As Dow† found, it is extremely difficult to judge how effective such cuts were in reducing the pressure of demand, and it cannot be said that the authorities themselves expected very much from such a policy. Indeed, given that the Government had only the vaguest idea at any particular time about the actual level of investment expenditures of the public corporations and Local Authorities, it is not surprising that little was expected from the cuts. Given the *size* of public investment relative to GNP, very substantial cuts in it would in any case have been necessary to produce sizeable effects on demand, and the authorities have never really envisaged more than a token effect from the cuts. Why, then, have they bothered at all? The answer to this lies in the belief that overseas speculators can only be convinced of the rightness of Government policy if it contains action on public expenditure, since most speculators attribute to public expenditure growth a causal role in any crisis.

Dow concluded that the action taken in 1960 to stabilise public investment, i.e., to hold the approved level of total public investment in 1961/1962 at the level of the previous financial year, was successful.‡ At constant 1958 prices public investment in 1961/1962 was some £120

* 'Public expenditure, notably public investment, will still rise rapidly this year. . . . It is quite justifiable that during a period when private investment is declining public investment should be allowed to advance quite rapidly, so expanding the infrastructure of society and raising the collective standard of living.' Mr. Callaghan, Budget Statement, *Hansard*, 11 April 1967, col. 990.

† J. C. R. Dow, *The Management of the British Economy 1945–1960*, Cambridge University Press, 216–221 (1965).

‡ J. C. R. Dow, *The Management of the British Economy 1945–1960*, Cambridge University Press, 221 (1965).

million above the 1960/1961 figure. However, the White Paper estimate of Public Sector (non-housing) investment for 1960/1961 made
in November 1960 was too high by 3 %–4 %, and too low in its forecast
for 1961/1962 by 2·5 %. Even the White Paper of October 1962 was

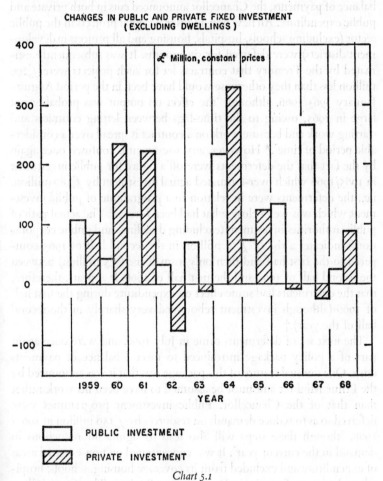

**CHANGES IN PUBLIC AND PRIVATE FIXED INVESTMENT
(EXCLUDING DWELLINGS)**

£ Million, constant prices

PUBLIC INVESTMENT

PRIVATE INVESTMENT

Chart 5.1

too low in its estimate of the out-turn for 1961/1962 and was way-out
in its forecast for 1962/1963. The conclusion to be drawn from these
data is that there was some partial achievement of public investment
objectives for 1961/1962 compared to 1960/1961, but this was due to
underfulfilment of programmes in 1960/1961 and a higher level of
expenditure than forecast in 1961/1962. But only over the two financial
years was there any kind of relative stability. What this case also illus-

trates is the great difficulty which the Government faces in forecasting public investment and the extent to which the timing of actual expenditures may differ substantially from that forecast.

In July 1965, as part of a package of measures aimed to strengthen the balance of payments, the Chancellor announced cuts in both private and public expenditure. All new non-industrial capital projects in the public sector (excluding schools, hospitals, housing and all projects in development districts) were deferred for six months. It was subsequently estimated by the Treasury that contracts let for such projects were £200 million less than they otherwise would have been in the period August–January 1965/1966, although 'the effect on output was probably not large in 1965, owing to the time-lags between letting contracts and starting work and because work on a contract is spread over a considerable period of time'.* However, any assessment is confused once again by the fact that the deferments were off a figure for public investment in 1965/1966 which over-estimated actual investment by £180 million, i.e., the deferments were in relation to a programme of public investment which was well below what had been forecast. The actual path of public authorities investment (excluding dwellings and public corporations) indicates a rise of £50 million in the second half of 1965 compared to the first half and then only a small rise (£5 million) between the second half of 1965 and the first half of 1966. It appears, therefore, that the deferments had some effect on expenditure during the first half of 1966 (although investment rebounded very sharply in the second half of the year).†

The next set of deferments came in July 1966, and were once again part of a policy package introduced to meet a balance of payments crisis. One unusual feature of this package was that it was announced by the Prime Minister and must be assumed to have been his work rather than that of the Chancellor. Public investment programmes were deferred so as to reduce demands on resources by £150 million in 1967/1968, 'though these steps will also lead to significant reductions in demand in the current year'. It was concentrated on non-essential areas of expenditure and excluded from its coverage housing, schools, hospitals and advance factories in Development Regions. The £150 million

---

* *Economic Report on 1965*, H. M. Treasury: H.M.S.O., 15 (1966).

† The path of Public Authorities investment excluding dwellings at constant 1958 prices was, 1965: I—£322 million, II—£372 million; 1966: I—£377 million, II—£404 million. The Treasury commented on this development in the *Economic Report on 1966*, page 16, 'Investment by public authorities (excluding dwellings) changed little up to the first half of 1966, by which time investment was being reduced by the deferments of July 1965, but it rose rapidly in the second half of the year.'

cuts were shared out between the Central and Local Authorities (£55 million in 1967/1968) and Public Corporations (£95 million in 1967/1968),* but were in relation to a public investment programme for 1967/1968 which had not at that stage been announced. The position was further complicated because investment in 1966/1967 was behind schedule and the National Institute commented at the time 'that there is always the possibility that cuts in the programme will not affect actual performance. . . . Finally, reductions of this kind in the past have frequently been ineffective . . . and [we assume] that the cuts will be roughly two-thirds effective.'† On this basis the Institute estimated the demand effects as negligible in 1966 and equal to about £90 million in 1967. This was also the Treasury's assessment of the outcome for 1966. Public investment (excluding dwellings) rose very rapidly (by more than 13 %) during 1967 and there must be considerable doubt as to whether the 1966 July deferments had much (if any) impact on investment and, therefore, on demand.‡

The final public investment cuts which we are interested in here were those taken post-devaluation. These included cuts of £100 million off nationalised industries investment made in November 1967 followed by a complete review of public expenditure in December and January. The cuts announced in January 1968 were forecast to cut public expenditure by £325 million in 1968/1969 and by £441 million in 1969/1970 (over and above the cuts announced in November 1967), so that 'public investment and public consumption are expected each to increase at a rate a little more than 2 % a year up to mid-1969'.§ The total effect of the November and January public expenditure cuts was estimated at £500 million in 1968/1969, i.e., public expenditure was expected to grow by £500 million less than planned during the financial year 1968/1969. The actual growth of public investment (excluding dwellings) in 1968/1969 compared to 1967/1968 at constant prices was 1·6 %, somewhat less than the 2 % forecast in the Budget of 1968. What is also particularly noticeable is the downward trend (continuously) of Public Authorities current expenditure on goods and services from the fourth quarter of 1967.‖ There can be little doubt that the post-devaluation cuts were effective and succeeded in bringing about a significantly

* *Hansard*, 20 July 1966, col. 632.
† *National Institute Economic Review*, 6 (August 1966).
‡ 'It is unlikely that there had been much effect on expenditure by the end of 1966.' *Economic Report on 1966*, H. M. Treasury: H.M.S.O., 16 (1967).
§ Budget Statement, *Hansard*, April 1968, col. 259.
‖ At constant 1963 prices, seasonally adjusted, public authorities' current expenditure was, 1967: second half—£2920 million; 1968: first half—£2936 million; 1968: second half—£2915 million; 1969: first half—£2903 million; 1969: second half—£2916 million.

slower growth in both public current and capital expenditure. The effects on demand during 1968/1969 must have been substantial, and the turn-round in the public sector's financial position associated with the cuts (and the swingeing tax increases in the 1968 Budget) powerfully assisted monetary policy during the post-devaluation period.

CONCLUSIONS

Experience in the sixties of the use of public investment cuts does not lead to any greater belief in their effectiveness. As a demand management technique, it suffers from many deficiencies, not least in the timing of its impact, and the authorities are clearly right to only resort to cuts when under severe pressure. More important, however, has been the development of systems of planning public investment and public expenditure in general which are concerned with the longer-term relationships of the public sector to the rest of the economy. It is undoubtedly more essential that the authorities develop better techniques for assessing the resource implications of expenditure programmes, and the implications of Government financing for monetary policy, than that they should concern themselves with public expenditure flexibility. If greater flexibility can be achieved in public expenditure then this is only to be welcomed. One improvement which is clearly desirable (which would improve flexibility) is greater control over, and knowledge about, the timing of investment expenditures by Local Authorities and Public Corporations. One of the most damaging criticisms that can be made of public investment programmes during the 1960s is that they were often inappropriately related to general demand developments, and more information about the progress of these expenditures would considerably have improved the quality of demand management.

6

MONETARY POLICY

Monetary policy has become increasingly important in recent years not only in Britain but also in other countries. This is due, at least in part, as a reaction against fiscal policy, which in the light of the conclusions of Chapters 3–5, is fairly founded. In Britain there is considerable awareness also of the weaknesses of monetary policy, due primarily to the findings of Radcliffe. However, much has changed since Radcliffe and the aim in this chapter is to introduce the reader to some of the developments in recent years. The treatment is inevitably selective, but it is hoped that the following sections, which cover the gilt-edged market, the market in Treasury bills, the rise of the Local Authority short-term market and the general problem of control of the money supply, will prove useful as an introduction to a changing and extremely complex system. Once again the aim has been to identify those elements of the whole which are particularly relevant for stabilisation policy.

THE GILT-EDGED MARKET

An understanding of the gilt-edged market is a pre-condition for any appraisal of British monetary policy during the past 10 years. In what follows only the barest outline is given of this complex problem which received a full analysis at the time of Radcliffe.* More recently the Bank

---

* Radcliffe *Report*, chapter 7 and Minutes of Evidence (especially Qˢ 11919–12065). In recent years the *Quarterly Bank Bulletin* has contained a regular commentary on developments in gilt-edged.

has itself stated in the clearest of terms its policy in relation to this key problem and its article on 'Official Transactions in the Gilt-edged Market'* is essential reading for understanding its behaviour. Management of the national debt is not merely a question of the cheapest way of meeting Exchequer financing requirements, but has a fundamental part to play in the execution of interest rate policy (along with Bank Rate) and an important role in effecting the credit policy of the banks and other institutions. However, neither credit policy nor interest rate policy has been the dominant long-term aim in debt management. The Bank has made it perfectly clear how it has assessed relative priorities: 'The dominant long-term consideration in debt management . . . is to ensure so far as possible that suitable finance is available, and will continue to be available in the future, so that there need be no excessive recourse to short-term borrowing from the banks on Treasury bills and accompanying increase in the money supply.†

The precedence given to this aim in debt management is itself the result of developments in the sphere of long-term finance of Government. One important element, which has for some time been exercising the mind of the Bank, has been the redemption of Government dated stocks. During the period 1963–1967 cash redemptions averaged some £870 million a year, and it was anticipated by the Bank that between 1966–1971 some £1000 million a year would fall due for re-payment.‡ A second factor has been the large net increase in the financial liabilities of the public sector, which averaged during 1961–1967 some £900 million a year. However, the amount the Central Government has had to borrow has been reduced by the increase in market debt of Local Authorities, leaving a net borrowing requirement of

1960	1961	1962	1963	1964	1965	1966	1967	1968	1969
307	220	−79	148	423	597	534	1134	755	1116

Source: *Financial Statistics*, H.M.S.O., Table 16, various issues.

Nevertheless striking changes have taken place with regard to Central Government financing in the period since devaluation. If in-

* *Quarterly Bank Bulletin* (June 1966).
† 'Official Transactions in the Gilt-edged Market', *Quarterly Bank Bulletin*, 141 (June 1966).
‡ The figure for cash redemptions was in excess of £1000 million in the years 1966–1968 (*Financial Statistics*, H.M.S.O.. Table 17, July 1969). This estimate of £1000 million a year is probably too low, and *The Economist* has put the figure nearer £1300 million a year ('Gilt Edged Market: The Crowded Years', *Economist*, 5 Aug. 1967), and at the present time the authorities put expected annual maturities at about £1500 million.

stead of taking calendar year figures for the Central Government's borrowing requirement (net balance) one looked at financial years, then the position shows a dramatic improvement. The Central Government's net balance in 1968/1969 was a surplus of £273 million—an improvement of £1608 million compared with the previous financial year. For the first time since 1962/1963 the Central Government repaid debt. This substantial change was mainly the result of a very large increase in revenue, due partly to the tax increases in the April 1968 Budget together with the additional measures taken in November (including the import deposit scheme). The year 1969/1970 saw a further improvement in the Central Government's net balance although nothing like as substantial as that of 1968/1969. This change in the Central Government's financial position has opened up an entirely new and more favourable background against which monetary measures can be operated—in particular in relation to policy in the gilt-edged market (a matter we return to below).

Only a very small contribution towards the financing of the Government has been forthcoming from small savings, which during the period 1962–1968 averaged only some £45 million, and in recent years (1965–1968) they actually raised the net borrowing requirement since they were negative to the extent of some £36 million a year. The recent behaviour of small savings would seem to be almost entirely due to a change in National Savings (negative during these four years as compared with large surpluses in the previous three years). There is clear evidence that certain forms of National Savings have declined in popularity, either through reduced liquidity relative to other forms of savings, or diminished popularity in other respects (one element in this is the tendency of interest rates on these savings media to lag behind increases in interest on other competing savings outlets).* Whatever the full explanation it is probable that very little contribution will be made by small savings towards the financing of Government during the next few years. It would seem unwise to think in terms of anything more than £50 million or so per year as their contribution to the financing of Central Government.

One further matter needs to be taken account of. During the sixties the Government has met part of its financing requirements through extensive overseas borrowing and through running down the foreign exchange reserves. The figures of direct borrowing (net) from

* On this point see E. V. Morgan, 'Gilt-Edged—Can the Budget Help?' *The Banker* (Aug. 1966). C. Goodhart suggests that certain statistical evidence throws doubt on this proposition, although 'high—but not rising interest rates may reduce the inflow of small savings'.

overseas Governments and institutions *plus* net change in gold and
currency reserves have been

1960	1961	1961	1963	1964	1965	1966	1967	1968	1969
−404	−293	−239	13	515	203	245	−35	467	−123

Source: *Financial Statistics*, Table 16, various issues.

Since the Government has set itself a balance of payments target of
£500 million a year so as to be in a position to repay debt and add to
foreign exchange reserves then simply to restore the position of 1961
would entail a substantial demand for funds—of the order of £250
million a year.

This, then, is part of the background against which to view debt
management policy. Firstly, the need to finance the redemption of
dated stocks which is expected to become an even bigger problem
(some £1500 million a year between 1968 and 1972). Secondly, the
need to find large sums of money to finance the capital programmes of
the nationalised industries and, through the Public Works Loan Board,
those of the Local Authorities. In the years 1960–1965 the Central
Government financed capital investment other than its own to the
extent of nearly £3000 million. Since 1964 the Local Authorities have
been encouraged to turn to the Public Works Loan Board (P.W.L.B.)
for more of their capital finance so that the Central Government's need
for funds for this purpose has increased sharply in recent years, and will
rise further.* For the next few years, therefore, the Central Government will have to find some £1200 million per year to meet capital
expenditure of Local Authorities and nationalised industries. In addition, there will be the need to pay off overseas debt (say £250–£300
million a year).† Against this there is the contribution from small savings
(£50 million a year), leaving a total demand for long-term finance of
close on £1500 million.

This is the size of the problem facing the authorities at the present
time. It is not, however, an entirely new problem and it has been
exerting its influence on the authorities' behaviour and attitudes at least
since the late 1950s.‡ It has led the authorities inevitably to believe that

* Local Authorities' borrowing from the P.W.L.B. averaged £480 million a
year during the period 1965/1966–1968/1969 Recently nationalised industries
have been encouraged by the Government to borrow abroad so as to reduce
their demands for Central Government finance.
† See the Appendix to Chapter 8.
‡ 'We have been faced with the problem of financing growing official borrowing needs . . . and of providing for the re-finance of large tranches of maturing

the 'chief purpose of debt management . . . is to maintain market conditions that will maximise, both now and in the future, the desire of investors at home and abroad to hold British Government debt'.* The Bank's case is, therefore, a relatively simple one. The amount of public sector debt is very large, although the volume of assets forming the base of the monetary system (market Treasury bills and currency) is relatively small, amounting to only some £3900 million in 1968. Any large movement of funds out of gilt-edged would lead to an excessive increase in the monetary base. Secondly, the Government's financial needs are such now (and will continue to be) a force making it essential to sell increased quantities of gilt-edged. It follows, therefore, that the maximisation of the long-term demand for Government debt, and the retention of existing debt in the hands of firm holders, should be the priority of debt management. How was this to be achieved?

Firstly, 'To ensure that dealings do not become seriously inhibited by the absence of buyers to match sellers, or that the market does not become too volatile due to the preponderance of buyers unable to satisfy their demands for stock.' Secondly, 'To slow down and moderate violent movements in the market unless there is likely to be a particular advantage in a rapid adjustment, as in a case of a change in Bank Rate.'† What kind of action would follow from an acceptance of these aims? Where the authorities believe a higher level of rates is desirable, and the market expects such an outcome then attempts will be made to sell stock. The deficiency of buyers will lead to stock being offered to the Bank, who will be able, through its buying policy, to bring about a change in market prices. Some level of prices will dissuade other market holders from selling further quantities of stocks. The adjustment in the price of bonds and the level of interest rates takes place smoothly and with little difficulty for the authorities.

However, this may not always be the case. A small change in prices may cause sellers to hold off (so that the downward movement in

* *Quarterly Bank Bulletin*, 142 (June 1966).
† *Quarterly Bank Bulletin*, 145–146 (June 1966).

debt. The total amount involved in both types of operation can approach £1500 million a year, and in the inflationary climate of the mid-1950s it was often difficult to persuade the gilt-edged market to absorb as much long-term debt as we would have wished. The consequent necessity for large-scale short-term borrowing created a situation in which the traditional market methods of controlling bank liquidity proved inadequate to the task of restraining the growth in bank credit.' Mr. L. K. O'Brien, Deputy Governor of the Bank. From 'Central Banking Developments', *Banking Trends in Europe Today*, International Institute of Banking, 25 (July 1964).

prices comes to an end). Alternatively, once a downward movement begins it may degenerate into a spiral, causing disruption of the market. In these cases the Bank's tactics will be different.

The Bank strongly held the belief, therefore, that it should not *initiate* movements in prices, i.e., it should not enter the market as a determined seller so as to produce a fall in prices nor, if sellers are already in the market, should the Bank forbear from buying stock until a new support level had been reached. Instead it should 'lean into the wind', and it has behaved consistently in this way during the period up to 1969. Its case for not attempting during this period a more active and positive role in producing a *downward* shift in prices was based on the following reasoning. In the first place it is, according to the Bank, impossible *ex ante* to say what the new support level is to be. This cannot be established in advance by the authorities because of uncertainty about market reactions, so that they can better judge what the support level is by staying in the market. Secondly, cumulative downwards movements in price are more likely to come about if the Bank withdrew from the market and to bring such a movement to a stop may entail 'disproportionate official support'.* This has the disadvantage that it will lead to a rise in bank liquidity at a time when restriction of credit is probably desirable. Thirdly, a downward movement in prices initiated by the Bank and left unsupported together with official intervention at some indeterminate level, may lead investors in gilt-edged to believe that the market is arbitrary, unpredictable and capricious. The development of this kind of attitude would in the long-term reduce the capacity of the Government to borrow long-term.

What is the Bank's case against the authorities initiating a *rise* in prices (fall in rates)? Any attempt by the Bank to produce such a movement when investors believe such a rise is unjustified in the light of economic conditions will be unsuccessful without excessive purchases of stock by the Bank. On the other hand, 'when conditions are right [the Bank] can stimulate the market's appetites for stock by selling at gently rising prices'.† However, any strong upward movement in prices should not be allowed to go too far, since any reaction by investors to the higher price of stocks may again lead to instability and reduce confidence in the gilt-edged market. To prevent this occurring the Bank will sell stock when prices are rising, and this is expected to lead to too high a level of prices. This may be equally inappropriate with respect to credit policy, since it will entail a reduction in liquidity

---

* *Quarterly Bank Bulletin*, 147 (June 1966).
† *Quarterly Bank Bulletin*, 147 (June 1966).

and rise in rates. The Bank's views on operations in the gilt-edged market can best be summed up by the following statement: 'Variations in demand in the market are therefore likely to lead to variations in supply at unchanged or only slowly changing prices, rather than to immediate variations in prices big enough to bring demand back into balance at nearly the same level of supply. Policy on interest rates can, and in all circumstances must, concentrate largely on fostering demand, in the future as well as in the present.'*

What have been the implications for monetary policy of following these rules? In the first place the authorities are no longer in control of either the amount of stock they can sell or of the level of interest rates. They are unwilling to reduce prices in order to stimulate demand for gilts unless they believe this is in line with market sentiment. The gain to be offset against this loss of freedom of action is the supposed improvement in expectations by investors which might lead to the market absorbing (and holding firmly) larger quantities of gilt-edged debt. This is based on the supposition (it is no more) that steady prices will maximise the long-term demand for gilt-edged, whereas it is perfectly conceivable that this aim could be achieved through actions leading to quite different price experience. Secondly, the authorities' ability to influence prices indirectly via changes in bill rates (more on this below) is likely to be slight. This follows from the fact that the linkage between short rates and long rates is relatively weak and that the Treasury bill rate is primarily adjusted for external reasons rather than for the purpose of influencing gilt-edged prices. The freedom to adjust the Treasury bill rate in order to influence prices of gilt-edged is, therefore, severely limited by the state of the external balance and international confidence in sterling.

Finally, the authorities in pursuing their long-term objective of maximising the demand for debt often find their activities acting in a contrary direction to short-term policy on credit control. For example, when confidence in sterling is low, overseas holders of gilt-edged will sell and in so doing increase pressure on reserves. The surrender of sterling to the Exchange Equalisation Account will reduce the Government's borrowing requirement at the same time as reducing the volume of exchange reserves.† Whether this leads to a reduction in the liquidity of the banks will depend on the extent of the reduction in the need of the Government for finance and the subsequent repayment of

---

* *Quarterly Bank Bulletin,* 147 (June 1966).
† For an analysis of the operations of the E.E.A. see 'The Exchange Equalisation Account; Its Origins and Development', in the *Quarterly Bank Bulletin* (Dec. 1968).

domestic borrowing. However, sales of gilt-edged will bring pressure on prices and the Bank, to prevent any drop in prices, will enter the market and buy stock. At a time, therefore, when the foreign exchange reserves are falling, the monetary authorities, because of their concern for the maximisation of the long-term demand for government stock, will buy gilt-edged and thus increase the liquidity of the system. Instead of a contraction of the monetary base when foreign exchange reserves fall (under a fixed rate, system), the authorities succeed in achieving quite the reverse.

Such, then, were the guiding principles of the authorities in the management of the gilt-edged market, but there is fairly conclusive evidence of a change in the beliefs of the authorities at the close of the sixties. For example, the *Quarterly Bank Bulletin*, March 1969, stated that throughout the period November to February 1969 'the authorities were, as always, prepared to deal in response to market offers, at prices judged by them both to conform with the underlying trend of interest rates and to be consistent with the underlying long-term objective of preserving market conditions favourable to maximum official sales of Government debt—particularly sales to investors outside the banking sector'. The aims of debt management have remained unchanged, but tactics show a clear break with the past (except during the international financial crisis of November 1968 when the authorities acted to steady the market). Statements in the *Bulletin* and the movements of gilt-edged prices themselves point to the conclusion that the authorities are now much less prepared to intervene in the market as buyers than they would have been in similar situations in the past. Maximisation of sales perhaps remains the guiding principle but this has been clearly reduced in importance and interest rate considerations significantly emphasised. This change in official policy has two proximate causes. Firstly, the International Monetary Fund Letter of Intent of November 1967 required the authorities for the year 1968/1969 to finance the Government's borrowing requirement 'as far as possible by the sale of debt to the non-bank public' and that interest rate policy would be used to achieve this. The May 1969 Letter of Intent was much more demanding, and set precise targets for Domestic Credit Expansion. To the extent that the Government finances its borrowing requirement by sales of gilts to the non-banks, the D.C.E. is restrained. In order, therefore, to meet the D.C.E. objectives set by the Fund the authorities have had to alter their approach to the management of the gilt-edged market. The second development has been the extraordinary swing into surplus of the financial position of the Central Government (noted above) which has considerably improved prospects for the gilt-edged market. For the time being, at least, interest rate considerations and control of the money supply, have become much more important determinants of official policy in relation to the gilt-edged market—a significant break with policy prior to 1968.

THE MARKET IN TREASURY BILLS*

That part of the financial needs of the Central Government which cannot be met by sales of gilt-edged, receipts of sterling from the Exchange Equalisation Account small savings or increase in currency, has to be met through the creation of market liquid assets. The authorities have, through their chosen policy, at least prior to 1969, deliberately limited their freedom to sell gilt-edged, and have even on occasion purchased gilt-edged stock during periods of sales by foreigners. As indicated above, the contribution to be expected from small savings is slight, while expansion of currency will often conflict with stabilisation objectives. By far the most important of the market liquid assets created to meet the Government's residual borrowing requirement are Treasury bills. In *Table 6.1* data are given on the Central Government's net borrowing requirement, the increase in liquid liabilities and the amount of these flowing to the banking sector. Since Treasury bills are conventionally accepted as part of the banking system's liquid assets ratio, it has become a fundamental aim of the authorities to control both the creation of market liquid assets and also the proportion of these flowing to the banking sector.

Several features emerge from *Table 6.1*. In the first place the size of the Central Government's borrowing requirement has often been largest during precisely those periods when it was pursuing restrictionary policies. That this conflict of policies should occur is explained, partly at least, by the fact that the net borrowing requirement is the outcome of diverse policy considerations—amongst which monetary policy is only one. The effect of this has been to reduce the authorities' control over the increase in market liquid assets. This is borne out by a comparison of rows 2 and 4, which shows clearly a conflict between the creation of liquid assets and the Treasury bill rate. Since the latter is supposedly within the control of the monetary authorities the changes

---

* For a description of the Treasury bill market see the following articles in the *Quarterly Bank Bulletin*: 'The Management of Money Day by Day' (March 1963); 'The Treasury Bill' (Sept. 1964); and 'The U.K. and U.S. Treasury Bill Markets' (Dec. 1965). This market and the critical role of the Treasury bill were fully investigated by Radcliffe; see especially pages 334–380 and 583–590 of the *Report*.

Table 6.1

CENTRAL GOVERNMENT
(£ million)

	1960	1961	1962	1963	1964	1965	1966	1967	1967	1969
1) Net borrowing requirement	307	220	−79	148	423	597	534	1134	755	−1 116
2) Increase in liquid liabilities	245	10	−516	146	150	306	182	647	862	−925
3) Increase in holdings of government's liquid liabilities by banking sector*	−67	134	−287	15	−315	235	−83	8	151	−325
4) Treasury Bill rate (average) %	4·88	5·13	4·18	3·66	4·61	5·91	6·12	5·81	7·03	7·6

* Net indebtedness to Bank of England Banking Department, Notes and Coin, Treasury Bills.
Sources: *Financial Statistics*, H.M.S.O., Tables 16 and 18 (various issues); *Annual Abstract of Statistics*, H.M.S.O., Table 358.

in its level will represent their view about desirable developments. There is observable in *Table 6.1*, however, a perverse relationship between either changes in the rate (or its level) and the creation of market liquid assets.

In *Table 6.2* the volume of market Treasury bills outstanding during 1960–1969 is given in column 1, and its distribution between different holders in the other columns. It is clear from column 1 that the authorities have been very successful in limiting the volume of market Treasury bills, and these have fallen continuously during 1960–1967 (1968 and 1969, however, represent quite a different story). Their success in this respect is not unrelated to developments in local authority finance (below). Of the main holders of Treasury bills the discount houses have only about one-third of their total assets in this form, which is to be compared with about a half in the mid-1950s, and represents a shift towards other bills and short-dated stocks.

The figures for the domestic banks are, of course, dominated by the London Clearing Banks, for whom Treasury bills are especially important as falling within the conventional liquid assets category. The Clearing Banks do not apply for Treasury bills on their own account at the weekly tender but obtain their needs later in the market. When a bank has cash to spare, but needs to use it for the purchase of liquid assets, it can either buy Treasury bills or commercial bills from the market or lend the cash at call to the market—the security being usually bills or short-dated stocks. It follows, therefore, that Treasury bills held by the banks are a direct alternative to Treasury bills held by the discount houses on call money lent by the banks, and the choice of policies lies with the banks. In fact, their holdings of Treasury bills, as a proportion of total liquid assets, has fallen from about a half in the mid-1950s to only 9 % in 1969 at the same time as their holdings of commercial bills have risen and a larger percentage of deposits has been lent at call to the discount market and to businesses outside this market.* At the same time the holdings of Treasury bills by the accepting houses and overseas banks have also fallen, and they now hold a much smaller proportion of their liquid funds in the form of Treasury bills.

Overseas central monetary institutions and international organisations hold Treasury bills, both because of their yield and also on account of their security and liquidity. They tend to be firm holders. Bill holdings outside the banks, discount houses and overseas monetary institutions have never accounted for more than a small percentage of the total. In March 1951 they totalled some £75 million (2·5 % of all Treasury bills held by the market). By March 1960 the figure had risen

* See *Table 6.4* page 123.

Table 6.2

MARKET TREASURY BILLS, ANALYSIS BY HOLDER

(End of March, £ million)

	Total outstanding	Banking Sector				Overseas Sector			Other holders
		Total	Deposit banks	Accepting houses and other overseas banks	Discount market	Total	Central monetary institutions	Other	
1960	3 267	1 500	959	91	450		995		772
1961	2 979	1 275	808	102	365		1 048		656
1962	2 759	1 275	812	92	371		988		
1963	2 585	1 124	675	83	366	1 127	1 061	66	334
1964	2 595	1 149	608	108	363	1 136	1 086	50	310
1965	2 094	736	430	91	215	1 205	1 173	32	153
1966	2 305	1 151	671	80	400	997	911	86	157
1967	1 723	701	425	57	219	903	822	81	119
1968	3 077	662	333	74	255	2 299	2 219	80	116
1969	3 217	628	297	69	261	2 515	2 428	87	74

Source: *Quarterly Bank Bulletin*, 191 (Sept. 1964)
Financial Statistics, Table 19 (July 1969)
Quarterly Bank Bulletin, Statistical Annex (various issues)

to £772 million (some 24% of the total), but has since fallen dramatically to only 6% (1968). In March 1964 the figure for 'overseas holdings' (in 'other' category) was only £50 million, since Treasury bills are not an especially attractive investment for overseas funds which typically prefer high yield to liquidity. Financial institutions (insurance companies, building societies, pension funds, etc.) are all small holders of Treasury bills (some £20 million in 1964) and in their case there exist other assets of a short-term kind providing a higher yield, if admittedly somewhat less liquidity, e.g., Local Authority temporary loans. The rest of the residual group 'other holders' consists mainly of industrial and commercial companies. Since holdings of Treasury bills provided a useful return on surplus cash, and given the rise in short-term rates during the 1950s, then holdings of Treasury bills proved attractive to these types of holders. However, in recent years the competition from the Local Authority temporary market and hire-purchase finance houses, where returns are higher, has reduced the demand from companies.

As noted above it has been part of Government policy to limit the amount of liquid market assets flowing to the banking sector so as to control the monetary base. However, attempts to increase the flow of market Treasury bills going to non-bank holders has not, as the table indicates, been successful. 'As the system works the banks and the discount houses between them inevitably hold the residual amount of bills necessary to bring into balance the Exchequer's cash position and the markets.'* This follows automatically from the informal agreement with the discount houses whereby their weekly tender, in aggregate, at least covers the amount of Treasury bills on offer so that they take up whatever has not been distributed to others (who bid higher prices). The discount houses are willing to do this since they know the Bank stands ready to act as lender of last resort so that they can always get money to cover their bid. If the banks are short of cash they will withdraw money at call with the discount houses, who will then borrow from the Bank.

What is the function of this process? Why should the Bank want to engineer a shortage of money in the first place? When the discount houses find themselves short of funds the Bank may take steps to relieve the shortage (usually by buying bills from them or from the banks or by forcing the discount houses to borrow from them at Bank Rate or higher. 'The enforcement of such borrowing increases the average cost of the houses' total borrowings and is one of the main ways (short of a change in Bank Rate) in which the Bank of England exerts an

* *Quarterly Bank Bulletin*, 192 (Sept. 1964).

influence on short-term interest rates and particularly on the rate at which the discount houses may be expected to bid for Treasury bills at the next Friday's tender.'*

It is easier, therefore, for the Bank to create an artificial scarcity in the market which it can then relieve as it wishes—perhaps forcing the discount houses to borrow from the Bank at a penal rate. If the market has a surplus of funds then the Bank does not have this power. In such a situation the Bank may sell Treasury bills but it cannot be expected that the market will purchase these in such quantities so as to put itself in the position where it needs to go to the Bank for money. In this case the Bank's influence lies in its ability to control the rate at which they offer to sell bills. In practice, the normal operation of the weekly Treasury bill tender will usually create an initial shortage of funds.

The initial aim, therefore, of this process is to change the Treasury bill rate. But what effect is this expected to have on the economy? If the authorities are forced, in order to bring about a change in the Treasury bill rate, to alter Bank Rate then this will lead to a change in the rates charged on advances and deposit accounts. But the demand for advances seems, from the evidence, to be relatively inelastic to a change in their cost, while the banks seem to think in terms of satisfying demand for these within some long-term planning horizon. There seems also to be little reason to expect much (if any) redistribution in the assets of the banks. Much more significant, if it occurred, would be the possibility of encouraging larger non-bank holdings of Treasury bills. This could happen through a change in the relative yields of short-term assets in that a relative improvement in the Treasury bill rate might induce the domestic non-bank public to buy more bills. If this happened, then the banking sector would suffer a cash shortage (and a reduction in liquid assets) which they could only relieve by borrowing from the Bank. Each time they borrowed from the Bank they would be charged a penal rate so that at the next tender they would reduce their bid on Treasury bills. If the outside bidders received a higher allocation at the next bid then the banking sector's initial cash shortage would reappear.†

The question which is relevant for policy is can the authorities through manipulating the Treasury bill rate persuade enough non-bank holders to behave in this way? There is a further problem (explained in

---

* *Quarterly Bank Bulletin*, 16 (March 1963).

† This is a fairly simple view of the position. On possible complications, plus some empirical evidence see A. B. Cramp, 'The Control of Bank Deposits', *Lloyds Bank Review* (Oct. 1967), pages 30–32, and a more extensive discussion in *Oxford Economic Papers* (March 1968), 'Financial Theory and the Control of Bank Deposits' by the same author.

detail by A. B. Cramp in several articles) in that it is also important to know the derivation of the funds which are used to take up additional Treasury bills. If the source is a reduction in expenditure or a fall in idle-balances then the effect of selling more Treasury bills to the non-bank public would be as postulated. But it is unlikely that expenditure is sensitive to movements in short-term interest rates or that financial institutions hold idle-balances. If this is so, then more money to buy Treasury bills will entail a reduction in the flow of funds to other short-term markets. One obvious competitor is the Local Authority temporary market, but it is most unlikely that rates in this market would be left unaltered in the face of an outflow of funds. What is much more likely is that there would occur an upward spiral in short-term rates which would effectively prevent any permanent tendency for funds to flow into Treasury bills.

In such a competitive struggle the increase in short-term interest rates could be large, and this in itself could raise problems for the authorities. Increasing short-term rates could influence inflows of foreign funds which might conflict with domestic monetary policy (e.g., a rise in foreign deposits with the banks would constitute an increase in their liquid assets). However, during most periods of rising short-term rates in recent years the authorities might well have welcomed inflows of capital for their assistance in financing payments inbalances, although they would prefer not to be put into a position of paying a rate in excess of such funds transfer earnings. Perhaps, more importantly, spiralling short-term rates might conflict with other aspects of short-term policy, e.g., through its effects on the flow of funds into the building societies and therefore on the level of the building programme. There is probably some limit also to the extent to which the authorities can force the banking sector to pay penal rates on money borrowed to cover the tender for Treasury bills, and the discount houses may react by trying to sell short-bonds. In such a situation, given the Bank's policy on the gilt-edged market, the Bank would purchase bonds so as to prevent the rise in short rates overflowing into the markets for medium- and long-term funds. In the event, therefore, the possibility of controlling the monetary base in this way has been limited.

What follows from the foregoing? In the first place, it is evident that the monetary authorities do not any longer have much control over the creation of liquid money assets, and the ability, via variations in Treasury bill rate, to alter the share of these taken by the non-bank sector has been considerably weakened by the development of other competing short-term money markets. Attempts to bring about an increase in non-bank holdings via changes in the Treasury bill rate are more likely to produce an upward spiral in short-term rates than to obtain this objective. Secondly, there remain doubts even about the ability of the Bank to raise the discount market's average money rate through making them borrow at Bank Rate, and Alford has found 'In our period [1960–1962] at least, the effect on the average money rate of borrowing at Bank Rate seems to have been too small to make this explanation convincing'.* This is completely at variance with the evidence given by the Chief Cashier of the Bank to Radcliffe, who had no doubts that forcing the discount market into the Bank would put up the rate for Treasury bills.†

THE LOCAL AUTHORITY MARKET

Local Authorities are very large spenders; in 1968 they undertook current expenditure of £4380 million and their capital expenditure came to £1745 million (out of a GNP of £36 690 million).‡ Only a small part of their capital expenditure is met out of revenue, and a further small part is financed by capital grants from the Government. The rest has to be met out of borrowing—either from the Government or from the private capital and money markets. In the post-war period up to 1953 the Local Authorities borrowed almost entirely from the Central Government, through the P.W.L.B., but from the beginning of 1953 they were permitted to borrow more freely from the private sector and from 1955 they were generally required to rely on private sources, and not on the P.W.L.B. Between October 1955 and March 1964 Local Authorities were not allowed to borrow from the P.W.L.B. unless they could demonstrate that they were unable to borrow funds on their own credit from the market on reasonable terms. The main argument advanced for the change in practice in 1955 was that the Local Authorities would, by borrowing on their own account, be able

---

* R. F. G. Alford 'Bank Rate, Money Rates and the Treasury-bill Rate', in *Essays in Money and Banking in Honour of R. S. Sayers*, Oxford University Press, edited by C. R. Whittlesey and J. S. G. Wilson (1968).

† 'Supposing we wanted to make short-term rates higher, we should keep money short in the market consistently, and as a result the discount market would be compelled to borrow from us quite heavily and quite often. This would have an effect upon the overall cost of the money which they are borrowing to finance their book of Treasury bills and short bonds. They would feel for that reason alone that they must put up the rate for the Treasury Bills they buy, in order to retain their profit margin. They would be influenced by obvious wishes of the authorities to move in this direction.' Radcliffe: *Report*, para. 360.

‡ *National Income and Expenditure*, tables 42 and 43 (1969).

to attract local capital which would otherwise not flow into the gilt-edged market. In so far as this did happen then the Central Government's borrowing requirement would be reduced and thus bank deposits and bank liquidity would be prevented from rising.* This argument (and others) did not find much favour with Radcliffe† and strangely enough the change introduced in access to the P.W.L.B. in 1955 was matched by a contrary requirement for the nationalised industries who at this time were required to borrow from the P.W.L.B. and not from the market.

Towards the end of 1963 it was announced that from the following April all Local Authorities would be able to obtain part of their long-term finance (borrowing for one year or more) from the P.W.L.B. at the Exchequer rate (plus small addition to cover Exchequer costs). It was intended that 50% of each authority's gross annual long-term borrowing requirement would eventually be met from the P.W.L.B. The reversal of practice was, according to the Bank, for two reasons. Firstly, to help Local Authorities meet their growing need for long-term finance resulting from their rising capital expenditure. And, secondly, 'because the Government were concerned about the continued use of very short-term finance for long-run expenditure—and wished to limit its growth'.‡ This latter development is of very considerable importance for understanding monetary developments during this period.

Since the mid-1950s interest rates had generally been high, and Local Authorities had been unwilling to burden themselves with high rates for many years ahead and had, therefore, borrowed on a temporary basis, i.e., loans with a maturity of less than one year. There developed during this period a temporary loan market run largely by money-brokers and some large stock-brokers. The majority of the loans to the Local Authorities are repayable at either two or seven days' notice, though some loans are initially for a longer period, such as three months. In practice the loans are often left for a considerable time. Rates paid for three months money have usually varied between 0·5% and 1% above the Treasury bill rate and have thus always been above the rate for prime bank bills, reflecting a slight loss of liquidity.

The main sources of temporary loans are shown in the following table. The predominance of banks (almost entirely the accepting houses and overseas banks in London) and of industrial and commercial

* On the development of the Local Authority markets and for the official reasoning see 'Local Authorities and the Capital and Money Markets', *Quarterly Bank Bulletin*, **VI** (Dec. 1966).

† Radcliffe: *Report*, paras. 596–600.

‡ *Quarterly Bank Bulletin*, **VI**, 338 (Dec. 1966).

concerns is evident; at March 1966 they held respectively about a third and a quarter of the total. The high returns in this market have encouraged the banks to bid for deposits (both sterling and currency) and lend these profitably. Industrial and commercial companies are clearly less concerned by the slight loss of liquidity and are interested in the high

Temporary Loans (£ million)	31 March 1966
Banks	560
Industrial and Commercial Companies	384
Overseas Residents	172
Building Societies	154
Insurance Companies	35
Pension Funds	37
Investment and Unit Trusts	43
Trustee Savings Banks	17
Persons (incl. net errors and omissions)	208
Total	1 610

Source: *Quarterly Bank Bulletin*, Table 3, 342 (Dec. 1966).

yield and security. An important feature of the market is the use of overseas funds. It is not possible to state accurately how big these are, since much of the funds have reached the market via intermediaries. In March 1966 direct overseas holdings amounted to £172 million, but apart from these holdings a large part of the temporary loans made by the overseas banks and accepting houses probably related to the investment of overseas funds held on deposit with the banks either in sterling or foreign currency. If the deposit was in sterling the proceeds will have often been placed for a matching period with a Local Authority. If it was in currency it will have been switched into sterling (such behaviour being profitable when short-term lending to Local Authorities, adjusted for forward cover, gives a higher return than would be earned by re-lending in the Euro-Currency market). In both cases the short-term nature of temporary loans and the continuing changes in relative yields (plus confidence effects) have meant a considerable movement of such funds into and out of Local Authority loans during the past few years (particularly in the winter of 1964–1965, the summer months of 1966 and the third quarter of 1967). The Bank has estimated that about half of all loans to Local Authorities by the accepting houses and overseas banks originated abroad so that in March 1966 about one-quarter of all

Local Authority temporary borrowing effectively came from overseas (some £400 million).*

In 1955, before the withdrawal of access to the P.W.L.B., the total of temporary debt outstanding was only about £170 million, 4% of total Local Authority debt at that time. By 1965 it had risen to £1800 million (more than 18% of total loan debt).† The growth of Local Authority short-term borrowing and the consequences had already been commented on by Radcliffe, but the Government ignored their warnings and recommendations on this point.‡ By 1963 the Government had itself recognised the dangers and from 1964 introduced restrictions on the growth in Local Authority temporary debt. Each authority's temporary borrowing was to be limited to not more than 20% of its total loan debt, and this reduction was to be operative from April 1968.§ By the end of the first year of this proposal the percentage of temporary debt to total loan debt had risen to 18·5% (compared with 17% in 1964 —31 March in both cases). The volume in 1967 was virtually the same as in the previous March, but the first quarter of 1968 showed a substantial rise in temporary borrowing (a large percentage in the form of advances from the Clearing Banks).‖ This was due to switching from other forms of finance (the high medium- and long-term rates deterred borrowing from the P.W.L.B. while there occurred substantial switching of sterling into foreign currency during this quarter creating a shortage of funds in the Local Authority market).¶ In the long-term, since the restriction is in the form of a percentage, the restriction will not reduce the volume of Local Authority temporary debt outstanding, but it will restrain its rate of growth.

What problems have the foregoing developments raised for the monetary authorities? In the first place, as was noted by Radcliffe, there

---

* *Quarterly Bank Bulletin*, **VI**, 343 (Dec. 1966). For a further discussion of the role of the overseas banks see 'Overseas and Foreign Banks in London, 1962–1968', *Quarterly Bank Bulletin*, **VIII**, 162–163 (June 1968).

† Radcliffe: *Report*, Table 38, p. 358, and *Annual Abstract of Statistics* p. 104, Table 348 (1967).

‡ Local Authorities 'have been borrowing on a huge scale at very short-term; they have been piling up short-term debt in a way which is clearly contrary to the funding policy of the monetary authorities and they have done it at rates much above Treasury bill rates' (Radcliffe: *Report*, para. 397). 'The monetary authorities enforced this restriction of long-term borrowing with the knowledge that it was causing a rapid accumulation of highly liquid short-term local authority debt' (*Report*, para. 398).

§ This was subsequently changed to March 1969. (See *Quarterly Bank Bulletin*, **VII**, 14 (March 1968).)

‖ From £1854 million in the fourth quarter of 1967 to £2007 million in the first quarter of 1968, and rose further in the second quarter (£2151 million). (*Financial Statistics*, H.M.S.O., Table 26 (Dec. 1968).)

¶ See *Quarterly Bank Bulletin*, **VIII**, 111 and 116 (June 1968).

has occurred an extensive amount of 'unfunding' on the part of the Local Authorities at a time when the aim of the monetary authorities was to fund, i.e., to lengthen the average life of the securities outstanding.* Indeed, part of the success of the authorities in reducing the volume of Treasury bills is related precisely to the growth in Local Authority temporary debt. Moreover, the Local Authority loan rate has always been higher than the Treasury bill rate and a large group of investors have clearly preferred to hold Local Authority debt in preference to Treasury bills. These investors have in the main not been constrained by traditional liquidity considerations, whereas the willingness of the clearing banks and the discount houses to take up this type of debt has been materially affected by this consideration. It follows, therefore, that small movements in the Treasury bill rate relative to the Local Authority rate will not persuade any substantial movement of funds into or out of Treasury bills (the clearing banks and discount houses being constrained by traditional liquidity considerations while other holders will stay in Local Authority debt because it yields a higher return). The important conclusion which follows from this is that one particular technique for controlling the reserve base of the system no longer exists. That is, the monetary authorities no longer have the ability to control the reserve base through sales of Treasury bills to the non-bank public.

The second main result of the above developments is that the Local Authority rate has become the most important rate in influencing the movement of short-term funds, and yet this rate has been virtually out of the control of the monetary authorities. A change in Treasury bill rate will affect the Local Authority rate but will not result in big shifts in the distribution of funds between the two types of assets. However, changes in the covered differential between Local Authority rates and those in the Euro-dollar market can result in large movements in short-term funds—with consequences for the foreign exchange reserves. There have been many occasions in recent years when banks have switched large amounts of foreign currency into or out of sterling, raising problems in the management of the foreign exchange reserves.

The attempt by the authorities in 1963/1964 to control the growth of this market will probably be successful, but there will remain in existence a large (and increasing) volume of Local Authority temporary debt which will inevitably prevent the monetary authorities from shifting

---

* 'Throughout the postwar period the dominant motive of the authorities in their management of the debt has been the desire to "fund".' (Radcliffe: *Report*, para. 533.)

substantial amounts of liquid assets into the hands of the non-bank public and will preclude the use of this technique for controlling the reserve base. Inevitably the Local Authority rate will retain considerable independence of the Treasury bill rate, and will continue to exert its influence on the movement of foreign funds.

CONTROL OF THE MONEY SUPPLY

In Britain control of the money supply means in practice the control of bank deposits (these accounted for about 80% of the official definition of the money supply in 1967).* There has been in recent years an extensive debate in the journals about the techniques available to the authorities in seeking to control the level of bank deposits. It has, on the whole, generated more heat than light. The whole question of whether the supply of money is an important variable has received a good deal of analysis, more so in the U.S.A. than here.† However, the authorities appear to be in the process of re-appraising the influence of this variable, partly as the result of pressure from the I.M.F., and their actions since devaluation would seem to be consistent with a reversal of the Radcliffe doctrine that 'the supply of money itself is not a critical factor'.‡

The discussion entered a new phase in the mid-1950s when the foundations were laid of the school of thought known as the 'new monetary orthodoxy'§ and their views were, in essentials, subsequently adopted by Radcliffe.

The Bank cannot restrain the lending operations of the clearing banks by limiting the creation of cash without losing its assurance of stability of the rate on Treasury Bills. It is because of this circumstance that the effective base of bank credit has become the liquid assets (based on the availability of Treasury Bills) instead of the supply of cash. The Bank of England has chosen stability of the Treasury Bill rate, and so cannot impose a fixed relationship between the amount of cash held and the amount of Treasury Bills held by the private

---

* *Financial Statistics*, H.M.S.O., Table 41 (Dec. 1968).

† See 'Regularities and Irregularities in Economics' by L. Harris in *Essays in Money and Banking in Honour of R. S. Sayers*, Oxford University Press, edited by C. R. Whittlesey and J. S. G. Wilson (1968).

‡ Radcliffe: *Report*, para. 397.

§ There were three basic texts: 'Should Liquidity Ratios Be Prescribed?' by Wilfred King in *The Banker* (April 1956); 'The Floating Debt Problem' by W. Manning Dacey in *Lloyds Bank Review* (April 1956); and 'The Determination of the Volume of Bank Deposits' by R. S. Sayers in *Banca Nazionale de Lavoro Quarterly Review* (Dec. 1955).

sector, which exercised the freedom of choice thus left to it. . . . If their deposits fall, the banks can exchange surplus cash for Treasury Bills; if their deposits rise (as they can if the liquid assets ratio is above the required minimum), the banks can obtain extra cash required to maintain the agreed 8 %, by holding less Treasury Bills (or lending less to the discount market so that market holdings of Treasury Bills are reduced).*

Open-market sales of bills or securities aimed at withdrawing cash from the market could always be replaced by last resort borrowing at the Bank, either at current market rates or at penal rates. If it did the latter then the cost of credit would rise, but its volume would not be reduced, although this conclusion is based on the assumption that the banks' liquid assets ratio was in excess of the required minimum. It follows that bank deposits could still be controlled if the authorities operated on the total holdings of the bank's liquid assets, i.e., cash, short-term loans, Treasury bills and commercial bills (although at the time of Radcliffe, for all practical purposes, the banks' liquid assets could be thought to consist of cash and Treasury bills). Since the banks were unwilling to let their liquid assets fall below the agreed minimum of 30 % (28 % after September 1963) then a reduction in this ratio close to the minimum would produce a multiplier reduction in bank deposits something like three times as large as the initial reduction in liquid assets. Such a reduction in liquid assets was to be achieved by the authorities through 'funding', i.e., the sale of long-term bonds to the non-bank public so as to both reduce the floating debt and also the growth of the banks' liquid assets.† As *The Economist* commented, 'Monetary policy became a facet of Exchequer financing; if the authorities were willing to shift the structure of their debt, i.e., sell bonds rather than bills, or to adapt their fiscal policies (to vary their total need for finance) they could determine the volume of bank deposits by determining the supply of Treasury Bills.'‡

The new orthodoxy, which was never fully accepted by the authorities, has subsequently been criticised by Newlyn and Crouch, and

* Radcliffe: *Report*, para. 376.

† 'It is as a result of these arrangements [continuous official operations in the bill market, the guaranteed covering of the tender and the syndicated bid at the weekly tender] . . . that cash and Treasury Bills have come to be practically interchangeable and, . . . the supply of Treasury Bills and not the supply of cash has come to be the effective regulatory base of the domestic banking system.' Radcliffe: *Report*, para. 583.

‡ 'Whatever Happened to Credit Control', *The Economist* (19 June 1965). This is an interesting and penetrating analysis of monetary developments, and well worth reading.

Table 6.3

MARKET TREASURY BILLS, ANALYSIS BY HOLDERS*

(£ million and %)

	(1) Total outstanding	(2) Total less†	(3) Holdings of London clearing banks	(4) Holdings of discount houses	(5) (3 + 4)	(6) Other holders	Col. 3 as % of col. 2	Col. 5 as % of col. 2	Col. 6 as % of Col. 2
1960	3 267	2 272	941	450	1 391	881	41	61	39
1961	2 979	1 931	790	365	1 155	776	41	60	40
1962	2 759	1 771	794	371	1 165	606	45	66	34
1963	2 585	1 524	667	366	1 033	491	44	68	32
1964	2 595	1 509	667	363	1 030	479	44	68	32
1965	2 094	921	559	215	774	147	61	84	16
1966	2 305	1 394	656	400	1 056	338	47	76	24
1967	1 723	901	403	219	622	279	45	69	31
1968	3 077	858	371	255	626	232	43	73	27
1969	3 217	789	310	261	571	218	39	72	28

* End March; sometimes mid-March for col. 3.

† Total (column 1) less holdings of Overseas Central Monetary Institutions.

Column 6 excludes Overseas Central Monetary Institutions.

defended at least in part, by Cramp.* However, the new orthodoxy contains two basic assumptions, both of which can be tested empirically. In the first place, it was believed that changes in the volume of market Treasury bills will lead to a reduction in holdings of Treasury bills by

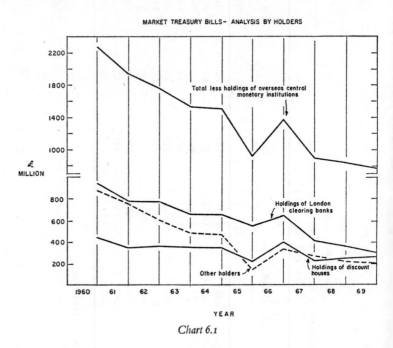

MARKET TREASURY BILLS- ANALYSIS BY HOLDERS

Chart 6.1

the banking sector. Secondly, that a change in the volume of Treasury bills held by the banks will lead to a similar fall in their liquid assets and therefore in their deposits. For the testing of both these hypotheses the volume of market Treasury bills outstanding has been reduced by subtracting the holdings of overseas central monetary institutions, who can generally be thought of as firm holders and whose demands can usually be forecast by the authorities. The volume of market Treasury bills and its distribution between the clearing banks and discount houses, and others, is given in *Table 6.3* and *Chart 6.1*. One thing is immediately obvious and that is the sharp decline in the total of market Treasury

* W. T. Newlyn, 'The Supply of Money and Its Control', *Economic Journal* (June 1964); R. L. Crouch, 'The Inadequacy of "New-orthodox" Methods of Monetary Control', *Economic Journal* (Dec. 1964). These authors' views have been extensively criticised by A. B. Cramp in 'Control of the Money Supply', *Economic Journal* (June 1966), 'The Control of Bank Deposits', *Lloyds Bank Review* (Oct. 1967), and 'Financial Theory and Control of Bank Deposits', *Oxford Economic Papers* (March 1968).

Table 6.4

LONDON CLEARING BANKS
(£ million)

	1960	1961	1962	1963	1964	1965	1966	1967	1968
A									
Total deposits	7 236	7 395	7 611	7 971	8 550	8 989	9 376	9 772	10 431
Total liquid assets	2 299	2 437	2 546	2 535	2 589	2 763	2 908	2 990	3 182
Money at call and short notice	562	606	718	748	738	910	1 006	1 136	1 335
of which to money market	490	507	524	532	533	675	731	806	896
Treasury bills discounted	1 007	992	933	842	790	653	689	564	468
Other bills discounted	142	233	272	298	365	461	446	492	527
of which U.K. commercial bills	121	180	202	224	283	368	343	357	341
Special deposits	74	174	159	—	—	56	137	194	208
Advances*	3 123	3 357	3 408	3 880	4 328	4 653	4 732	4 725	5 075
B Assets as % of total deposits									
Total liquid assets	31·8	33·0	33·5	31·8	30·3	30·7	31·0	30·6	30·5
Coins, notes and balances with B. of E.	8·1	8·2	8·2	8·1	8·1	8·2	8·2	8·2	8·2
Money at call on short notice	7·8	8·2	9·4	9·4	8·6	11·0	10·7	11·6	12·8
Treasury bills discounted	13·9	13·4	12·3	10·6	9·2	7·3	7·3	5·8	4·5
Other bills discounted	2·0	3·1	3·6	3·7	4·3	5·1	4·8	5·0	5·1
Investments	19·5	15·2	15·7	15·6	14·3	12·1	12·1	13·7	13·2
Advances*	43·2	45·4	44·8	48·7	50·6	51·8	50·5	48·5	48·6
C									
1) Liquid assets less cash	1 711	1 830	1 923	1 888	1 893	2 024	2 141	2 192	2 331
2) Treasury bills (directly held) as % of 1	59	54	49	45	42	32	32	26	20
3) Commercial bills (directly held) as % of 1	7	10	11	12	15	18	16	16	15

* Excludes advances to nationalised industries.
Sources: *Annual Abstract of Statistics*, Table 35, and *Financial Statistics*, Table 35, (Dec. 1968).

bills from £2272 million in 1960 to £789 million in 1969. Over the same years the holdings of the banking sector (clearing banks and discount houses) fell from £1391 million to £571 million, which is a rate of decline somewhat less than that of the total supply (one explanation of this must have been the attraction of other short-term money markets for certain types of investor). Nevertheless, there is observable a close relationship between the total of market Treasury bills and holdings of the banking sector, although the series do diverge in 1958–1961 when outside bill holdings rose sharply. Broadly speaking, the first hypothesis is borne out by the facts.

The second hypothesis, a change in Treasury bills held by the banks

LONDON CLEARING BANKS – ASSETS AS % OF TOTAL DEPOSITS

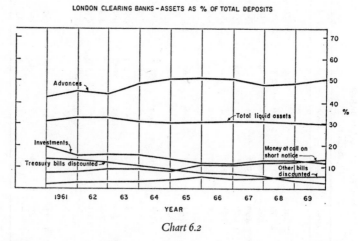

Chart 6.2

will cause a similar change in their liquid assets, is disproved by the data. *Table 6.4* provides data on the structure of the liquid assets of the banking sector (London clearing banks and the discount houses), and this is shown diagramatically in *Chart 6.2*. Up to about 1958 the total liquid assets of the clearing banks moved fairly closely with the banking system's Treasury bill holdings. Since 1958 the two series have diverged markedly (although during 1959–1961 the direction of change of the two series was the same). In 1960 the direct holdings of Treasury bills of the clearing banks was £1007 million, and money on call to the discount market was £490 million. In that year the discount market held £574 million of Treasury bills (some 48% of total assets). Applying this percentage to the money lent at call to the discount market by the clearing banks yields a total holding (directly and indirectly) for the clearing banks of £1242 million. Liquid assets of the clearing banks (minus cash) in 1960 was £1711 million, so that total (direct and indirect holdings of Treasury bills accounted for 73 % of total liquid assets. By 1969 the total direct and indirect holdings of Treasury bills of the clearing banks had fallen to a mere £633 million, whereas liquid assets (minus cash) had increased to £2572 million. In that year they accounted for only 25 % of the clearing banks' liquid assets. Clearly, therefore, a reduction in the flow of Treasury bills had not reduced the banks' liquid assets and they have increased the supply of alternative assets which satisfy their liquidity requirement.

That this was a possibility had long been recognised—even by the Bank itself in its evidence to Radcliffe.* That the clearing banks were able to increase the supply of liquid assets is dependent on two factors. In the first place, the decision on what constitutes assets suitable for inclusion in the liquid assets ratio rests largely with the banks, and not with the authorities. As the Bank put it (rather plaintively) in 1962, 'By accepting the bankers' definition of "liquid assets" certain constituents of the Ratio are more under the bankers' than the authorities' control.'† In the second place, the bankers were willing to substitute other assets for Treasury bills, in spite of the fact that these were less liquid, because of their belief that the minimum liquidity ratio (30% subsequently reduced to 28 % in 1963) was excessive purely in terms of normal banking requirements. Attempts by the authorities to reduce bank deposits by shifting more Government debt into the hands of the public (so putting pressure on the bank's liquid assets ratio) can be frustrated by the banks in several ways.

The bankers' first avenue of escape is through the sale of short-dated Government stocks, since a large proportion of the clearing banks holdings of gilt-edged is in this form and can usually be realised without substantial loss. In this way they can either increase their advances or add to their liquid assets. However, the scope for doing this has now been substantially reduced. Whereas in 1958 the ratio of the London clearing banks' investments to their total deposit liabilities was about 32%, it had fallen to 10% in 1969, and by no means can all of these investments be regarded as available for sale in order to increase advances or add to liquid assets. The banks resorted on a large scale during the 1950s to this practice, as was noted by Radcliffe: 'If the demand for advances is expanding when total deposits are not rising, they sell bonds in order to comply with their customers' demands. . . . Since October 1958 the banks have sold investments on a considerable scale and the

* Q 2732 Minutes of Evidence: *Chairman* 'Owing to the uncertain boundaries of the word "liquidity", you have a subject in which ingenuity is particularly liable to defeat your purposes? . . .' *Mr Cobbold* 'I would back myself at defeating it much more easily than imposing it.'

† 'Bank Liquidity in the U.K.', *Quarterly Bank Bulletin*, 254 (Dec. 1962).

resulting change in their portfolios may have brought them a little nearer to a position where they would become sensitive. . . .'* However the Bank of England's chosen policy in relation to the gilt-edged market actively assists the banks in behaving in this way. Attempts by the banks to sell short-bonds would tend to depress prices, and the Bank would enter the market as a buyer so as to maintain them ('lean into the wind'). From the bankers' viewpoint this would be welcome since it would tend to minimise capital losses.

The initial effect of the stock sales by the clearing banks on the total of their liquid assets will depend on who takes up the bonds. If they are taken up by the authorities, then the banks' liquid assets will be raised by the amount of the sales, and deposits would be unchanged. Secondly, sales can be made to the discount market, who may finance the increased holdings of Government stock either by selling Treasury bills to the banks or by borrowing more call money from the banks. In this case also the banks' liquid assets would rise by the volume of the stock sold, with no change in deposits. There will, however, be a limit to the amount of stock the discount houses are willing to hold in relation to their total assets. Finally, the banks' sales may be to the public, reducing bank deposits by the amount of the sales but leaving liquid assets unchanged. This will raise the liquidity ratio, although to a lesser extent than if the sales had been made to the authorities. However, sales to the public may have a secondary effect. If such bank sales replace sales that would otherwise have been made by the authorities to the public, then the fall in bank deposits which would have occurred does not take place. Again, if the public finances its holdings of stock (bought from the banks) through reducing its holdings of Treasury bills then the banks' deposits will be unchanged and the final result would be the same as if the stock had been sold by the banks directly to the authorities.

There is a second alternative open to the clearing banks, and one which they have availed themselves of on a large scale. This is to accommodate industrial and commercial customers by discounting commercial bills rather than through advances. This will raise the banks' liquid assets (advances do not qualify for inclusion), and the same result would be achieved if the banks raised the volume of funds lent at call to the discount market and they held a larger volume of commercial bills. From the point of view of the customers, borrowing on bills would be more clumsy, and would be perhaps slightly more costly. On the other hand, these factors have not been sufficiently powerful to deter the growth of demand for accommodation, and resort to the commercial

* Radcliffe: *Report*, para. 145.

bill has shown a dramatic increase during the last decade. The changing structure of the liquid assets of the clearing banks is detailed in *Table 6.4* and the changing relationships are shown very clearly on the Chart. In 1960 the clearing banks held £121 million of commercial bills and £21 million of other bills. In the same year the discount houses' holding of bills (commercial and other) amounted to £117 million. Their total bill holdings were £259 million in 1960. By 1969 the commercial bills held by the clearing banks had grown to £274 million, and other bills to £294 million, while the total holdings of bills by the discount houses had increased to £627 million. Total bill holdings came to £1195 million; an increase of approximately 460% over the 1960 level. It appears that this particular feature of monetary developments was actually encouraged by the Bank, who felt that it would constitute a 'structural improvement'!*

What conclusions emerge from the foregoing? In any situation where the authorities are faced by both rapid inflation and a large net borrowing requirement of the Central Government, then their ability to control the volume of bank deposits is slight. In the short run the supply of money has largely got out of control. Because of developments in alternative short-term money markets, particularly the Local Authority temporary market, the authorities are not able to affect the cash base of the banks through sales of Treasury bills to the public. The belief that the authorities can squeeze the liquid assets of the banks at will through their control over the supply of market Treasury bills has been shown to be totally unrealistic. The banks, through innovation, have put themselves in such a position that a reduction in the supply of Treasury bills can relatively easily be offset through the expansion of alternative liquid assets—particularly commercial bills. What is left to the authorities is the possibility of maximising the long-term demand for debt by sales to the non-bank public as and when the demand in the market is favourable to such sales. And, finally, the authorities can, and do, via their choice of rates at which to relieve cash shortages (lender of last resort functions), affect a wide range of short-term interest rates (although how effective they are in achieving the structure of rates they would prefer has been questioned recently by Alford). But in the period relevant for conjuncture policy the level of bank deposits, and therefore the money supply, has not been under the control of the authorities.

In what ways have the authorities tried to re-establish control over the money supply? One technique which has been used in recent years is to call for Special Deposits. These had been looked at by Radcliffe, but

* There is a further alternative open to the banks and that is to increase their cash through attracting foreign deposits.

Table 6.5

SPECIAL DEPOSITS WITH THE BANK OF ENGLAND

Announced		London Clearing Banks			Scottish Banks	
		Called	Released	Cumulative total	Called	Released	Cumulative Total
1960	28 April	1		1	½		½
	23 June	1		2	½		1
1961	25 July	1		3	½		1½
1962	31 May		1	2		½	1
	27 September		1	1		½	½
	29 November		1	—		½	—
1965	29 April	1		1	½		½
1966	14 July	1		2	½		1

Source: *Financial Statistics*, Table 33.

Note: Date of payment of Special Deposits does not coincide with date of announcement, e.g., the increase by 1% of S.D.s on 23 June 1960, was paid in two equal instalments on 20 July and 17 August 1960, so that the cumulative total of 2% is correct as of the last payment.

were not used until 1960. The view of Radcliffe is instructive, since they also pointed towards a possible source of dissension between the clearing banks and the Bank. Special Deposits have been called for on various occasions during the last 10 years (see *Table 6.5*) and in varying amounts. These deposits do not count towards the clearing banks' liquidity ratio, although they do earn a rate of return. They are compulsively deposited with the Bank of England, and in effect reduce the Exchequer's market borrowing requirement. Radcliffe did not report very favourably on the proposal for Special Deposits: 'Any proposal of this kind ... would have to be drastic if it was to influence the banks in their lending operations, as opposed to inviting them to make compensatory adjustments in their portfolios of Government bonds. We should find it difficult to justify drastic action of this kind, unaccompanied by general restrictions on all classes of lenders.'* Radcliffe has focused attention on two important points. Firstly, when a demand for Special Deposits is made on the clearing banks then how do they find the cash? The answer would seem to be through a reduction in their Treasury bill holdings. This is usually possible since at any point in time the clearing banks will have holdings of Treasury bills which are close to maturity. While this will reduce temporarily the banks' liquid assets ratio this will not necessarily reduce their deposits by more than the initial amount of the Special Deposits. Whether it does so will depend on their initial liquidity position (were their liquid assets in excess of the minimum requirement) and on their ability to create further liquid assets. As has been indicated above the banks have found little difficulty in expanding the supply of liquid assets satisfying the requirements of the ratio. It must, therefore, be concluded that Special Deposits have not yielded satisfactory results, at least in the way the authorities have used them.

The second point raised by Radcliffe, that Special Deposits may entail an element of injustice in that other financial institutions will escape this control, has not been lost on the banks themselves. There have been numerous occasions (see below) when the banks have complained about the restrictions placed on them as lenders which are either not applied to other (competitive) institutions, or, if applied, are inadequately policed. In respect of Special Deposits the authorities have recently announced a scheme, similar in form, which will apply to banks in the U.K. other than the clearing and Scottish banks. The sterling deposits of these banks rose from £1000 million in 1958 to £3000 million in

* Radcliffe: *Report*, para. 508. See also 'The Procedure of Special Deposits', *Quarterly Bank Bulletin* (Dec. 1960). It is perhaps worth noting that in 1969 the interest payable on a Special Deposit was arbitrarily cut by 50%. This was a penal act intended to make clear the authorities' displeasure with the clearing banks, who had failed to comply with the ceiling on bank advances.

1967, while their sterling lending to the private sector rose by some £800 million (some 20% of the total increase in such lending). It is intended that the new proposal* will both plug this particular gap in the authorities' control over bank lending, as well as go some way towards placating the clearing banks.

The traditional techniques of central bank control have, therefore, largely failed to prevent the expansion of bank deposits. Attempts to apply what is in effect a variable liquidity ratio (the imposition of Special Deposits) seem also to have been fairly ineffective. In the end the authorities have been led to interfere more and more directly in the affairs of the banks, and, finally, of other financial institutions. Requests for restraint in lending were made in July 1961 as part of the measures introduced to deal with the sterling crisis. These included a call for Special Deposits of an additional 1% (plus a request that this fall primarily on advances) together with a request to the banks that they 'be particularly severe towards proposals for new advances, or the renewal of existing commitments, for purposes of personal consumption, including hire purchase, speculative building. . . .'† This request was drawn to the attention of other banks in the U.K. (including overseas banks) and the Accepting Houses who were requested to reduce the rate of growth in their advances and apply the same general criteria. They were requested (all banks) not to increase the amount of bill finance, while similar requests for restraint on lending were made to insurance companies and the finance houses (hire-purchase companies were requested not to borrow further from the public in order to finance expansion). Such restraints remained in force until October 1962, although some Special Deposits were released at the end of May (at this time the request of the previous year was reaffirmed and the institutions were specifically instructed to give precedence to the needs of exporters).‡ In December 1964 further requests were made setting out criteria for lending, and in this case the building societies were brought within the area of control.§

---

* The proposal is outlined in 'Control of Bank Lending; The Cash Deposits Scheme' in the *Quarterly Bank Bulletin* (June 1968). The Bank explains the purpose of the scheme as 'for use at times when it may be desired to influence the banks' lending policies, but when something less is called for than strict quantitative controls of the "ceiling" type. Although quantitative controls tend to be employed on occasion, they suffer from a number of well-known disadvantages, including in particular the restriction of competition among banks' (pp. 167–168). Penalty aspects (higher deposits and/or lower interest on these) are included in the scheme 'to underline any official guidance, which it may seem desirable from time to time to offer to the banks, concerning the growth and direction of their lending' (p. 168).

† *Quarterly Bank Bulletin*, 6 (Sept. 1961).
‡ *Quarterly Bank Bulletin*, 87 (June 1962).
§ *Quarterly Bank Bulletin*, 263 (Dec. 1964).

At the end of April 1965 the existing restraints were reinforced by calls for Special Deposits and a further letter was sent by the Bank to the main banking and financial institutions requesting a restriction in credit expansion and its confinement to specialised classes of borrowers.* Subsequently the Bank approached a number of other leading financial houses which were not members of the various associations written to in April, and they were asked to comply with the Governor's letter. In July a further letter was sent to the banking institutions emphasising the need for credit restraint and for selective discrimination; in this case the letter identified for special mention the need to restrain the growth in the supply of finance for imports.† The April request was different in kind from any earlier requests in that it imposed for the first time a quantitative ceiling on credit, and this has continued in operation ever since.

On 1 February 1966 a further letter was sent to the clearing banks. This asked (additionally to the previous May's ceiling on advances) that their advances, acceptances and commercial bills, taken separately, should not rise above the levels set for March 1966. No change was introduced about lending. Similar letters calling for continued restraint were sent to other financial institutions.‡ The ceiling remained in force, and was confirmed on several occasions during 1966, with emphasis on the continuance of the 105% limit at least until March 1967. In the Budget of 1967 the Chancellor announced that the ceiling on lending to the private sector by the clearing banks and Scottish banks was discontinued, 'although continued restraint will be needed in credit to the private sector'. Priority categories were again identified, although 'there should be no appreciable increase in lending for the finance of personal consumption [etc.]. . . . Credit given by way of discounting commercial bills . . . should be treated as subject to the same priorities and restrictions as credit given in the form of loans and overdrafts.' The Bank's instructions contained an explicit threat: if there was too rapid an expansion of credit then the Bank would not hesitate to call additional Special Deposits and they intended to act more frequently than in the past to adjust the control of credit. In relation to other banks and finance houses the 105% ceiling remained in force.§

* *Quarterly Bank Bulletin,* 111 (June 1965). In this respect the authorities impressed on the London clearing banks the necessity for the impact of Special Deposits to fall on bank lending and that they should not try to mitigate the effects of the Special Deposits via a liquidation of investments. On advances the clearing banks were asked to restrain the growth in advances to an annual rate of increase of 5% during the year to March 1966. At the same time the banks should limit their acceptances and purchases of commercial bills.

† *Quarterly Bank Bulletin,* 218 (Sept. 1965).

‡ *Quarterly Bank Bulletin,* 3 (March 1966).

§ 'Credit Restraint in 1967/1968', *Quarterly Bank Bulletin,* 164–165. (June 1967).

Freedom was short lived. On 19 November further measures of credit restriction were introduced. Lending was to be restricted to the current level, and priority given to certain classes of borrowers. Commercial bills were introduced within the restraint. The Bank realised its demands might prove troublesome: 'The authorities recognise the difficulties that the banks may encounter. . . . The Bank of England will therefore be inviting all the main banking groups to regular and frequent discussions with the Bank, so that progress may be better examined and difficulties more easily surmounted.'* In May 1968 further instructions were given to the banks, in the usual terms and the ceiling was fixed at 104 % of the November level (the actual May level). Quite clearly the authorities had introduced an unworkable principle in their November letter (which excluded the finance for exports from the ceiling) and they had been forced to permit a rise in overall bank lending between November 1967 and May 1968. The May instruction gave up the attempt to isolate lending for exports as a failure, and reverted to an overall ceiling.† However, this decision was relatively soon revoked. In November special export finance was taken outside the ceiling again after representations from the banks. A new ceiling was introduced; after exclusion of fixed-rate lending the clearing banks were asked to reduce their lending to 98 % of its mid-November level by mid-March 1968 (other banks were to work to a ceiling of 102 % of the November 1967 level). Instructions were particularly specific in relation to lending to finance imports (the restriction was announced at the same time as the introduction of the Import Deposit Scheme). The restrictions were extended to other financial institutions (as usual), but this letter clearly entailed a substantial repayment of outstanding advances and inevitably caused an uproar (in this case one which developed within the public arena).‡

How effective have these measures been in restricting the growth of credit? One is again up against that most formidable problem in economics of not knowing what the alternative might have been. On the other hand, our investigations of these measures leads us to the conclusion that the requests did not have substantial effects on the giving of credit to the private sector. Monetary developments during the 1960s

* 'Credit Restrictions: New Measures', *Quarterly Bank Bulletin*, 348 (Dec. 1967).
† 'Credit Restriction, May 1968', *Quarterly Bank Bulletin*, 120 (June 1968).
‡ 'Credit Restriction', *Quarterly Bank Bulletin*, 358–359 (Dec. 1968). For the details of the bankers' case against the restriction see *The Financial Times* and *The Economist* of that date. The failure of the clearing banks to get within the 98 % ceiling during 1969 remained a source of embarrassment to the authorities, although the banking sector as a whole did finally comply with the ceiling. However, the opposition to ceiling control became stronger, and more public, in 1969 and some alternative form of control has become a matter of considerable urgency.

have contained a major contradiction. Whereas the supposed advantage of monetary policy lies in its impersonal *market* characteristics, instead we have witnessed the failure of traditional market weapons of control and the birth of a whole web of restrictions and instructions. Within the past few years the authorities have been put in a situation where there is nothing left for them to do but write letters. Inevitably this has placed great strains on the relationships between the authorities and the clearing banks (which overflowed into public acrimony during January 1968), and between one financial institution and another. The operation of such restraints, quantitative controls, requests, etc., have had an unequal effect on the business of different institutions and has, therefore, favoured the growth of some institutions more than others. Monetary policy during the past 10 years has been a far cry from the models in the textbooks.

7

THE IMPACT OF
MONETARY POLICY

Monetary measures have been extensively used by the authorities in Britain as short-term stabilisers since the revival of monetary policy in the early 1950s. Very rarely have monetary measures been allowed to have a gradual impact on the economic system since policy action has typically been a response to compelling circumstances, usually falling reserves. Quick results have always been demanded by the authorities. But it has been argued, particularly by Friedman, that monetary action of a discretionary nature is undesirable on the grounds that the 'outside lag'* is of considerable length and highly variable. Friedman is not alone in his views and recent econometric studies in the U.S.A. of monetary lags have confirmed some of his conclusions.† Even Radcliffe, while not denying the usefulness of monetary policy, concluded that it alone cannot 'be relied upon to keep in nice balance an economy subject to major strains from both without and within'.‡ This is not merely a

---

* The 'outside lag' refers to the time lapse between, say, a change in the money supply and credit and a change in real output. Friedman has suggested that this lag is of the order of eighteen months and while monetary policy is highly powerful it is because of the length of the lag, and its variable nature, that discretionary monetary action is highly dangerous. See Milton Friedman 'The Role of Monetary Policy', *American Economic Review*, **LVIII** (March 1968).

† For a survey of recent research on lags in monetary policy see W. H. White 'The Timeliness of the Effects of Monetary Policy: The New Evidence from Econometric Models', in *Banca Nazionale Del Lavoro Quarterly Review* (Sept. 1968). He finds much of the econometric research unconvincing and reaches more favourable conclusions on the time-lags involved. For a similar conclusion, on the basis of U.S. evidence, see Ando *et al.* 'Lags in Fiscal and Monetary Policy', in *Stabilisation Policies*, Commission on Money and Credit: Prentice-Hall (1963).

‡ Radcliffe: *Report*, para. 514.

question of the length of the relevant lags, but is also a question of the quantitative impact of the alternative monetary measures. In what follows *The Role of the Money Supply* deals with the changing attitude of the monetary authorities to the importance of the money supply and to what appears to have been a recent fundamental change in their thinking on this topic. *The Effects of Credit Restrictions on Persons* surveys the influence of credit controls on personal expenditure, and is followed by *The Determinants of Investment*, an analysis of the impact of monetary variables on investment. The final section, *The Control of Short-term International Capital Movements* looks briefly at the influence of interest rates on international short-term capital movements.

THE ROLE OF THE MONEY SUPPLY

It was a matter of great astonishment to many to discover in the Government's Letter of Intent to the International Monetary Fund in November 1967 an undertaking by the authorities of a limit to the growth in the money supply. This was strangely at variance with what were known to be the beliefs of the authorities—beliefs which had been largely derived from their experiences during the 1950s. That the undertaking of November 1967 was no passing aberration has been confirmed by subsequent policy statements by the Government, including a more tightly defined target for the growth of the money supply (domestic credit expansion) in the May 1969 Letter of Intent. This change of attitude on the part of the monetary authorities, while it falls right at the end of (and to some extent outside) the period we are dealing with, is sufficiently important to devote a certain amount of space to it.

Even prior to Radcliffe, the authorities had formulated a view of the importance of money which came very close to that finally adopted in the Report. Sir Edmund Compton, the main Treasury Witness, explained that in 1955 'Everyone told us and we believed ourselves that we ought to be looking primarily at the level of deposits. We thought we were doing quite well during those months . . . simply because the money supply as measured by bank deposits was going down. It was the fact that that had no effect that really caused us to go back to what had been perhaps an earlier doctrine, that the level of advances was decisive, and to ask for that ingredient of the banks' assets to be brought down.'[*] This attitude to the money supply was clearly the result of practical experience and in no way reflected the acceptance of any particular theory. The doctrine had two other elements. Firstly, that the income velocity of money was unstable, at least in the

[*] Radcliffe: para. 2435 of the Minutes of Evidence.

postwar period, and secondly, that the influence of changes in the money supply on expenditure depended critically on the cause of the change in money supply.

Such then were the views of the authorities as put to Radcliffe and these were found mainly acceptable by the Committee. It is worth repeating the Radcliffe findings since these broadly reflected the attitude of the authorities and remained their guiding principles during the post-Radcliffe period. They concluded that, firstly, while the supply of money was not unimportant, its importance lay in being part of the structure of liquidity.* Secondly, that the income velocity of circulation of money, while not a useless concept, is still not a relevant concept in that it has both proved unstable and also 'tells us nothing directly of the motivation that influences the level of total demand'.† It follows, therefore, that 'the authorities thus have to regard the structure of interest rates rather than the supply of money as the centre piece of the monetary mechanism'.‡ In this view of things the banks are specially important precisely because of their position as the main lenders in the system, and not because of their role as the creators of money.§

These conclusions have not gone uncriticised—both in England and elsewhere. Nevertheless, for our present purpose what is important is that they are a succinct statement of the monetary beliefs of the authorities. Indeed, it is precisely because of their 'acceptance' of the Radcliffe doctrine on the importance of the structure of liquidity as a factor determining the level of expenditure that the authorities have pursued a particular set of policies during the 1960s. Given either their inability or unwillingness (depending on one's point of view) to manipulate interest rates they have, logically, ended up in constructing a complex of controls over financial institutions which have been largely ineffective.‖ Undoubtedly, the failure of these instruments to achieve their objective has played some part in the conversion of the authorities' views on the importance of the money supply, although this is clearly related to other important factors. It is not due to any theoretical

* Radcliffe: *Report*, para. 389.
† Radcliffe: *Report*, para. 391.
‡ Radcliffe: *Report*. para. 397.
§ 'It is the level of bank advances rather than the level of bank deposits that is the object of this special interest; the behaviour of bank deposits is of interest only because it has some bearing, along with other influences, on the behaviour of other lenders.' Radcliffe: *Report*, para. 395.
‖ This was foreseen by Radcliffe: 'If for other reasons the authorities are inhibited in their manipulation of interest rates. . . . The authorities are likely . . . to be driven either towards a comprehensive structure of financial controls or to reliance on non-monetary measures as the effective regulations of total demand.' *Report*, para. 394.

revolution within the Treasury or the Bank of England, nor is it because officials have succumbed to the views of these American economists who believe most passionately in the Quantity Theory.* Indeed, most of the research on the significance of the quantity of money has been confined to the U.S.A., and even so there has been no general acceptance of its results.† In Britain there has been virtually no research, and again there is dispute about the validity of the results of even the few pieces of work which have been done.‡ This empirical work lends little, if any, support, for a belief in the hypotheses of the quantity theorists.§ The conversion of the authorities is due, therefore, primarily to the need to meet I.M.F. demands in terms of policies essential to achieve internal balance as a condition for receiving assistance.

That differences in approach to monetary matters existed between the Fund and the authorities has been apparent for some years. The Fund, in any case, has a reputation for being a strong believer in the role of money as a determinant of the level of activity and it is not surprising that clashes on policy should have emerged between the British authorities and the Fund officials in the discussions concerning the post-devaluation strategy.‖ While the Fund was able to write into the 1967 Letter of Intent a clause on the money supply, and other conditions relating to the Government's borrowing requirement, this did not of itself indicate any conversion by the British Government to a money supply doctrine. Indeed, the authorities permitted a substantial rise in

---

* The most powerful defender of the Quantity Theory is Milton Friedman; see his *Studies in the Quantity Theory of Money*, University of Chicago Press (1956), and more recently 'The Role of Monetary Policy', *American Economic Review* (March 1968).

† Robert Solow's comment seems apt: 'My own experience is that the hard scientific evidence one is always hearing about as proving the Chicago School's case has never materialised. Indeed the School's utterances too often have a Delphic quality that makes it difficult even after the event to know whether a given statement has proved true or false. . . .' R. M. Solow 'Putting the Money-supply Dispute into Its True Perspective', *The Times Business News* (28 Oct. 1968).

‡ See 'Two Aspects of the Monetary Debate', *National Institute Economic Review*, No. 49, 41 (Aug. 1969). One of the conclusions reached was that for U.K. 'it is fiscal measures . . . rather than monetary measures which are the more powerful and certainly the quicker acting'.

§ Two important tests of the Quantity Theory in Britain are the works by A. A. Walters and C. R. Barrett, 'The Relative Stability of Monetary and Keynesian Multipliers in the U.K.', *Review of Economics and Statistics, 1966*, and A. A. Walters, 'Money in Boom and Slump', *Hobart Paper*, No. 44 Institute of Economic Affairs (1969). Professor Walters' conclusions on the Quantity Theory are based almost entirely on the downturn of 1955–1956, although other non-monetary explanations are equally plausible.

‖ For an early statement of the views of the I.M.F. see J. Polak 'Monetary Analysis of Income Formation and Payments Problems', *I.M.F. Staff Papers*, **VI** 1957–1958.

K

the money supply during 1968 (by £987 million, an increase of 6·5 %), of which a large proportion of the rise occurred during the fourth quarter when the Bank, following its traditional approach to the gilt-edged market, bought large quantities of gilts. Since the balance of payments showed an adverse balance of some £460 million, the figure for domestic credit expansion (the money supply definition favoured by the Fund) for the year was £1904 million, larger even than during the devaluation year of 1967.

The year 1968 represented an unacceptable outcome and the I.M.F. officials obviously bargained more strongly, and demanded more specific commitments in the negotiations leading up to the May 1969 loan. The result was an agreed definition on DCE, together with quarterly and annual ceilings on DCE, written into the Letter of Intent. This has amounted to the acceptance by the British authorities of control of the money supply as an important policy aim. With this, and essentially linked, has occurred a change in the attitude of the authorities to the gilt-edged market. While the 1967 Letter of Intent included an undertaking that the Government's borrowing requirement would be financed as far as possible by the sales of gilt-edged to the non-bank public, this did not prevent the Bank's supporting on a sizeable scale the market during the fourth quarter of 1968. It is clear from their actions since then that, while the basic policy remains one of maximising sales of gilts, the authorities are now significantly less willing to support the market than they have been previously. This implies both more emphasis on interest rates as variables affecting demand, and, secondly, a determination to limit the growth in the money supply.

That monetary factors are being taken more seriously has been explicitly stated by the Treasury, which has noted that 'given the developments that have taken place in recent years, it is now becoming more practicable to make more use of money supply and particularly domestic credit expansion statistics during the year, as indicators of economic developments and guides to policy. . . . The fact that more use is being made of monetary indicators does not affect the choice of instruments of economic management in a particular situation.'* Nevertheless, from the tone of this article, it is perfectly clear that control of DCE has become a critical policy objective because of the assumed relationship between credit expansion, the level of domestic activity and the balance of payments. By accepting a target for DCE, the authorities have accepted the basic relationships of the supporters of

---

* 'Money Supply and Domestic Credit; Some Recent Developments in Monetary Analysis', *Economic Trends*, xxiv (April 1969).

the concept and are committed to the pursuit of certain types of policies essential to the achievement of the DCE target. Whether the relationships are valid, only time, and a great deal more research than has already been done, will prove. For the moment, what is important is that the authorities have accepted a money supply concept and within the limits set by a ceiling on credit expansion are adjusting their policies on debt management, fiscal policy and the growth of public expenditure. The year 1969 has become a watershed in British post-war monetary developments.

THE EFFECTS OF CREDIT RESTRICTIONS ON PERSONS

The consumption function has been the subject of extensive research by economists, and other social scientists, during the last 20 to 30 years, and there exist a number of excellent surveys of their results.* Most of this research has emphasised some form of income concept as an explanatory variable—either absolute, relative or permanent—but has broadened the determinants to include many other variables, including financial (liquid assets, credit availability, etc.), expectational (those factors which affect *willingness* to buy as opposed to *ability* to buy) and socio-economic. Income has retained its primacy in most of the recent models of the consumption function, but its role has been substantially modified in the light of empirical research. In particular, analysis of the short-run behaviour of consumption has confirmed that the relationship between income and consumption is not a stable one, and that other factors play a substantial part in explaining consumer behaviour. Much of this short-run instability in the consumption function is due to variations in purchases of durables, a form of expenditure of a highly discretionary nature. Indeed, as an increasing proportion of durable expenditure takes the form of replacement demand, then the discretionary element (when is the optimum time to replace) becomes more rather than less important.

Expenditure on consumer durables is about 8% of all consumer expenditure, equal to about 5% of total domestic expenditure. Almost 40% of sales of durables are financed by hire-purchase or by other credit instalment means. The authorities have long recognised that control over the supply of credit, including bank advances and

---

* See G. Ackley, *Macroeconomic Theory*, chapters X–XII, Macmillan (1961); M. J. Farrell, 'The New Theories of the Consumption Function', *Economic Journal*, **69**, 678–696 (Dec. 1959); and R. Ferber, 'Research on Household Behaviour', *Surveys of Economic Theory*, **III** Macmillan (1966).

hire-purchase credit, is important precisely because of the critical role of credit availability in the financing of durable expenditures. It is availability which is emphasised, and not the cost of credit. This distinction is not a new one, and figured prominently in the discussion of this problem by Radcliffe. On cost they concluded that 'private persons are as a rule quite unconscious of the rate of interest upon which their hire-purchase charges are based, and are governed in their hire-purchase commitments only by the amount of the down-payment and of the monthly (or weekly) instalment'.* The interest cost of personal borrowing from the banks is more obvious, but during the inflationary conditions of the 1960s (and given the existence of tax relief on bank interest charges) the effective interest charge has been insufficient to deter borrowing.†

Both the Treasury and the National Institute in their short-term forecasts identify a 'credit effect' as being a significant factor in determining consumers' expenditure. In the case of the Treasury, a guideline equation of the following basic form is currently used:

$$C_{(t)} = a + bC_{(t-1)} + cYw_{(t)} + dYw_{(t-1)} + eY_{G(t)} + Yo_{(t)}$$
$$+ g(\Delta \text{ h.p. debt}) + h(\Delta \text{ bank credit}) + iT$$

Where C_t = consumers' expenditure at time (t),
  Yw = disposable wages and salaries,
  Y_G = current grants,
  Yo = other personal disposable income,
  T = time trend
and changes in h.p. and bank debt are measured in the current quarter.

Since hire-purchase credit is linked directly to the purchase of goods a change in hire-purchase debt will probably be matched almost entirely by a change in consumers' expenditure (although there may be some change in savings). The relationship between bank advances to persons and consumption is likely to be less direct and less easy to identify since the statistics of advances did not, until 1967, clearly distinguish personal borrowing. Nevertheless, most personal bank advances will be made in the light of specific acquisitions and there is unlikely to be any significant lag between the granting of an advance and expenditure. Statistical analysis indicates that the long-term debt coefficient (for hire-purchase debt and bank advances) is close to 0·9 (this coefficient is not very different from that used by the National

---

* Radcliffe: *Report*, para. 465.
† The relief on personal bank loans was abolished in 1969.

Institute who have argued that the credit effect is equal to roughly 80 % of the change in hire-purchase debt and 80 % of the change in 'other personal bank advances').*

This belief by the authorities in the importance of credit availability as a factor determining consumption in the short-run has led them frequently in recent years to limit its supply—either in the form of hire-purchase restrictions and/or in requests to the banking sector to limit personal advances (see *Table 7.1*). There has been guidance on priorities to be observed in bank lending continuously since May 1965, usually making it clear that finance for consumer spending should either receive low priority or be positively restricted. Since November 1967 the banks have been asked to ensure that personal loans, where related to goods subject to hire-purchase control, should be on terms no easier than those allowed on hire-purchase contracts. Since 1965 (May) not only banks but other members of the Finance Houses Association have been asked to operate within fixed ceilings and to observe priorities in personal lending. While the authorities have little idea of the quantitative importance of these additional requests they obviously believe them to be essential as a reinforcement of the hire purchase controls and as a complement to the restrictions on bank credit restriction. Indeed, since 1967 Chancellors have exhorted other lending institutions to exercise similar restraint, but once again there is little evidence as to how effective such requests have been. Any substantial shift in the direction of personal loans (as against hire-purchase finance) would substantially weaken the effect of hire-purchase terms control as a short-term economic regulator, and the authorities are clearly seriously worried by the possibility that this may happen (and indeed may already be the case).

Hire-purchase controls have been extensively used during the 1960s (particularly since 1965) and have generally taken the form of changes in the minimum down-payment and changes in the maximum repayment period (see *Table 7.1*). Such controls have one great merit, as a short-term regulator of demand, in that they have an immediate impact on expenditure. This follows from the fact that increases in the minimum deposit entails an immediate increase in cash outlay associated with any given expenditure (there are no lags as in the case of changes in indirect taxes which have no effect while existing stocks last). On the other hand, hire-purchase controls have a diminishing impact through time as consumers build up their liquid balances to a level where they can now meet the higher minimum deposit and therefore undertake expenditure. In this respect hire-purchase controls serve only to delay

* *National Institute Economic Review*, table 3, footnote c, 10 (Nov. 1968).

Table 7.1

CHANGES AFFECTING MAIN CATEGORIES OF GOODS, HIRE-PURCHASE AND CREDIT SALE RESTRICTIONS

Date of order	TV, Radio, Domestic Appliances, Cameras, etc.		Furniture		Carpets		Cars & Motor Cycles	
	% Dep.	Months	% Dep.	Months	% Dep.	Months	% Dep.	Months
(A) 4/1960	20	24	10	24	10	24	20	24
(B) 1/1961	20	36	10	36	10	36	20	36
(C) 6/1962	10	36						
(D) 6/1965	15	36			15	36	25	36
(E) 7/1965	15	30			15	30	25	30
(F) 2/1966	25	24	15	30	25	24	25	27
(G) 7/1966	33·3	24	20	24	33·3	24	40	24
(H) 4/1967							25*	27*
(I) 6/1967							30†	30†
(J) 8/1967	25	30	15	30	25	30	25	36
(K) 11/1967	33·3‡	24‡					33·3†	27†
(L) 11/1968	33·3	24	20	24	33·3	24	40†	24†
							33·3*	24*

* 3-wheeled cars & motor cycles.
† Cars other than 3-wheeled.
‡ Cameras and binoculars.
Note: Cookers and water heaters have remained at 10 % deposit and 48 months repayment period throughout the period.

expenditure, although other outcomes are possible. It has been suggested that consumers, who are prevented from purchasing durables
through a tightening of restrictions, may not increase their savings, but
instead divert expenditure to other goods. This may well happen,
although there is little evidence to suggest that this is an important by-
product of terms control. It seems more than likely that the effect of

HIRE PURCHASE DEBT OUTSTANDING AND NET BORROWING EACH QUARTER

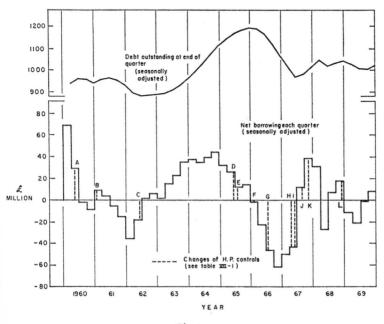

Chart 7.1

hire-purchase control is not asymmetrical. They are usually imposed at
or near the top of the cycle when consumers may find their liquidity
position stretched and at a time when consumer demand is high.
Restrictions will, as can be seen below, be very effective in curbing
demand. On the other hand, relaxation of the restrictions on hire-
purchase may be less effective in stimulating demand, since they will be
operating in an environment where demand is growing slowly, if at
all—they will simply be a passive factor.

Changes in hire-purchase debt in the periods immediately following
changes in controls provide some quantitative information on the
initial effects of such measures. On the other hand, not all of the change
in expenditure on durables can be attributed to changes in hire-purchase
controls, since other measures influencing demand (taxation, bank

credit restriction, etc.) have often been taken simultaneously (or nearly so). The existence of a 'package deal' inevitably makes it difficult to identify the precise contribution of each of the individual measures. In *Chart 7.1* the main developments in hire-purchase debt can be observed. The total debt rose rapidly after the abolition of controls in 1958 to a figure of £878 million at the end of 1959. It then grew more slowly (and was slightly reduced after the imposition of controls in April 1960 and a further tightening in January 1961) and then began a long period of growth after the relaxation of controls in June 1962. By the early months of 1965 the rate of increase in debt had begun to fall off, although the level of debt continued to rise until the end of the year. From then on successive tightening of controls led to a fall in debt with the maximum rate of fall following the July 1966 measures to reach a low point in mid-1967 some £200 million below the 1965 peak.

As well as the level of hire-purchase debt the chart also plots changes in debt. A rise in debt in a period means that credit being extended on new business is more than current repayments, and this indicates the extent to which consumers are adding to their disposable funds. As can be seen there is a clear relationship between changes in the controls and changes in the rate of net borrowing. This can be seen more clearly, for

Table 7.2

NET BORROWING IN PERIOD

	Actual (seasonally adjusted) (£ million)	As annual rate (£ million)	Change in net borrowing as annual rate (£ million)
1/1965–5/1965	+50	+120	—
8/1965–1/1966	+27	+54	−66
2/1966–7/1966	−40	−80	−134
8/1966–5/1967	−187	−224	−144
6/1967–8/1967	−6	−24	+200
9/1967–11/1967	+44	+176	+200
12/1967–9/1968	+16	+19	−157

Note: Relates to hire-purchase sales of durable goods shops, finance houses and department stores.
Source: Treasury and Board of Trade Memorandum, 'Hire Purchase Controls', submitted to the Crowther Committee on Consumer Protection.

the years since 1965, in *Table 7.2* by comparing the rates of net borrowing in the periods between changes. The figures in the final column cannot be taken as an estimate of the effects of the controls since other changes were simultaneously occurring. Nevertheless, the controls (along with other measures) have had a marked effect on net borrowing.

What relationship is there between changes in net borrowing and expenditure on durables? One would expect this to be close since the occasion for net borrowing is expenditure on durables. *Chart 7.2* provides data on changes in net borrowing and changes in consumer's expenditure on durables on a quarterly basis. Some connection is apparent, although clearly other factors are affecting durable expenditure apart from net borrowing. This is most clearly observable in the

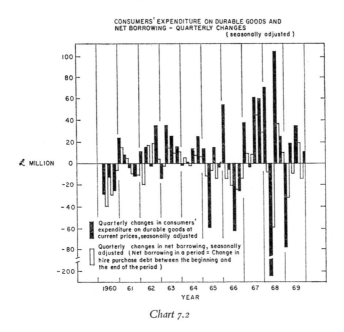

Chart 7.2

large rise in durable goods expenditure between the fourth quarter of 1967 and the first quarter of 1968, when net borrowing actually fell. This was clearly related to anticipatory buying on the part of consumers who had had fair warning from the Chancellor that a tough Budget was likely in April (1968), and consumers were prepared to reduce their savings in order to forestall purchase and other tax increases. Nevertheless, it is still reasonable to assume that changes in debt outstanding are a reasonable indicator of the scale of the total effect on durable and non-durable expenditure and that the controls have an impact on demand, at factor cost, of the order of £100 million, at an annual rate.

An estimate of this size is broadly in line with earlier estimates of the effect of hire-purchase controls. As Radcliffe observed, a regulator is only useful if it can have reasonably sizeable effects within a relatively short period of time. They found that hire-purchase controls did have a minimum effect of the order of £100 million but that these 'sizeable effects on total demand have implied major directional effects, which, though sometimes deliberately sought, have in general been detrimental to economic efficiency'.* Dow reached similar conclusions, and was equally critical of the directional impact of terms control.† These criticisms have been repeated over and over again during recent years in many private and semi-official reports on the operation of terms control. They have, as everyone admits, severely interrupted the flow of sales in certain industries and this has certainly had unfavourable effects on the growth of capacity. On occasion this shortage of capacity has undoubtedly worsened the balance of payments and terms control has contributed to the problem of regional unemployment. On the other hand, from the point of view of the Treasury, the use of credit controls (and particularly hire-purchase control) is highly desirable on balance. A sizeable impact on demand can be achieved relatively easily, with fair certainty, and quickly. Such controls do not have the disadvantage (as with indirect tax changes) of pushing up the price level, but they also have the disadvantage (in the case of terms control) of having a diminishing impact. For the moment the Treasury is concerned to keep its powers over terms control as a major weapon in the management of demand, in spite of its side effects. Nevertheless, they are undoubtedly perturbed by the growth of other forms of credit, a development partly due to the continuous use of terms control since 1965, and the fear that this alternative source of credit will greatly weaken terms control as a regulator of demand.

THE DETERMINANTS OF INVESTMENT

BUSINESS FIXED INVESTMENT

Many theories have been advanced by economists to explain the behaviour of fixed investment but in spite of a vastly increased amount of empirical investigation the quantitative importance of different variables remains a matter of academic dispute. A great deal of econometric testing of investment functions has occurred in the last 10 to 15 years,

* Radcliffe: *Report*, para. 469.
† Dow considered it likely that a very rapid expansion of credit (including bank advances and hire-purchase credit) could add something like £100 million or more to consumer expenditure in two to six months. The effect on consumption during a year of transition from tight to very easy credit might be to add a maximum of £200 million to demand.

but these have not resulted in conclusive results. The aim of such studies ought not, of course, be to lead to the espousal of any particular *theory* of investment but rather to identify the precise quantitative size of the relevant variables. As yet neither the statistical techniques, nor the theories of investment, have permitted economists to produce these answers so that the analysis of investment has been largely confined to the question of which variables (change in profits, in sales, in monetary variables and so on) are important or unimportant. From the point of view of economic policy such results are of more value, but the authorities are inevitably much more interested in the size of the coefficients. Also important for our present purpose is the fact that most of the econometric and non-econometric research into investment has been undertaken in the U.S.A., and that very little recent work has been undertaken in the U.K. Two conclusions follow from this. In the first place, statistical results which are based on American research which themselves have not produced conclusive results even in relation to American conditions are a poor indicator of the importance of factors affecting investment in U.K. Secondly, as will become apparent later, the British authorities have very little empirical evidence on which to base their policies; they have beliefs about the importance of alternative variables, but do not have any precise quantitative information on the values to be attached to these.

One of the more important theories of investment* is the neo-classical theory of optimal capital accumulation. According to this theory businessmen will undertake investment up to the point at which the internal rate of return is equal to the rate of interest. Such behaviour entails calculations of the factors influencing the yield of investment, including the expected life of the asset, the price of the capital good, expected revenue from sales and so on. The best-known theory in this form is that of Keynes, who held both that the marginal efficiency of capital is a decreasing function of the stock of capital and that 'the actual rate of current investment will be pushed to the point where there is no longer any class of capital asset of which the marginal efficiency exceeds the current rate of interest'.† On the other hand, Keynes was extremely sceptical of the powers of the monetary authorities to influence investment through variations in the rate of interest, although recognising clearly that the interest elasticity of investment would not be constant through the cycle.

* For a convenient survey of the various theories see chapters 1 and 2 of J. R. Meyer and Edwin Kuh's, *The Investment Decision: An Empirical Study*, Harvard University Press (1957).

† J. M. Keynes, *General Theory of Employment, Interest and Money*, Macmillan, 136 (1936).

A number of criticisms have been levelled at the neo-classical theory. In the first place, a large number of non-econometric investigations of the *motivations* of firms (usually business surveys) suggest that marginalist considerations are largely irrelevant in the investment decision. This was certainly the conclusion of one of the earliest investigations of investment by Henderson⋆ in 1938–1939, subsequently confirmed by later studies both in Britain and in the U.S.A.† The argument is based on the assumption that firms have short planning horizons and typically expect investment to pay for itself in a relatively short period of time (say four to five years). This view results from uncertainty about the future partly caused by expectations of rapid technological obsolescence, so that small variations in the rate of interest do not materially affect investment demand. On these grounds those capital goods with the longest life and the greatest certainty attaching to them would be the most responsive to interest rate variations, and this effect would be at its minimum where the economic life of the investment is short and uncertainty greatest.

Radcliffe, which is, surprisingly, for the U.K. the only recent reasonably comprehensive investigation of the impact of monetary variables on investment, investigated the direct effect of the rate of interest on business investment. They found general scepticism. 'The insignificance of interest charges in relation to other costs and to the risks involved was emphasised to us again and again, in relation not only to fixed investment but also to stocks of commodities.'‡ They asked the directors of large companies how they reacted to changes in interest rates and received replies which made it clear that in manufacturing industry they assumed a more or less constant interest charge and 'would not alter their existing plans even if they thought somewhat higher rates had come to stay'. Similar independence of investment decisions from

---

⋆ H. D. Henderson, 'The Significance of the Rate of Interest' in T. Wilson and P. W. S., Andrews, *Oxford Studies in the Price Mechanism*, O.U.P. (1951). He concluded, 'It is hard to suppose that a difference in interest rates, which could only represent a small item in the calculation, could play a material part in the decision reached.'

† These survey results are conveniently summarised by W. H. White in 'Interest Inelasticity of Investment Demand—The Case from Business Surveys Re-examined', *American Economic Review* (Sept. 1956), and again in 'The Changing Criteria in Investment Planning', materials submitted to the Joint Economic Committee, 87th Congress, 2nd Session, Part II (1962). In his view much of the survey data have been misinterpreted and he holds firmly that 'when buttressed by other neglected considerations, to establish at least a borderline case for significant effects on a big company's investment from interest rate changes having the magnitude of cyclical variation recently observed'. He tends to be in a minority in holding this view.

‡ Radcliffe: *Report*, para. 451.

interest rates appeared in the answers of smaller businessmen and representatives of Local Authorities and nationalised industries. However, there were exceptions, and Radcliffe noted that in some cases changes in interest rates which amounted to changes of 'gear' were sometimes influential in changing expenditure. In all these exceptional cases the changes in expenditure were mainly in response to changes in short-term interest rates. However, the Radcliffe assessment of the direct effects of interest rates on business investment has been criticised mainly on the grounds that the questionnaire evidence available to the Committee was deficient. This is probably an inevitable problem where one is asking *ex post* about the importance of different variables on a particular act—in this case investment—and many firms must have found it impossible to determine the importance of one monetary variable from another, or distinguish between economic policy and other considerations. Nevertheless, Radcliffe were completely confident in their final assessment of the direct effects of interest rates on investment: 'We have not found sufficient evidence to justify a conclusion that in the conditions of the 1950s the rise in interest rates would by itself have directly provoked a worthwhile curtailment of demand.'*

However, Radcliffe did note that firms who sought alternative sources of credit (during credit squeezes) usually had to pay more for it. Most of these did not flinch, but in some cases 'the stiffer terms evidently led to a reconsideration of the project, especially where this was in a very preliminary stage. . . . In short, the hindrance to customary channels of borrowing, though it left various avenues of escape open, had real effect in checking projects in their early stages.'† In the Radcliffe analysis the impact of interest rates on current investment expenditure was typically slight, and that effect lay mainly on the length of the investment cycle.‡

There appears, therefore, to be little evidence to support the marginalist approach, and the data suggest that interest rates in themselves are probably not an important influence *directly* on the level of investment. Nevertheless, the data were imperfect and many of the econometric studies which have thrown up negative results are in various ways

---

* Radcliffe: *Report*, para. 453.

† Radcliffe: *Report*, para. 457.

‡ 'The monetary instruments employed left untouched the large industrial corporations that control more than half the investment in manufacturing industry; and neither their planning nor that of the public corporations appears to have responded seriously to changes in interest rates. In the more fractionally organised parts of the private sector there has been pressure here and pressure there, though nothing of great moment.' Radcliffe: *Report*, para. 472.

deficient. In particular the market interest rate used in many such studies may be a poor indicator of the actual cost of money to firms wishing to invest. Other studies which have identified positive results for the interest rate variable have all indicated that this effect is small. However, such investigations have typically concentrated on the *direct* effects and have ignored their *indirect* impact, a point to which we return later.

The neo-classical theory has come in for rather heavy criticism. Meyer and Kuh and Simon* have attacked it as being far too narrow in its interpretation of firms' motives. They have shown that research into the behaviour of firms has identified many alternative hypotheses apart from profit maximisation. In the place of a single aim they have suggested the substitution of utility maximisation. These much more complex theories of the firm focus attention on the multitude of factors which effect the investment decision. For example, some writers have suggested that maintenance of existing systems of control in the firm are important constraints on investment. This arises from the fact that in certain situations a conflict may arise between investment which is expected to be profitable but which would require access to external sources of finance and maintenance of control. In such situations some investments which are profitable would not be undertaken. Alternatively, it has been suggested, notably by Duesenberry† that investment in certain market situations may be undertaken for defensive reasons. The argument is applied specifically to oligopolistic markets where firms cannot afford to let their costs get out of line with each other. If they did, then the firm with lowest costs could cut prices and increase its market share. In the event, therefore, the firm which is prepared to accept the highest risks will probably set the pace for both investment and research with the probability that such industries will exhibit high rates of technological obsolescence and high gross levels of investment.

Other writers, of which Meyer and Kuh are the best known, have stressed the importance of financial variables as affecting the investment decision. According to these theories financial flows place a constraint on the pace of investment. They believe that there exists a 'clear tendency for liquidity and financial considerations to dominate the investment decision in the short-run, while, in the long-run, outlays for plant and equipment seem geared to maintenance of some relation between out-

---

* H. A. Simon, 'Theories of Decision Making in Economics and Behavioural Science', *Surveys of Economic Theory* ,Vol. III, Macmillan, London (1966).
† J. S. Duesenberry, *Business Cycles and Economic Growth*, McGraw-Hill (1958).

put and capital stock'.* They emphasise, as many other writers have done, the high ratio of self-financing which is typical of manufacturing firms. The role of profits in such a theory is multi-faceted. Typically investment will only be undertaken when it is expected to be profitable and so profits become an important expectational variable. However, expectations of rising profits will not always lead to investment where the increase in profits will be due to rising sales which can be met from existing capacity. The *previous* flow of profits is also felt to be relevant since this will make it possible to finance internally a higher level of investment (and so avoid 'control' conflicts). This factor will be more important for some firms than for others—for example, it will be more critical for the firm which has been growing fast and whose liquidity may be stretched and for small firms who find it expensive to try to raise external sources of finance. That liquidity factors may be important has been denied by some researchers (Eisner in particular), while Barna in his investigation of manufacturing investment in the U.K., found that financial obstacles were rarely mentioned by firms as important constraints.

Certainly the authorities, during early 1966, behaved as if liquidity factors were important in determining investment. At that time the payment of S.E.T. by firms was expected to tighten company liquidity (in the case of manufacturing companies only temporarily since repayments plus the premium would occur later in the year) and the Chancellor promised to watch the situation closely in order to act with regard to bank lending restrictions should the squeeze on liquidity endanger investment expenditure. (Action was effectively overtaken by the changes in Government policy associated with the July 1966 measures.) Again in 1968 the Treasury believed that one effect of the Import Deposit Scheme would be on the liquidity of firms, who, denied access to the banking sector for finance for imports, would have to meet the deposits on imports from their own resources. It was expected that the resulting squeeze on companies' cash flow would affect investment. Once again this expectation proved unfounded. Evidently firms managed to finance the import deposits (often through the provision of credit by overseas suppliers) without great difficulty, so that no observable impact was made on company investment. At a more recent date

* J. R. Meyer and Edwin Kuh, *The Investment Decision: An Empirical Study*, Harvard University Press, 192 (1957). In a later study, prepared for the Commission on Money and Credit they asserted that 'financial supply conditions entering into manufacturers' investment decisions are such that manufacturers' plant and equipment outlays would be little influenced by monetary policy even if the demand for manufacturing investment were highly interest elastic.' *Impacts of Monetary Policy*, Prentice-Hall, 346 (1964).

still, towards the end of 1968, it appeared to the authorities that pressure on the cash flow of companies would, during a period when bank borrowing was severely restricted by the 98% ceiling together with high interest rates, lead to substantial reductions in investment by firms during 1969 and 1970—particularly in the latter year. It was considered most unlikely that firms would actually undertake the amount of investment indicated by the investment intentions inquiries given the tightening of liquidity foreseen by the authorities. For firms to persist with their investment plans would entail a substantial running down in their liquid assets during 1969 and 1970 on a scale not previously experienced by companies, and from a liquid assets base which was itself more inadequate than usual.*

The Bank of England has certainly accepted the thesis that liquidity is an important determinant of business investment and by the mid-1960s had come to believe that monetary policy, particularly control of bank lending, was becoming a more critical factor, rather than becoming less important, with the development of alternative sources of finance for companies. This belief in the power of monetary policy to substantially influence investment is nothing new for the Bank, who expounded these views most strongly in its evidence to Radcliffe, although it did not support its evidence by any empirical research.

There are some grounds for thinking that the Bank may be right in attributing more influence to monetary measures in determining investment during the second half of the 1960s. It is, however, quite a different thing to demonstrate this, and the Bank can be criticised not so much for its beliefs but for its failure to substantiate them. During the years 1952–1958 the internal funds of companies as a proportion of funds from all sources was 93%, while in the period 1959–1965 internal funds accounted for 85%. There has occurred, therefore, in recent years a greater recourse to external funds, entailing more borrowing from the banks (and other financial institutions), more capital issues, and a running down of some types of liquid assets. In the period 1952–1958 the capital expenditure of companies was financed by internal funds to the extent of 85%, whereas this figure was 71% during 1959–1965. In the cyclical peak of investment in 1960 external borrowing plus running down of liquid assets met 24% of capital expenditure. In the next cyclical peak (1964) this figure had risen to 32%. Borrowing by companies from all sources as a percentage of total capital expenditure rose

* Liquid assets of companies rose more slowly than GNP (as a measure of transactions) during the 1960s. For an account of developments in company finance and an explicit statement of the hypothesis that liquidity is a critical factor in determining investment see Bank of England *Quarterly Bank Bulletin* (March 1967).

from 15 % per annum in 1952–1958 to 26 % per annum in 1959–1965, and that from banks for the same period from 1·3 %/annum to 12·0 %/annum. While there occurred little change in the proportion of total capital expenditure of companies financed by capital issues or non-bank borrowing in the two periods, the increase in bank borrowing is clearly concentrated in this second period. During 1959–1965 bank borrowing was equal to half of total company borrowing (12 % of total capital expenditure) compared to only 9 % of total borrowing during 1952/1958. Furthermore, companies added less to their liquid assets in 1959/1965 (plus 2 % per annum) than in 1952–1958 (plus 5 % per annum) and thus while failing to maintain the build up in such assets, they were better able to accelerate capital expenditure.

The above date, while not conclusive, lend some support for the official view. Company liquidity is now less favourable than in the 1950s. This is not to say that all companies have insufficient liquid assets, and it is probable that some companies are affected more by tight monetary conditions on their cash flow position than others because of the inadequacy of their liquid assets. On the distribution of liquid assets among companies little is known. It is believed, and this seems reasonable, that liquid assets are distributed unevenly and that tight monetary policy (as seen during 1968/1969) had a differential impact. Unfortunately for policy, it is not known in advance where the impact will fall, and this makes nonsense of certain other aspects of Government policy. Monetary policy in this respect becomes too blunt an instrument and its effects may fall on precisely the wrong sectors of the economy. Moreover, part of the pressure on companies with few liquid assets may be partly offset by extensions of trade credit.

How important is this effect likely to be? Very little evidence is available on which to base any firm conclusions, although this does not prevent there existing several fairly-well-defined views on this topic. As Radcliffe noted: 'An expansion of trade credit . . . is unlikely to affect every sector of the economy in the same way; some sectors will find themselves net takers and others net givers of credit, and the resulting change in relative liquidity may reinforce or thwart the policy of the authorities, especially if the two groups are not equally dependent on bank and other forms of credit. . . . Moreover trade credit is so large in relation to bank credit that a comparatively small lengthening of trade credit would normally offset quite a large proportionate reduction in bank credit.'[*] Radcliffe further found that small firms are more dependent on trade credit than large firms, and that the volume of trade credit is largely unaffected by changes in interest rates. They were

[*] Radcliffe: *Report*, paras. 299–300.

L

agnostic in their conclusion: 'The evidence at our disposal is insufficient to allow us to say how far trade credit took the place of bank credit during the credit squeeze.'* A later investigation by Brechling and Lipsey found that the activation of idle balances is a 'strong potential frustrator of monetary policy',† mainly through the channelling of idle funds from liquid firms to firms suffering from the tight monetary conditions.

The views of Radcliffe, and the conclusions of Brechling and Lipsey have come in for a certain amount of criticism. Dow considers it likely that 'restrictions on bank lending may induce further restrictions on the giving of private credit'.‡ This follows from the behaviour assumption (it is no more than this) that an initial restriction on bank credit 'makes each firm anxious to maintain its own liquidity, and with any given degree of liquidity, more reluctant to lend to others'.§ W. H. White‖ concluded that trade credit expansion would 'not nullify much of a tight money programme'. There can be no firm conclusions on the point and what is needed, as Radcliffe suggested, is more research. There is an additional requirement—a great improvement in the quality of the figures relating to trade credit collected by the Government. At present these are so inadequate as to prevent any worthwhile analysis. The problem remains—how elastic is the supply of trade credit, and to what extent can expansion of it frustrate the operation of bank credit controls. It is evident that the authorities believe this force to operate and to be quantitatively significant (even if not at present quantifiable).

No firm conclusions on the importance of liquidity (and particularly of profits) seems possible. The Meyer and Kuh conclusions, which have been particularly influential, can be variously interpreted and Eisner and Strotz have shown that their results can be explained better by other factors.

One of the points made by those who stress the importance of financial variables is the relationship of financial variables, monetary policy and the cycle. According to these writers the early part of the cycle is characterised by ample and rising liquidity. As demand begins to rise from the floor of the cycle, firms find profits per unit of output

---

* Radcliffe: *Report*, para. 311.

† F. R. Brechling and R. G. Lipsey, 'Trade Credit and Monetary Policy', *Economic Journal*, 641 (Dec. 1963).

‡ J. C. R. Dow *The Management of the British Economy 1945–1960*, Cambridge University Press, Cambridge, 324 (1965).

§ J. C. R. Dow, *The Management of the British Economy 1945–1960*, Cambridge University Press, 323 (1965).

‖ W. H. White, 'Trade Credit and Monetary Policy: A Reconciliation', *Economic Journal*, 945 (Dec. 1964).

increase rapidly at the same time as dividend payouts remain low and monetary policy is easy. During this phase of the cycle internal finance is typically not a constraint on fixed investment, although difficulties may arise in the financing of inventories. In the later phase of the cyclical upswing firms will have undertaken fixed investment and will want to add further to their capacity. The ratio of their liquid assets to sales may well have fallen and they will probably have become more dependent on external sources of finance. Monetary policy at this stage will be more influential in affecting investment either directly (the higher cost of borrowed funds to the firm plus reduced elasticity of supply of these) or indirectly (through the control of monetary parameters the authorities may affect other components of expenditure— of consumers or local government) and thus have an unfavourable impact on profit anticipations. Capacity utilisation rates may fall (actual sales less than expected sales), which will lead to cuts in planned investment in plant and equipment. The cyclical down-swing will be characterised by an easing of monetary policy which will not be sufficient to prevent the demand for capital goods falling. In this phase of the cycle the main motives for capital investment will be cost reduction and/or the introduction of new products. There will be little resort to external finance, and internal finance will be sufficient to meet the low levels of investment. Indeed, there may be even disinvestment, and thus a rise in the supply of liquid assets. At this stage of the cycle monetary policy will be ineffectual.

A considerable amount of research (described by Eisner and Strotz) has stressed the importance of sales as a variable determining investment. The results do not indicate the existence of any simple accelerator relationship, but they do suggest that investment can best be explained by a lagged accelerator, adjusted for downswings and conditions of excess capacity. There will be no single accelerator coefficient, and no one believes that the real value of the coefficient has yet been found. These less rigid formulations of the accelerator (usually characterised as capital stock adjustment models) have found increasing favour in recent years. They set at the centre of the stage as the most important variables recent and expected sales and throw considerable light on the process whereby the actual capital stock is adjusted to the desired capital stock— taking account also of the variable lags involved in the production of capital goods.

What conclusions can be drawn from the foregoing about the determinants of investment and the influence of monetary policy? In the first place the weight of the evidence does seem to be in favour of some form of lagged accelerator, although the precise size of the coefficients are unknown. The importance of financial flows has been emphasised by many writers, but has also been denied. The evidence on this point is inconclusive, although it is clear that in recent years that British monetary authorities have considered changes in liquidity to have important effects on investment expenditure. Thirdly, little weight has been placed by most commentators on the direct effect of interest rates on investment. However, such conclusions on interest incentive effects are based on studies which have often inadequately expressed the investment-interest relationship. Furthermore, these results only refer to the direct effects and neglect the indirect effects of monetary policy on investment. These could operate either through their influence on expectations (which are important in all theories of investment) or through their effects on other components of expenditure (and thus on sales and profit forecasts). Such indirect effects include the impact of changes in short-term rates on the behaviour of financial institutions, including in particular the impact on the mortgage market and thus on housing expenditure. However, there is little evidence that such indirect effects are very powerful, and the factors which have frustrated the direct effects have probably operated to frustrate the indirect effects as well. Attempts to control not only the terms of credit but also its quantity are likely to be frustrated by the high elasticity of supply of non-bank credit. Periods of bank credit control are thus likely to lead to an increase in trade credit and to a redistribution of liquid balances between firms which will permit larger expenditures to take place. If the authorities wish to influence investment expenditures then it is long rates which are relevant, but to operate on these may entail major policy changes, which relate not only to stabilisation over the cycle but also to longer-term considerations about the balance of demand for resources. It is much more difficult for the authorities to change long-term rates than to change short-term rates, and as we saw in the previous chapter there exist powerful constraints on the ability of the authorities to produce much wider swings in long-term rates.

INVENTORIES

Turning now to inventories, i.e., reserves of materials and fuel, intermediate goods and work in progress in factories needed to maintain and increase output, together with finished goods for delivery to customers. Variations in stock levels play an important role in the fluctuations in economic activity and are probably the main cause of the four-year short-cycle.* Such variations in the volume of stocks take place not only because of variations in demand (both final demand and intermediate demand) but also because of changes in supply and expectational variables. One role which they play in the economic system is that of a 'buffer', in that they cushion variations in sales on output so that changes in the rate of stockbuilding are often involuntary and result from unexpected developments in sales. Changes in stockbuilding directly lead to increases or decreases in real expenditure, and while changes in stocks are typically small (some 1%–2% of the total *level* of stocks) they tend to be a very volatile component of demand. Since 1960 the change in stockbuilding (i.e., the change in the change in the volume of stocks) between successive years has varied from an increase of more than £400 million (1960) to a decline of £270 million (1961), both at constant 1958 prices. These figures compare with an average annual change in Total Final Expenditure of about £1000 million (1960–1968), and in some years the change in stocks has been particularly large. In 1960 the change in stocks accounted for 23% of the rise in Total Final Expenditure, and in 1964 to 18%, both years of rapid increases in imports.

Manufacturing is both the most important sector in terms of share in total stocks, and it is also the most volatile. This can be seen clearly in *Table 7.3*, and it is immediately apparent that fluctuations in

Table 7.3

STOCKBUILDING 1960–1968
(£ Million and %)

	(1)	(2)	(3)	(4)	(5)
1960	595	+416	86	1 789	+585
1961	325	−270	69	805	−40
1962	73	−252	30	328	+104
1963	206	+133	55	1 360	+207
1964	581	+375	61	2 125	+523
1965	365	−216	59	768	+55
1966	227	−138	57	669	+98
1967	140	−87	−29	977	+371
1968	185	+45	−8	1 478	+459

Col. (1) Value of Physical Increases in Stocks and Work in Progress at 1958 Prices.
Col. (2) Change in Stockbuilding (1958 prices).
Col. (3) Manufacturing Industry: % Share of Col. (1).
Col. (4) Change in Total Final Expenditure (1958 prices).
Col. (5) Change in Imports (goods and services, 1958 prices).

* For example of the way in which different assumptions about the sales-output lag can lead to dynamic sequences see L. A. Metzler, 'The Nature and Stability of Inventory Cycles', *Review of Economics and Statistics* (Aug. 1941).

stockbuilding by manufacturing industry have been substantial. Between 1960–1968 manufacturing quarterly stockbuilding in volume, seasonally adjusted, varied between *minus* £140 million (first quarter 1968) and *plus* £148 million (third quarter 1960). (This is equal to about 3 % of total manufacturers' stock at the time of the stock change.) This is to be compared with variations in *total* stockbuilding of *minus* £111 million (first quarter 1968) and *plus* £170 million (second quarter 1964). Furthermore, manufacturing output is distinctly more cyclical than output of other sectors and this leads to a different pattern of stockbuilding. In particular there exists, for manufacturing industry as a whole, a lag of about three quarters between an upturn in production and an upturn in the level of stocks. However, the lag is not constant for all branches of manufacturing industry and a different pattern and rate of stockbuilding is apparent for production based on a rise in consumer demand from that which occurs when the expansion is led by increased investment in fixed capital equipment. This follows from the fact that the engineering industries typically produce capital goods to order (with generally a long production period), while consumer goods industries tend to produce in anticipation of demand. The result is a different response of stockbuilding to rising demand and production, with a greater likelihood of involuntary stock accumulations/decumulations in consumer goods industries.

Four general reasons can be discerned for holding stocks both in manufacturing and trade sectors. Firstly, there are transactions arguments, e.g., it may only be possible to order stocks in discrete 'lumps' so that given the time pattern of the outflow from stock there will exist through time a balance of stocks. During the process of production the firm will require stocks, and trading organisations clearly need to hold stocks for quick delivery to customers, goods in process of distribution, etc. Secondly, there exist precautionary motives. Uncertainty prevails in relation to the inflow of materials supplies, the production time schedule is uncertain and delivery times to customers are variable. Stocks in these situations reduce uncertainty and act as buffers. Thirdly, there is the possibility of price speculation in inventories and expectations of rising prices on the part of firms will lead them to hold larger stocks. Finally, holding stocks entails costs and these costs will limit the desired level of stocks. Such costs include the opportunity (interest) cost of funds tied up in stocks, their overhead/storage costs and the costs entailed through obsolescence.

It is this final factor which is relevant to monetary policy, what Radcliffe called the interest incentive effect. But it is not the only way in which monetary policy can affect stock levels, and variations in credit availability may also be important. Usually restraint on credit and changes in the opportunity cost of funds tied up in stocks will occur together, while other factors affecting stock decisions may also occur simultaneously. Of these other factors clearly changes in sales is probably the most important. Decisions to add to or reduce stock are usually, therefore, the result of many different variables and it is difficult (if not impossible) to separate out the relative importance of these variables in relation to specific stock decisions. Attempts to do so (either through surveys or through econometric research) have not yet produced generally acceptable conclusions on the importance of financial variables for inventory holdings, and there clearly exists a conflict between the authorities and other commentators (including Radcliffe).

Since Radcliffe there would appear to have been little or no research into the factors determining stockbuilding in general or the importance of financial variables in particular, although a good deal of research has been undertaken in the U.S.A. However, the results of American research may not be especially relevant to British conditions and there remain considerable doubts about the validity of their results.* One particular U.S. study is perhaps worth noting, that by Darling and Lovell, which specifically introduced the interest cost of holding stocks into their regression equations. For stocks held in trading sectors they found 'that the interest rate variable remained as a (marginally) significant factor for retail trade but was found to be insignificant for wholesale trade. It may be that the interest variable operated as a proxy for variations in the severity of credit rationing which affects principally the smaller firms found in the retail trade.'† However, in their analysis of both durable and non-durable manufacturing inventories the interest rate variable appeared with positive coefficients. Both this study, and others surveyed by Eisner and Strotz, contain serious technical deficiencies, particularly the problems associated with multicollinearity and interdependence (i.e., the tendency for the rate of interest, the rate of capacity utilisation and the change in order backlogs to rise and fall together when measured by deviations from a linear trend). The functional forms of the equations are often incomplete and could be better specified. The estimates, therefore, tend to be subject to simultaneous equation bias.

While the American econometric work can be criticised, at least

* For a survey of U.S. Research on inventories see Eisner and Strotz, 'Determinants of Business Investment', *Impacts of Monetary Policy*, Commission on Money and Credit: Prentice-Hall, 192–223 (1964).

† P. G. Darling and M. C. Lovell, 'Factors Influencing Investment in Inventories', *The Brookings Quarterly Econometric Model of the U.S.* (Ed. by Duesenberry, Fromm, Klein and Kuh), p. 153.

research has been undertaken, which would not appear to be the case in the U.K. Little empirical work has been done since Radcliffe, and several inventory forecasting models used in the U.K. do not include financial variables. The official Treasury model is based on the belief that there exists a tendency for stocks to be adjusted to some 'normal' ratio so that there exists some desired level of stocks and stocks are gradually adjusted to this level. In the Treasury's view, changes in Bank Rate may lead to some modification in stockbuilding, but the effect is likely to be weak.* Occasionally the Treasury has noted in the Economic Report the impact of credit restraint on stockbuilding, so this effect is supposed to operate, although the quantitative importance of this factor (and interest effect) is unknown.† The forecasting model used by the London Business School contains a stock equation which is a very simple model relating stockbuilding to sales and the existing volume of stocks. No financial variables are included in the equation, and the equation as at present set up produces poor results even when using *actual* values.‡

The Bank of England remains convinced that financial variables do affect stockbuilding, and its commentaries in the *Quarterly Bank Bulletin* often contain statements to this effect.§ For example, the commentary in December 1961 says, 'The prospective easing of demand in some sectors, the weakness of some material prices, the restriction of credit and the high level of short-term interest rates suggested that the rate of stock accumulation would continue to be moderate'. In its evidence to Radcliffe the Bank was even more emphatic in its views on the effectiveness of high short-term rates in reducing the rate of stockbuilding.‖ There seems, however, to be no reason to believe that these views of the

---

* See *Fourth Report of the Estimates Committee Session 1966–1967, on Government Statistical Services*, H.M.S.O., para. 28 of Appendix 7 (Dec. 1966).

† A typical statement is that in the *Economic Report on 1967* page 16, where the Treasury observed that 'the volume of stocks held by manufacturers and distributors fell. This may owe something to businessmen having adapted themselves to holding smaller stocks during previous periods of tighter money and credit restrictions and to the restrictive effect of the temporary import surcharge.'

‡ The model is described in an article by R. J. Ball and T. Burns, 'An Econometric Approach to Short-run Analysis of the U.K. Economy, 1955–1965', *Operational Research Quarterly*, **19** (1968).

§ For comments see the *Quarterly Bank Bulletin*: Dec. 1961, p. 6; Sept. 1962, pp. 168–169; June 1964, pp. 90–91; and March 1965, p. 11.

‖ Bank of England Memoranda to Lord Radcliffe, Vol. 1, para 24, reads as follows: 'A rise in interest rates can be sufficient to tilt the balance in decisions of holders of commodity stocks whether to run down stocks or at least to cease from making further additions to them. This is most likely to be so when the rise in interest charges is imposed on a situation in which there has been some speculative buying accompanied by a rise in commodity prices and by relatively large dependence upon short-term borrowing by holders of such stocks.'

Bank are based on any deep investigation of the relationships, but instead seem to be derived from historical attitudes. Dow reached similar conclusions in his analysis of the impact of monetary policy during the 1950s and while the 'interest elasticity of stockbuilding must at best be small, it seems reasonable to conclude that credit restrictions if vigorously pushed may have some effect on stockbuilding . . . particularly if it comes at a time of falling profits or general uncertainty and financial stringency'. While the effects of financial variables might be slight in relation to the total demand for stocks, nevertheless even a small percentage change (say, 1 %) would affect the level considerably (by £100 million).*

Now the views of the authorities, Dow and other commentators (such as White and Hawtrey†) that financial variables do affect stockbuilding is both contrary to Radcliffe's conclusions on this point and would appear to be based on little empirical evidence. Radcliffe is the only recent attempt to discover how important were the interest rate and credit effects on stockbuilding, and they were categorical in denying that such effects were significant. On the effect of short-term rates on the incentive to hold stocks, the Committee found that 'stocks of commodities are extremely insensitive to interest rates, and in any case they are often financed with long-term capital, and could be much more widely so if firms found this much cheaper'.‡ Their view was that credit restraint was equally ineffective: 'We have not been able to find that the squeeze had any marked effect on holdings of stocks of commodities.'§ However, the empirical basis for these views is also not very convincing and it would appear that they reached their conclusions on a fairly cursory appraisal of the evidence presented to them.

This evidence consisted of the views given by the directors of eight large firms plus the results of surveys carried out for the Committee by the F.B.I. and A.B.C.C. The Committee found the survey results to be inadequate on account of the low response rate to the questionnaires and the belief on the part of the Committee that the results were subject to bias.‖ White¶ has suggested that the Committee was cavalier in its

* J. C. R. Dow, *The Management of the British Economy 1945-1960*, Cambridge University Press, 294, 296 and 298 (1965).
† W. H. White, 'Inventory Investment and the Rate of Interest', *Banca Nazionale del Lavoro Quarterly Review*, No. 57 (June 1961); R. G. Hawtrey, 'Stocks of Commodities, Fixed Capital and the Interest Rate', *Bankers Magazine* (May 1960).
‡ Radcliffe: *Report*, para. 489.
§ Radcliffe: *Report*, para. 460.
‖ 'The response rate of both inquiries was relatively low, and it may well be that the answers came for the most part from those who had some positive reaction to report.' Radcliffe: *Report*, para. 453.
¶ W. H. White, *Banca de Lavoro Quarterly Review*, June 1961.

attitude to these survey data and failed to take on board many of the points raised by the F.B.I. in their evidence. One point made in particular by the F.B.I. was that the response from large firms was high, and that they accounted for a large proportion of stocks held in industry. A second criticism of the survey was that it asked a highly specific question on whether the Bank Rate change in 1955 was the *major* reason for decisions on stocks. Two criticisms are possible here. Firstly, it is possible for interest rates to be a significant factor even if not the *major* factor, so that many firms who were affected by the rise in interest rates did not in fact reply. Secondly, the Bank Rate change referred to (in 1955) was a large one of 1·5% points but at a low *level* of interest rates (an increase of Bank Rate from 3% to 4·5%). However, as Radcliffe itself noted, the normal rate on bank loans is 1% above Bank Rate with a minimum of 5% so that the effective rise in borrowing costs in 1955 was probably much less than 1·5% (perhaps only 0·5%) and firms would typically be insensitive to an increase in borrowing costs of this size.

One of the main factors which led Radcliffe to deny the importance of both the interest incentive effect and the credit effect was the belief that companies were not very reliant on bank credit for financing their activities in general or stockbuilding in particular. This was certainly the conclusion of Tew and Henderson,[*] which was partly due to the inadequate nature of the data available. Nevertheless, in 1956 Lydall[†] had found that 70% of manufacturers with 200–500 employees had used overdrafts during a five-year period and it would seem that the Committee's dependence on balance-sheet data for information on bank lending to companies led them to underestimate its extent. Indeed, data now available on bank lending to industrial and commercial companies indicate that whereas in the period 1954–1959 bank borrowing was equal to only 28% of total borrowing, in the period 1959–1967 it equalled 40%.[‡] Clearly, therefore, firms have become more dependent on bank credit during the last 10 years and are on *a priori* grounds likely to be more sensitive to credit controls. A second feature of company finance in the 1960s is that companies have failed to maintain their liquid assets so that their savings have been much smaller as a proportion of total capital formation in the 1960s compared with the 1950s. Firms are, therefore, both more dependent on bank credit and simul-

---

[*] B. Tew and R. F. Henderson, *Studies in Company Finance* (1960).

[†] H. F. Lydall, 'The Impact of the Credit Squeeze on Small and Medium Sized Manufacturing Firms', *Economic Journal*, 424–425 (Sept. 1957). (Quoted by White.)

[‡] 'Company Finance 1952–1965', *Quarterly Bank Bulletin*, Table D, 39 (March 1967), plus data from *Financial Statistics*, H.M.S.O. Table 68 (Dec. 1968).

taneously rather less liquid, both developments which would strengthen the impact of monetary policy on expenditure of firms.

The foregoing section contains little which is new, but it brings out at least one fact with great clarity. Virtually no research has been undertaken in the U.K. into the factors determining stockbuilding, and that there is a general belief that the only empirical work (that of Radcliffe) was inadequate. U.K. research has usually not been concerned to identify the financial variables, and when it has done so the research has often suffered from technical deficiencies. On the other hand, the views of Radcliffe were presented in the light of monetary experience in the 1950s and as they recognised a changing environment might lead to modification of their conclusions. Certainly in at least two respects the 1960s have been different from the 1950s; the level of interest rates has consistently been higher and firms are both less liquid and more dependent on bank credit. Both these developments would suggest that inventories are sensitive to tightening credit and more expensive credit, but that it is impossible as yet to identify the quantitative importance of such effects. What is required is econometric research which takes account of the complex simultaneous relationships which are involved.

HOUSING INVESTMENT

In 1968 capital expenditure on housing by Local Authorities amounted to 10% of gross fixed capital formation. Whereas they accounted for only a third of investment in dwellings in 1960, by 1968 the proportion had risen to almost a half (total expenditure on housing rose during the same period from 18·3 % of gross fixed capital formation to almost 20 %). Subsidies are payable only in respect of houses for which the tender has been approved by the Ministry of Housing and Local Government and the number of houses to be approved each year is settled as a matter of policy by the Government. If a Local Authority was prepared to build without a subsidy, it would still require a loan sanction—but the subsidy is too important for such a situation to arise. As Radcliffe noted, 'The central authorities by virtue of social legislation in effect determine the scale and direction of investment by Local Authorities in most of the main fields of expenditure (notably housing and education).'* The 1967 Housing Act provided much larger housing subsidies so that the Government pays the difference between the actual capital charge (annual interest and amortisation) and the hypothetical

* Radcliffe: *Report*, para. 90.

charge if the rate of interest was 4%. Under this system the subsidy is, given the interest rate, proportional to the capital cost. In order to control capital cost the Ministry has introduced 'cost yardsticks' and will only pay subsidies on costs which fall within these limits. In effect this system leaves Local Authorities with even less freedom than they had previously. What is also of note is that the proportion of new investment in dwellings undertaken within the public sector is now larger (and the total itself has grown) so that a larger percentage of housing investment is within the field of administrative action and, therefore, largely unaffected by monetary policy.*

On the other hand, is there any evidence that private housing investment is affected by changes in monetary policy? The authorities clearly believe that a sizeable and worthwhile impact on real expenditure can be achieved through a tightening of monetary policy and that 'the effect on real demand and output of changes in Bank Rate is thought, at least in the short-term, to be seen mainly in the mortgage market, which strongly influences the demand for private housing'.† Building Societies are by far the most important institution in the U.K. concerned with the finance of private expenditure on housing (during the period 1958–1967 they provided about two-thirds of the finance for private building). They have followed a general policy on interest rates which implies a steadiness in their rates both to borrowers and also to lenders (on shares and deposits). A change in Bank Rate, or any other indicator, does not automatically lead to the adjustment of Building Societies' rates and instead the 'Building Societies rather sit up and take notice when Bank Rate is changed, but do not themselves move until a general movement of interest rates in competitive channels causes an uncomfortable change in the flow of funds'.‡ *Chart 7.3* brings out the lagged relationship of Building Society rates to Bank Rate (which is taken as a proxy for other relevant short-term rates), and the lower part of the Chart brings out clearly the effect on the net inflow of money into shares and deposits of Building Societies when there occurs a widening in the gap between the Building Society rates on deposits and other short-term rates. Such a widening of the differential (a

---

* Radcliffe had noted this tendency: 'The removal of investment decisions relating to some of these capital works [home-building, public utility constructional works, etc.] from the market to the administrative sphere has obviously tended to reduce the automatic, market effect of interest rate changes on the total pressure of demand' (para. 386). Nevertheless, Radcliffe did cite the exception of a local authority which in autumn 1957 had cut the housing programme because interest rates were high. Radcliffe: *Report*, para. 452.

† Treasury Memorandum to the Estimates Committee on *Government Statistical Services* 1966/1967, p. 478, para. 27.

‡ Radcliffe: *Report*, para. 292.

worsening) during 1961/1962, 1964/1965 and 1966 led to sharp falls in the net inflow of shares and deposits and inevitably affected the Societies' ability to lend, although changes in lending typically lag changes in inflow with liquid assets providing a cushion. The decline in their receipts was particularly noticeable during the second half of

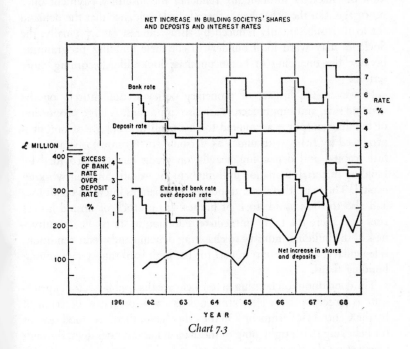

NET INCREASE IN BUILDING SOCIETYS' SHARES
AND DEPOSITS AND INTEREST RATES

Chart 7.3

1964 and the first half of 1965, when there developed a 'mortgage famine'. However, by the second half of 1965, although credit conditions remained tight, the relatively favourable rates offered by Building Societies attracted a large inflow of funds.

The Societies have typically reacted in three ways in periods when the net inflow of funds has fallen. Firstly, they have tended to discriminate against old houses, and in evidence to Radcliffe the Building Societies referred to their policy, during periods of restraint on their lending capacity, to favour new houses in order to help the building industry.* Secondly, the proportion of valuation which is lent may be dropped from its normal level and this may have significant effects on

* Minutes of Evidence, Question 7294. This attitude surprised the Radcliffe Committee who did not see it as part of the Building Societies' function to behave in this way towards the building industry.

the demand for mortgage finance.* A rise in the loan to value rates will bring in a whole new class of potential house-buyers, and an increase in the ratio from 70% to 85%, for example, reduces the down payment on a house by a half. In the same way a reduction in the rate of interest, or any extension in the period of repayment (or both) can have the same kind of effect by substantially reducing the monthly payment on a mortgage. On the other hand, there is little evidence that the demand for loans is substantially reduced by rising interest rates.† Finally, the Societies may warn local builders to cut their building programmes because the financing of house purchase looks like becoming more serious.

However, the impact of monetary policy is not entirely on the demand side, and supply factors are also important. A large proportion of building output is accounted for by small firms (44% of output is produced by firms with under 25 persons—1958 census) operating on little capital and depending heavily on credit facilities provided by building materials firms and utilising bank overdrafts for their working capital. They are, therefore, responsive to changes in credit conditions and also to the unsold stock of houses. If the stock of unsold houses rises then there is a fairly immediate reduction in starts. The sensitiveness of the building industry to changing demand and credit conditions is legendary, and accounts in part for the high bankruptcy rate among building firms.

The conclusions on housing investment are that public sector expenditure is largely interest insensitive and its size is primarily determined by the Central Government. On the other hand, there are good reasons for believing that a tightening of short-term interest rates does, through its effect on the mortgage market, affect building construction. This is so even though a large proportion of money borrowed is not for new houses since the sale of one house often produces the money for the purchase of another so that money lent for the purchase of an existing house frequently finds its way into the new housing market. There is, therefore, a fairly immediate reaction in the form of a reduction in housing starts to a decline in the flow of funds into the building

---

* The importance of changes in the loan to value ratio has been emphasised in several recent studies of the demand for housing. See particularly the Commission on Money and Credit, *Impacts of Monetary Policy*, Research Study 4, 'Determinants of Residential Construction: A Review of Present Knowledge' (Prentice-Hall 1964). For the U.K. see A. R. Nobay, 'Short-term Forecasting of Housing Investment', *National Institute Economic Review* (Aug. 1967) (especially pages 46 and 47 and Appendix).

† This was certainly the view of the Building Societies Association in evidence to Radcliffe, e.g., Question 7295: 'The result of the raising of the Bank Rate and higher interest rates has not been to damp down the demand for home loans.'

societies. However, the impact of monetary policy is not entirely on the demand side, and there are important effects on the supply side as well. These conclusions are broadly in line with Radcliffe (although they said little about supply factors) who found 'any persistent movement of interest rates tends not merely to drag building societies rates behind it, and to produce effects on the demand for building, . . . but also to force, during the lag period, a considerable tautening (or loosening) of the purse-strings; the impact on the pressure of demand in the building industry can thus be quite direct'.*

THE CONTROL OF SHORT-TERM INTERNATIONAL CAPITAL MOVEMENTS

During the sixties, and particularly during the last four to five years, the authorities have been continually concerned about international short-term capital flows and the effect of outflows on a reserve position which was generally considered inadequate. It always seemed likely, and frequently came about, that basic balance of payments weakness led to speculative outflows of capital due to the expectation that the authorities would not be able to maintain the exchange parity of sterling. The traditional response to this kind of situation has always been to raise domestic interest rates so as to improve interest arbitrage comparisons. However, the authorities in their evidence to Radcliffe, obviously did not believe that direct profit incentives arising from interest rate differentials in themselves would lead to any appreciable net improvement in the reserve position. Radcliffe concluded that 'we have had little evidence of actual movements of funds in response to changes in short-term rates, or of any other measurable effects on the exchanges'.†
Nevertheless, the authorities believed that an increase in Bank Rate was essential as one element in any 'package' of measures aimed at rectifying an unfavourable balance of payments position because of its effects on overseas confidence. These confidence effects arose not from any widely-held belief in the effects of Bank Rate on real demand, but from its symbolic role as an indicator that the authorities were taking steps to remedy the situation. Such confidence effects occurred only if an increase in Bank Rate took place alongside other economic measures. Any improvement in confidence led to a reduction in forward speculation against sterling and further improved the reserve position through altering the timing of leads and lags.

* Radcliffe: *Report*, para. 294.
† Radcliffe: *Report*, para. 695.

Clearly within recent years there has been a revision of the authorities' views about the importance quantitatively of short-term capital flows and the extent to which movements of funds are determined by interest rate differentials. Indeed, since 1961 the Commentary of the *Bank Bulletin* has consistently noted, and commented on, movements of short-term capital in response to arbitrage considerations. However, the arbitrage comparison which is relevant is not the uncovered differential between the bill rate and overseas short-term rates, but the covered comparison between the Local Authority three-month rate and the Euro-dollar rate. On a number of occasions in recent years, looked at more closely below, unfavourable movements in the covered comparison between Local Authority rates and Euro-dollar rates have led to substantial switching of funds out of sterling by banks with consequent pressure on the reserves.

Several factors have contributed to the greater importance attached to short-term flows by the monetary authorities. In the first place the expansion of foreign trade has increased the size of leads and lags effects on the reserve position. Secondly, many non-official holders of sterling balances have become less prepared to hold these—or less prepared to be firm holders—given the increasing risk during the sixties of exchange depreciation. Such an attitude was not confined entirely to non-official holders of sterling and for some years prior to devaluation some official holders of sterling balances had been diversifying their reserves. Such diversification did not have any substantial effect on the U.K. gold and convertible currency reserves mainly because only net accruals to national reserves were held in/converted into non-sterling currencies. After devaluation the process of diversification proceeded swiftly and it became essential to lessen the strain on U.K. resources. The Basle Agreement of 1968 was intended to do this through a gold (really a dollar) guarantee of 90% of each sterling area countries' reserves held in the form of sterling. A third factor increasing the importance of short-term capital flows has been the growth of the Euro-dollar market. Very substantial amounts of dollars (and other currencies) have been placed in London, and the whole complex of financial arrangements which is the Euro-dollar market has been concentrated there. Dollar balances placed in the Euro-dollar market are highly responsive to changes in international interest rate comparisons, and the switching of substantial funds in and out of sterling has raised new problems for the authorities. This was especially evident in 1966 (and again in 1968) when a tightening of U.S. monetary policy led to large-scale borrowing by U.S. banks in the Euro-dollar market in order to increase their dollar deposits and thus expand their domestic lending activities. One result of the extension of the Euro-dollar market has been to increase the volatile component of U.K. reserves.*

While the importance of controlling short-term capital flows has increased, the ability to do so has diminished. In the first place the relevant arbitrage comparison is between the Local Authority temporary rate and the Euro-dollar rate (covered comparison) and not the Treasury bill rate. But, unfortunately for the authorities, the Local Authority rate is only tenuously under control although movements in it are linked to changes in bill rate. Secondly, an increase in Bank Rate (with the intention of raising the Treasury bill rate and other short-term rates), has become associated with periods of exchange weakness (generally speaking decisions to raise Bank Rate have been taken in response to reserve losses caused by an unfavourable balance of payments). This action, instead of being considered as part of a corrective process aimed at removing the cause of external imbalance, has increasingly been interpreted as a sign of weakness and has increased speculative activity rather than diminished it. The increase in Bank Rate (rise in bill rate) has had, therefore, perverse effects on capital flows. The increased speculation has led to a rise in the forward discount on sterling so that this exceeds the margin on inward covered arbitrage (which the increase in Bank Rate was intended to bring about).

An example of what can happen when the authorities do not act purposefully and raise Bank Rate in the face of falling reserves and speculative pressure is November 1964. The new Government, which came into office in October, found itself with a huge external deficit and decided to fully inform the nation of the grave economic situation it had uncovered. Short-term capital outflows had already been substantial (before the change of Government) and these increased as a result of the Government's statements and in anticipation of the expected policies (including expectations of a devaluation). In general a rise in Bank Rate was expected and when no change was announced on Thursday, 19 November, speculation increased further. Precisely why the Government made no change in Bank Rate has never been explained: it was probably related to a desire to hold down domestic

---

* See Chapter 8 for details of short-term capital movements in recent years. The outflow prior to devaluation was especially large and amounted to £417 million during the second half of 1967. It was only partially reversed in the few weeks following devaluation, and took mainly the form of reductions in net liabilities in sterling and in foreign currencies to residents of N.S.A. countries, together with a large negative balancing item in the third quarter. Both of the international exchange crises of 1968 (in March and November) led to large outflows of funds, providing clear indication of the effects of confidence factors on their movement.

M

rates in order to fulfil promises to home owners, etc. But it also owed something to a doctrinaire unwillingness to use monetary policy; an attitude certainly held by Dr. Balogh, the most important outside economic adviser brought in by the new Government. Whatever the explanation, the result of the Government's inactivity was a vast capital outflow and so critical did the position become that an increase of 2% (to 7%) in Bank Rate was announced on Monday, 23 November. Unfortunately, the Bank Rate change was not strengthened by any other measures and was interpreted as heralding financial collapse. The speculative outflow increased further and was only brought to an end some two days later with the announcement of a $3000 million loan from other Central Banks.

During the course of the crisis of confidence in November 1964, the Bank began, on a continuous basis and on a substantial scale, to operate in the forward exchange market. This action cannot be attributed to any fundamental change in the Bank's attitude to forward dealings and can only be understood as being a panic reaction to the crisis. This policy departure was totally at variance with the views put to Radcliffe by the Bank and Treasury on the usefulness of supporting the forward rate. Radcliffe partly concurred with this view—at least in so far as agreeing that forward exchange dealings would be an ineffective method of countering speculation against the pound.* It was precisely under these conditions that the Bank's new policy began to operate!†

How successful has action in the forward market been in limiting the extent of short-term capital flows? Has the Bank been an able operator —in a purely technical sense? How large specifically was the cost to the reserves of the large forward commitments entered into prior to devaluation? All these questions must largely go unanswered. It is thought that the Bank has shown great technical expertise in its forward dealings, but since its actions are shrouded in secrecy, it is impossible to validate this claim. Only the authorities, because they have the data, can assess whether action in the forward market reduced short-term outflows and that its cost (it has been costly) was justified. The extent of the pre-devaluation commitments were very sizeable indeed, and it follows, therefore, that forward support for a rate which was never really defensible in the weeks leading up to 25 November 1967 proved exceedingly

---

* Radcliffe: *Report*, para. 707.

† There has been a certain amount of discussion of the desirability of this policy in the *Westminster Bank Review*. See the articles by Oppenheimer, Goldstein and Einzig in the issues of February 1966, August 1966 and February 1967. One aspect of this practice, and similar forward dealings by the U.S. Federal Reserve System, has been a massive expansion of central bank co-operation during the 1960s.

costly to the reserves—and to the nation as a whole.* It is to be hoped that the Bank will at some stage defend its record in its otherwise admirable Quarterly Bank Bulletin.

CONCLUSIONS

It is perhaps worthwhile to try to draw together some of the conclusions of the previous sections on the impact of monetary policy.

1. Little evidence has been produced to change the prevailing belief that monetary measures operate on demand with a considerable time-lag. But this is not equally true of all monetary measures. Hire-purchase terms control has a substantial (if diminishing) impact on demand virtually immediately, although the lags vary at different points in the cycle. Again there is some research which attributes a fairly quick effect of availability of funds (and sometimes cost) on stockbuilding, and the British authorities clearly believe this is an important way in which monetary policy has an effect. Furthermore, expenditure on new housing starts is fairly quickly responsive to changes in the inflow of funds to building societies and this can be influenced by the monetary authorities. On the other hand, all the evidence points to very slow effects on business fixed investment, and monetary variables operate (if at all) only with an extended lag.

2. For most of the period under review the authorities concentrated on the structure of liquidity, and did not express any belief in the money supply as such. However, in spite of the fact that virtually no research has been undertaken in Britain on this topic, the authorities have recently accepted targets for DCE which will determine their economic strategy. This is unfortunate, although perhaps inevitable, and it should be fully recognised that there is no convincing evidence to support such a change of attitude.

3. Sizeable effects on consumers' expenditure have been achieved through the operation of credit controls. Hire purchase terms control has been extensively used and has affected expenditure by perhaps £100 million at an annual rate. However, such controls have a diminishing impact (perhaps no bad thing) and their impact is being eroded by the development of alternative sources of consumer credit. As an economic regulator terms control has very undesirable side-effects—particularly

* The Treasury estimated the loss due to the Exchange Equalisation Account's forward commitments entered into before devaluation at £105 million in 1967 and £251 million in 1968. Source: *Economic Trends*, No. 194, table 9 (Dec. 1969).

on the growth in capacity and on employment in that narrow group of industries primarily subject to control. The timing of changes has continued to be poor.

4. Controls on bank lending have probably been more effective in reducing consumers' expenditure than in altering expenditure levels of firms since the sources of finance available to firms are more extensive. Nevertheless the high and growing stock of liquid assets held by the personal sector has permitted consumers to maintain rising expenditure even in the face of strict ceilings on personal bank borrowing. Terms control has probably been more effective in restraining personal consumption than has bank credit control, and has the advantage, from the authorities' point of view, of being under more immediate control.

5. Very few firm conclusions can be reached on the determinants of business fixed investment although lagged capital stock models are favoured by many economists. While the use of investment appraisal techniques using a discount rate is now fairly general, there is little evidence that interest rates have become a more important element in the investment decision. On the other hand, the British authorities have emphasised in recent years the importance of liquidity factors in determining investment. Certainly developments in the financing pattern of British industrial and commercial companies would lend some proof for the hypothesis that they are now more sensitive to pressure on their cash-flow position. The effect of liquidity factors would not be general, and would affect particularly those companies with few liquid assets. Even for these companies the high elasticity of supply of non-bank credit—especially trade credit—has probably blunted the impact of monetary policy. Indirect effects of monetary policy on investment also appear weak.

6. A number of investigators have found some short-term effects of monetary policy on inventory accumulation. Clearly the authorities believe that interest effects and changes in the supply of credit have a substantial effect on this type of investment—with perhaps 50% of the effects of monetary policy coming through within six months. Many other variables, other than financial variables, have been identified as important and on occasions these variables will swamp the impact of policy on inventory accumulation.

7. Again a fairly immediate impact is achieved through monetary policy on housing investment. New housing starts respond fairly quickly to changes in the supply of funds into mortgage institutions, although there is little evidence that changes in the cost of borrowing have much effect. Changes in monetary conditions will also affect the supply side of the industry through their impact on credit availability.

8. Short-term international capital movements have presented a continuous problem in recent years. While the movement of such funds is partly determined by interest arbitrage considerations other factors, particularly confidence in the ability to hold the exchange rate, are also important. Unfortunately confidence effects have considerably offset interest effects, and the authorities' ability to control the movement of such funds has been substantially weakened. Previously increases in Bank Rate intended to lead to favourable changes in interest rate comparisons, and thus to an inflow of funds, have been interpreted during the sixties as signs of weakness and produced speculative outflows. The policy of forward intervention probably had only partial success in preventing speculative movements of short-term capital.

These conclusions are not generally so unfavourable as to invalidate the use of monetary policy. While the lags may be uncertain they are not nearly so long or unstable as Milton Friedman would have us believe and some of the impact of monetary measures comes through fairly quickly in terms of its impact on real expenditure. Unfortunately, a good deal of the impact is derived from the exercise of credit controls which have well-known drawbacks, and through effects on the mortgage market which are perhaps also undesirable for other reasons. But such criticisms are far from a wholesale condemnation of discretionary monetary action and an active role for the monetary authorities can be supported. However, the current preoccupation by the authorities with money supply questions is much more open to criticism, and they can be further criticised for failing to quantify the effects of policy. In many respects the situation found by Radcliffe has remained unaltered; the supply of financial statistics has improved dramatically but the failure to identify the quantitative impact of monetary measures has continued to be a persistent source of weakness in the conduct of stabilisation policy.

8

THE BALANCE OF PAYMENTS

The balance of payments has been almost continuously at the centre of the British economic problem during the sixties, and much of economic policy is explicable only in terms of the imperatives imposed by the state of the external balance. And not only economic policy, but also policy in respect of Britain's wider international and diplomatic role. At the beginning of the decade the Government held a number of policy aims which were directly relevant to its balance of payments policies, and in certain years these goals proved to be inconsistent, so that the authorities were forced into trade-offs between a better external balance and achievement of other policy aims.

First among these policy goals was the achievement of full-employment and a faster rate of economic growth, but years of fast growth (1959/1960 and 1963/1964) have usually been accompanied by massive deteriorations in the balance of payments, leading to pressure on the reserves and finally to the sacrifice of employment and growth targets. Thus the 'stop–go' cycle had its origin in the persistent weakness of external payments. For a while, between 1963 and 1964, the Government attempted to maintain a high rate of growth in the face of a deteriorating external position in the hope that this could be financed through borrowing from international organisations, increasing sterling liabilities, running down the reserves and so on.* If only, so it was believed by Chancellor Maudling, the external deficit could be financed, then the purely temporary factors acting to raise imports, mainly the rise in imports of goods for stock purposes, would be overcome,

* For a statement of the arguments in favour of this strategy, see the Budget Statement, *Hansard*, 3 April 1963, cols. 470–473.

while exports would rise as the result of the favourable effects of sustained growth on productivity and export competitiveness. It was odd that the Treasury should have espoused such a policy since there could have been no conclusive evidence in its favour even at the time. The recorded data lend no support for the Maudling thesis. The ratio of total stocks to GDP was if anything below trend between 1963–1965, and a substantial part of the sharp rise in imports in 1964 was of finished manufactured goods (23 %) and not merely imports intended for stock. Similarly, export expectations were not fulfilled, and, as was to be expected, raising the domestic pressure of demand served mainly to divert resources away from export markets on a very substantial scale.*
It was naive to have expected any substantial improvement in export performance as a result of raising the rate of economic growth, in excess of potential capacity, for any very short period of time. The result of the Maudling policy was a massive external deficit, immense pressure on the reserves, and the partial abandonment of the policy by the new Government in October 1964. The episode is instructive as an example of the dilemma facing the authorities—an economy caught in a vicious circle of low growth, low productivity, high export costs, poor export performance leading inevitably to payments deficits whenever policy aimed at faster growth.†
However, the above has to be viewed against the background of other strongly-held commitments. This included a determination to maintain London as an international financial centre together with a belief in the sanctity of the sterling rate of exchange even though by the mid-sixties there was fairly abundant evidence that this was overvalued. The tardy recognition of this fact entailed a substantial cost in terms of resources under-utilised, a massive increase in short-term debts, and, during the second half of 1967, huge reserve losses as the monetary authorities attempted to hold a forward rate which was clearly unsupportable. While the devaluation opened up new problems for the authorities, it also opened up new possibilities for the economy. It amounted, nevertheless, to a failure of the balance of payments policies pursued by both Conservative and Labour Governments, and gave a sharp twist to the, by then, weak relationship between Britain and the rest of the Sterling Area.
Britain has traditionally been a large exporter of long-term capital and Conservative administrations have always maintained that this was eminently desirable even though it may, on occasion, amount to the

* See below (pages 187–191.)
† Not necessarily inevitable, but the commitment to liberalisation of trade and payments in general precluded the extensive use of import controls.

substitution of increased short-term liabilities for increased long-term assets. However, this was certainly not the view of officials and even before the accession to power of Mr. Wilson the Treasury had decided that the costs of maintaining this traditional role of exporter of long-term capital exceeded the benefits. We have witnessed since 1965, therefore, substantial changes in Britain's role as a provider of long-term capital, which has entailed a weakening (as did the devaluation) of the bonds perpetuating the Sterling Area.

While all Governments have believed that British interests are best served through further liberalisation of international trade and payments, and thus participated fully in the Kennedy round, they have nevertheless since 1964 followed policies which were directly restrictive in their impact on current account transactions. This marked a distinct and decisive change in approach to the problem of adjusting the balance of payments. A willingness to experiment with import surcharges, export rebates, import deposit schemes, and the use of shadow exchange rates in Government procurement, in the pursuit of both short-term and long-term policy aims.

With the above changes has also gone a fundamental reappraisal of Britain's position in the world. The persistent balance of payments difficulties, themselves partly the result of sharply rising expenditures overseas for military and aid purposes, has led to a decisive break with history and tradition. A belief that henceforward Britain would benefit more from higher domestic living standards than from pursuing its traditional 'pax britannica' role.*

Such then have been the main commitments of Government, and, as we have seen, during the sixties they have had to modify, sometimes reverse, strongly-held traditional attitudes as a direct result of balance of payments weakness. Policy makers were faced, almost continuously, with having to choose between one set of policy objectives and another, or in economists' jargon, to concern themselves with the trade-offs between economic variables such as the rate of economic growth, the level of full employment, preservation of the value of the currency extension of control over private capital and current transactions, and far-reaching decisions about the wider political and military role of Britain. Such decisions could not, and were not, taken lightly and not without considerable dissent. Nor were they taken on the basis of economic considerations alone, although these were clearly important.

* The role has not, of course, been entirely relinquished and within the Conservative Party there remains a hankering for a continued presence 'East of Suez'. On the other hand the resumption of an active military and diplomatic role would prove extremely costly and it is not at all clear how any Conservative administration would finance it.

The aim in this chapter after a short analysis of the balance of payments out-turn in the sixties, is to focus the discussion on the main changes in policy as they affected the balance of payments with emphasis given to the measurement of the benefits to the balance of payments of the policy trade-offs. In general, those policies which aimed at strengthening the balance of payments in the long-run (rationalisation of industry, development of import substitutes, raising the skill-level of the work force, incomes policy, etc.) are not considered. No doubt they have a value in the long-run, but, consistent with our emphasis throughout the study, the focus remains on short-term policy. Six types of policy action are discussed below; *Movement to a Lower Pressure of Demand* confines itself to an analysis of the trade-offs between employment and the balance of payments. *Commercial Policy* examines the impact of changes in commercial policy; the *Balance of Payments Cost of Military Expenditures Abroad and Overseas Aid* is then looked at; in *Capital Export* recent changes in policy regarding private capital outflow are examined; the next section attempts an analysis of *Devaluation*; and *Sterling Balances* concludes with a few remarks on the future of the Sterling Area.

SURVEY OF THE BALANCE OF PAYMENTS, 1960–1969

Table 8.1 and *Chart 8.1* present the main components of the balance of payments for the years 1958–1969. Several trends are immediately obvious and deserve attention. Firstly, the visible balance continued in deficit in every year except 1958 with very large deficits in 1960 and 1964, both years of fast economic growth, in 1967, a year when exports actually declined, and in 1968 when import values rose as a result of the devaluation together with an unanticipated increase in import volume. More striking perhaps than the pattern of visible deficits (a traditional feature of Britain's balance of payments) was the very substantial growth in both exports and imports. In volume exports increased at an annual compound rate of 5·0% between 1958–1969 (by 7·7% in value) and imports by 5·1% in volume (7·1% in value). Over the same years British imports of total manufactures rose at a rate of 14% per annum and finished manufactured imports by no less than 17% per year. This very fast increase in imports of manufacturers reflects in part a general force at work in international trade—a secular upward drift in the propensity to import manufactures on the part of consumers in industrial countries as their tastes become more sophisticated—but it also reflects a lack of price and non-price competitiveness on the part

Table 8.1

U.K. BALANCE OF PAYMENTS 1958-1969

(£ million)

	1958	1959	1960	1961	1962	1963	1964	1965	1966	1967	1968	1969
Exports and re-exports (f.o.b.)	3 406	3 522	3 732	3 891	3 993	4 282	4 466	4 777	5 122	5 042	6 143	7 013
Imports (f.o.b.)	3 377	3 639	4 138	4 043	4 095	4 362	5 003	5 042	5 214	5 576	6 801	7 152
Visible trade balance	+29	−117	−406	−152	−102	−80	−537	−265	−92	−524	−664	−139
Net adjustment for recording of exports							+20	+40	+60	+80	+130	+43
Payments for U.S. military aircraft							−2	−12	−41	−98	−109	−61
Visible balance	+29	−117	−406	−152	−102	−80	−519	−237	−73	−552	−643	−157
Invisibles												
Government (net)												
Military	−126	−129	−172	−198	−224	−237	−268	−268	−282	−267	−265	−268
Other	−93	−98	−110	−134	−136	−145	−164	−179	−188	−197	−197	−191
Private services and transfers (net)	+241	+227	+192	228	+241	+184	+161	+165	+202	+325	+486	+531
Interest, profits, & dividends (net)	+293	+260	+231	+252	+333	+392	+397	+438	+381	+369	+322	+500
Invisible balance	+315	+260	+141	+148	+214	+194	+126	+156	+113	+230	+346	+572
Current balance	+344	+143	−265	−4	+112	+114	−393	−81	+40	−322	−297	+415
Official long-term capital (net)	−50	−124	−103	−45	−104	−105	−116	−85	−80	−57	+21	−98
Private long-term capital (net)	−146	−131	−89	+113	+6	−44	−238	−112	−27	−82	−120	+81
Balance of long-term capital	−196	−255	−192	+68	−98	−149	−354	−197	−107	−139	−99	−17
Balance of current and long-term capital transactions ('basic balance')	+148	−112	−457	+64	+14	−35	−747	−278	−67	−461	−396	+398
Basic balance adjusted for Euro-borrowing						−30	−732	−268	−55	−393	−220	+468
Balancing item	+67	−22	+299	−25	+75	−72	−15	+31	−37	+227	−125	+219
Balance of monetary movements	−215	+134	+158	−39	−89	+107	+762	+247	+104	+234	+521	−617
Change in reserve position*	−303	−5	−328	+343	−196	+58	+479	+246	+265	−18	+619	−74
Change in U.K. external liabilities in sterling†	+84	+133	+402	−356	−23	+115	+48	+64	+140	+186	+185	−584

* Includes change in U.K. position in E.P.U. and I.M.F. Also includes the transfer of £316 million in 1966 and £204 million in 1967 from the dollar portfolio to the reserves.

† U.K. total liabilities in sterling excluding I.M.F.

of British output, together with shortage of domestic capacity in certain years.

Secondly, while the invisible balance (net) continued in surplus its ability to offset the visible trade deficit declined over the period. Whereas its contribution averaged some £215 million a year on average between 1955 and 1960, this subsequently fell to an average annual figure of £174 million between 1960 and 1967. This deterioration was due partly

BALANCE OF PAYMENTS

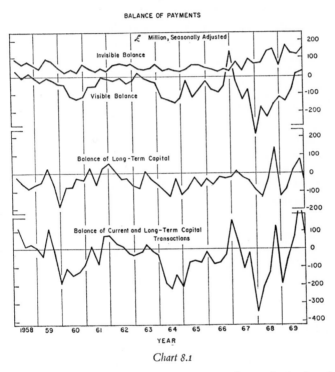

Chart 8.1

to the sharp rise in Government overseas expenditures for both military and non-military purposes, which more than doubled (net) between 1958 and 1965, although it then levelled out in later years at a sum rather less than 1965. Private services and transfers (net) irregularly declined over the period, excluding the post-devaluation years when there was a substantial increase in sterling terms. The most important elements in this decline were the movement into deficit of shipping earnings in 1960, and the sharp rise in overseas expenditure which increased (net) fourfold between the late 1950s and 1965. A trend which was later reversed by the tourist expenditure restrictions introduced in 1966. The contribution of interest, profits and dividends (net) rose very substantially from an annual average of £242 million (1955–1959) to one of £362 million for 1960–1969, reflecting the build up of long-term assets during the fifties.

Finally there is the long-term capital account which consists mainly of Direct Investment. Outflows for this purpose were considerably higher in the sixties than in the fifties, some £300 million a year between 1960 and 1969, rising throughout the period. However, the net outflow was significantly less than this averaging only some £100 million a year during the sixties. Portfolio investment continued relatively unimportant although a change in trend is noticeable from the middle of the decade following the 1965 changes in policy.

For a country running a reserve currency it is difficult to find any entirely satisfactory measure of the overall balance of payments. Perhaps the most suitable for this purpose is the identified balance, i.e., the balance of current and long-term transactions.* Between 1958 and 1969 this was in surplus in only four years, and the accumulated deficit, 1960–1968 amounted to £1971 million. Of this accumulated deficit £512 million was due to private long-term outflow and the rest (£778 million) to official long-term capital outflow. The sixties managed only three years of surplus, 1961, 1962 and 1969, with 1961 only in surplus because of a positive balance on long-term capital arising from the huge inward Ford transaction. Deficits were continuous from 1963 until 1968 and were particularly large in 1960, 1964, 1967 and 1968. The pattern of sterling crisis was slightly different from that of large deficits, and both deficits and crises have become almost commonplace in recent years (major sterling crises occurred in 1961, 1964, 1966 and 1967). Even at the opening of the decade the reserves, including the International Monetary Fund position, were inadequate by almost any economic criteria and proved hopelessly insufficient during the sixties in the face of the size of payments imbalances which emerged. In some years the reserves suffered very severe losses, in 1961, 1964, 1965, 1966 and 1968.†

Table 8.2 re-arranges the normal balance of payments figures in order to demonstrate how the external financing requirement arose between 1964 and 1968 and how it has been met. The total financing requirement includes the deficit on current and long-term capital account, and other financing movements which affected the reserves.

* The 'basic balance' is particularly misleading for 1968, and the deficit is reduced to £252 million when account is taken of Euro-dollar borrowing to finance outward investment. On this point see *Economic Trends*, p. 12 (Sept. 1969).

† Recorded reserves rose by £34 million in 1966 but only because of the liquidation and transfer to the reserves of £316 million of Government-owned dollar securities. A further £204 million was transferred in 1967

Table 8.2

FINANCING OF U.K. DEFICIT 1964–1968

£ million (rounded)

1.	Current account	1 300	6.	Change in account with I.M.F.	1 100
2.	Long-term capital	800	7.	Other official borrowing	2 000
3.	Net sterling balances	1 200	8.	Sale of Treasury dollar portfolio and change in reserves	500
4.	Other, including balancing item	300			
5.	Total to be financed	3 600	9.	Total financing	3 600

Source: *Financial Statement and Budget Report, 1969–1970*, H.M.S.O. (15 April 1969).

Net sterling balances fell by £1200 million, of which £500 million was a reduction of balances held in Britain by overseas residents and £700 million an increase in U.K.'s sterling claims (mainly export credit given by British banks, much at long-term). Line 4 includes other trade credit, exchange adjustments after devaluation plus Euro-dollar finance for U.K. outward investment.* This adds up to a total financing need of £3600 million—very substantial indeed. It was met by borrowing £1100 million from the I.M.F and by other official borrowing of £2000 million (line 7), which consists of official borrowing in foreign currencies plus changes in sterling balances held by central monetary institutions in North America and Western Europe. The rest of the financing need was met by the transfer to the reserves of the proceeds of the sale of the Treasury dollar portfolio and change in reserves. As can be seen from the table almost all of this borrowing is short-term and therefore faced the Government with a severe debt repayment problem in the early seventies.†

However, the recorded balance of payments data are deficient as an *ex post* measure of external performance in that they reflect the impact of measures taken to prevent an even worse balance of payments position and reflect inadequately the underlying position. For example, unemployment during the sixties varied from a low of 1·32% (1965) to a high of 2·37% in 1969 and the recorded balance of payments figures reflect these fluctuations in employment which were themselves policy induced. In both 1961 and 1965/1966 the Government deflated demand, raising unemployment in later years to levels in excess of 2%, and in the second half of the sixties reduced the pressure of domestic demand (raised the acceptable level of unemployment) in order to improve the external position. The recorded data also include the effects of other adjustment policies, including the temporary import surcharge, restrictions on capital outflows and on travel expenditure, cuts in Government military expenditures abroad, and changes in oversea aid policy (in its volume as well as in the terms of assistance).

* A substantial proportion of U.K. outward investment in recent years has been financed by Euro-dollar borrowing from U.K. banks (£150 million in 1968). This is in line with the Government's policy operated through exchange control and the Voluntary Programme since it avoids any call on the reserves and is in effect self-financing.

† This seems in fact to have been somewhat less of a problem than earlier envisaged. In the 15 months since the beginning of 1969 $4·1 billion of external debt has repaid and reserves increased by almost $300 million. However, $1·4 billion of the repayment was accounted for by rolling forward an I.M.F. loan which had come due. This was made possible by the very strong current-account position by the S.D.R. allocation ($410 million), together with the large short-term capital inflow attracted by high domestic interest rates and a replenishment of trading balances.

Nevertheless, the recorded data make it perfectly plain that, even including the effects of adjustment measures, the balance of payments has remained in deficit for most years in the past decade.

There are undoubtedly many reasons for this very poor performance and what follows is in no way intended as a complete explanation. However, it does focus on some of the main forces affecting the external position. It can be seen from *Table 8.3* that Britain failed to maintain

Table 8.3

VOLUME OF WORLD AND U.K. EXPORTS OF MANUFACTURES. 1956–1968
1956 = 100

	World	U.K.	U.K. Share %
1956	100	100	19·3
1957	107	102	18·6
1958	105	99	18·1
1959	114	102	17·2
1960	128	108	16·3
1961	133	111	16·1
1962	142	112	15·2
1963	153	118	14·9
1964	172	123	13·8
1965	188	129	13·3
1966	205	134	12·6
1966 IV – 1967 III	216	136	12·2
1967 IV – 1968 III	239	140	11·3

Source: R. L. Major, 'The Competitiveness of British Exports since Devaluation'. *National Institute Economic Review*, No. 48, Table 1 (May 1969).

its share in world trade between 1956–1968. The data are at constant 1963 prices and thus provide a volume estimate of world and British export growth (a volume measure was used so as to be in a position to analyse share in the post-devaluation period when, as was to be expected, there was an acceleration in the rate of decline of the U.K.'s share in the value of world trade in manufactures). Over the whole period 1956–1968 the volume of world trade increased at an annual average rate of about 7·5 % although British exports rose at less than half this rate (3 % per annum), so that Britain's share declined by more than two-thirds. However, the decline in share, while continuous, did not take place at a constant rate and was especially rapid in 1960, 1964 and 1968, all years when world trade rose at a very fast rate. This lends some support to the argument that loss of share was fastest when world trade expanded rapidly and that capacity limitations in both 1960 and 1964 must have been a factor in producing loss of share.

Part of the loss of export share has been ascribed to changes in the pattern of trade, i.e., to a tendency for demand to grow relatively slowly in trade in which U.K.'s share is relatively high. *Table 8.4* throws

Table 8.4

DISTRIBUTION OF THE U.K.'S LOSS OF SHARE IN TRADE, 1954–1966, IN RELATION TO
THE VALUE OF EXPORTS IN 1954

	Share in U.K. Exports 1954	Contributions to the net loss of shares 1954–1966	
	%	%	£ million
By commodity group			
Chemicals	9·7	7·9	193
Textiles	15·1	11·9	289
Metals and metal goods	13·8	12·3	300
Electrical equipment	8·2	13·3	325
Other machinery	19·2	16·5	404
Transport equipment	19·1	22·8	557
Other manufactures	14·8	14·3	350
Change in pattern of trade		0·9	21
Total	100	100	2439
By area			
U.S.A.	4·9	1·0	25
Canada	5·6	6·1	150
Japan	0·4	−0·3	−7
EEC	11·4	21·4	521
EFTA	10·1	6·9	168
Other OECD Europe	5·1	5·1	125
Non OECD sterling area	48·5	39·8	970
Latin America	4·9	0·7	18
Other	9·8	1·2	29
Change in pattern of trade		18·2	440
Total	100	100	2439

Source: R. L. Major, 'Note on Britain's Share in World Trade in Manufactures, 1954–1966' *National Institute Economic Review*, No. 44, Table 2, 52 (May 1968).

some light on this argument. It confirms the results of several earlier studies by N.E.D.C., N.I.E.S.R. and the Board of Trade which found that very little of the loss of share was due to either the commodity structure of exports or to market pattern.* As can be seen from the table,

* See particularly *Export Trends*, N.E.D.C.: H.M.S.O. Table 5, p. 7, London (1963), and 'Fast and Slow Growing Products in World Trade,' *National Institute Economic Review*, No. 25 (Aug. 1963). The conclusions of the latter study were denied by Professor Tibor Barna who found that Britain's comparatively poor export performance was due to a low proportion of technically advanced products in her export structure (*The Times*, 3 April 1963).

the fall in share has been widespread and was greatest in those sectors of trade in which share had been highest—particularly trade with the overseas sterling area and trade in textiles. But the fall in share was not confined to this trade alone; falls in share occurred in all the main commodity groups and in all the major trading areas except the Sino-Soviet. According to Major the combined effects of market pattern and commodity structure account for only some 9% of the total loss of share between 1954 and 1966 and that 'The remainder results from net losses of share in individual sectors of trade and must, therefore, be attributed to declining competitiveness in the broadest sense . . . it seems probable that the bad performance in 1960 and 1964 should be attributed to the exceptionally rapid increase on the pressure of demand in the U.K., which was taking place on each occassion.*

A multiplicity of reasons have been put forward stressing both price and non-price factors (marketing deficiencies, poor design, long and unreliable delivery dates, high cost export credit and so on). It is difficult, if not impossible, to estimate the quantitative significance of these variables on export performance, but they undoubtedly contributed (more at some times than at others) to the decline in the U.K. export share. On the other hand it is unquestionably true that British export prices rose faster, relative to her main competitors in the sixties, than in the second half of the previous decade, but with no close correlation of year to year movements of relative prices and year to year movement in Britains' export share. Over the period 1958–1967 British export prices (unit values) rose more than twice as fast as world export prices.†
One important study completed in the early 1960s found a significant correlation between export prices and export performance, yielding a short-term price elasticity of substitution of 1·86 and a long-term elasticity of 2·29.‡ However, the I.M.F. study stressed the importance of other factors which they believed had not been fully eliminated by their techniques of analysis. A later piece of research, by J. R. Parkinson, confirmed that prices were an important factor although it varied in importance from commodity to commodity. His conclusion was later confirmed by G. R. Ray who found, in a study on exporting to Eastern

---

* R. L. Major, 'Note on Britain's Share in World Trade in Manufactures, 1954–1966', *National Institute Economic Review*, No. 44, 56 (May 1968). G. A. Renton 'British Exports of Manufactures to Industrial Countries', *National Institute Economic Review*, No. 42, 42–43 (Nov. 1967) reached a similar conclusion about the effects of capacity on exports in 1960 and 1964 (see below pages 190–191 for further consideration of this point).

† *National Institute Economic Review*, No. 48, Table 23 (May 1969).

‡ Helen B. Junz and R. R. Rhomberg 'Prices and Export Performance of Industrial Countries, 1953–1963', *I.M.F. Staff Papers*, **12**, 246–247 (July 1965).

N

Europe. 'The fairly unanimous view that British prices were too high, but British quality superior . . .'[*]

By the mid-sixties it was fairly clear that special factors (market pattern/commodity/structure/aid flows, etc.) could only explain a small part of loss of export share: that perhaps a further 20%–30% was due to unfavourable relative changes in costs and prices, with the rest accounted for by a multitude of non-price factors.

However, while it is possible to identify the most significant factors affecting export performance (and implicitly, therefore, the trends on the import side), the point needs to be made that there is no necessary relationship between the cause of a country's external difficulties and its solution. It may well be the case that an external deficit is due to rising Government expenditures overseas, but it does not follow that this should be cut back. Instead the authorities should aim at eliminating the deficit so as to minimise costs in terms of policy objectives foregone. On the other hand where the proximate cause of a deficit is an excessive pressure of domestic demand, then securing a better balance between demand and resources will also reduce, perhaps eliminate, the external deficit. The importance of this consideration is seen most clearly in relation to the decision to devalue in November 1967. This was criticised by some on the grounds that Britain's cost/price position was not out of line with her main competitors (a view that is difficult to reconcile with the evidence) and therefore wrong to devalue. But the decision to devalue was not taken on the basis of cost/price comparisons alone (it was one factor) but was the result of a balancing of the costs and benefits of following alternative policies. Deflation had been tried, in July 1966, and had failed, and a change in the exchange rate was preferable to further massive deflation. Exports may have been competitive, but they had proved insufficiently competitive to yield the size of surpluses considered essential to the achievement of strongly-held economic, social, political and military aims.

It is interesting to try to estimate what the underlying balance of payments position was in the first half of the sixties in order to throw some light on the magnitude of the payments problem, of its trend, and, therefore, of the size of effects required from the policies introduced in

[*] J. R. Parkinson, 'The Progress of U.K. Exports,' *Scottish Journal of Political Economy*, **XIII**, No. 1, 5–26 (Feb. 1966) and G. R. Ray, 'Export Competitiveness: British Experience in Eastern Europe', *National Institute Economic Review*, No. 36, 59 (May 1966). In general, however, attempts at measuring statistically the relative importance of prices on the value of U.K. exports (as opposed to export share) have not been very successful. In part this reflects the defective nature of the export (unit value) series which can change without any movement in price but simply as a result of a change in the composition of trade. See sources quoted by G. A. Renton, *National Institute Economic Review*, No. 42, 41–42 (Nov. 1967).

the later 'sixties'. There is little point is asking the question what the balance of payments would have looked like at a different pressure of demand, i.e., a higher unemployment rate than actually existed, although below an estimate is given of the trade off between employment and the balance of payments. Instead the procedure followed here is to take the recorded data and, on the basis of a number of critical assumptions, to smooth these. The objective has been to estimate what the balance of payments in each year would have looked like if the development of the economy had proceeded at a smooth rate rather than fluctuating. This entailed adjusting GDP, stockbuilding and imports in each year to the average rate for the period. Since import prices first rose and then fell this meant a critical assumption about import prices, which were assumed to have their average level over the period in each year. Exports were adjusted so as to have their trend values in each year (which tended to raise exports in the earlier years and reduce them in later years). Further adjustments of a relatively minor kind were made to the long-term capital account in order to smooth certain large transactions over the whole period, e.g., the large Ford investment in 1961. The basic procedure, therefore, was to take recorded data and redistribute the results between the years.

This is a very speculative procedure, particularly with respect to import prices, and there is the obvious objection that if growth, etc., had proceeded at a smooth rate then other items in the balance of payments would have looked rather different. However, for what it is worth, the exercise indicated a continuous deterioration in the current balance, especially large at the turn of the sixties (related to growing military and aid expenditures overseas plus unfavourable changes in shipping earnings) and in deficit between 1960–1965. The position on long-term capital account deteriorated throughout the period, the deficit being especially large in 1964 and 1965. The identified balance is in deficit continuously from the late fifties, small in the early years, worsening during the sixties with an average basic deficit of some £200 million (1960–1965). By 1964–1965, however, the basic deficit was closer to £300 million.

MOVEMENT TO A LOWER PRESSURE OF DEMAND

During the first half of the sixties, with an average unemployment rate of about 1·7% there existed an underlying balance of payments deficit of at least £200 million. Inevitably, therefore, the question was raised, both in the journals and also within official circles, of what would be the gains to the balance of payments of operating the economy at a lower pressure of demand. What was envisaged was not merely a temporary increase in unemployment but a permanent shift of emphasis in the unemployment target from say a target level of 1·7 or 1·8 % to 2 % or even higher. Since the July measures of 1966 this is precisely what has happened so that the level of unemployment has been rather higher at an average level of 2 % in the second half of the decade, and even higher than this (2·3 %) between 1967 and 1969.

What size of balance of payments relief could have been expected as a result of running the economy at a lower pressure of demand in the mid-sixties, and what level of unemployment would have been necessary to eliminate the underlying deficit entirely? The analysis is somewhat complicated but is perhaps worth setting out in some detail. In the first place there are the relationships between unemployment (or employment) and output, and also that between output and imports. Shepherd has estimated that at the margin an increase of 1 % in output gives rise to a fall of 0·2 % in unemployment when unemployment is already low (300 000) but to a larger fall of 0·33 % when unemployment is somewhat higher (500 000).* The relatively small fluctuations in employment compared with output are explained primarily by the comparative stability of the overhead labour force in the short-term and by fluctuations in hours worked. In the longer term it would be reasonable to expect little change in the rate of growth in productivity, for a small change in the pressure of demand, so that in the year of transition to a higher level of unemployment output might react in the ratio 5:1 (at an unemployment level of 300 000) or at 3·3:1 (unemployment at 500 000). In the following years output would, on this assumption, be lower only to the extent that employment is lower— perhaps 2·5 % times the change in the percentage of unemployment.

For example, in 1965 raising the unemployment rate of 1·3 % (300 000) by 0·2 % would have reduced output in that year by 1 % and in subsequent years by 0·5 %. This would have led to a reduction of imports, goods and services, of approximately £60 million in 1965 declining to only perhaps half that amount within a couple of years. In addition, in the year of transition to a higher unemployment rate, but not thereafter, there would be further reduction in imports through a once for all adjustment in the rate of stockbuilding. This might be equal to 1 % of total stocks, say a reduction of £100 million, and with an import content of 50 %, a saving on imports in one year only of about £50 million. On the basis of these estimates the reduction in imports

* J. R. Shepherd, 'Productive potential and the demand for labour'. *Economic Trends*, No. 178, 26 (Aug. 1968).

would be about £100 million in the first year, declining to about £30 million in later years due to a permanent rise in the unemployment rate of 0·2 %, implying a trade-off in the first year of 0·1 % of unemployment for £50 million of imports at 1965 prices, but in later years of only £15–20 million for a 0·1 % rise in unemployment.* However, at a higher level of unemployment (500 000) a 1 % change in output is accounted for by a 0·3 % change in unemployment, so that the trade-off in the first year would be £30 million of imports for a 0·1 % change in unemployment declining to only £10 million for the same change in unemployment in later years.

There is a second element in the calculation and that is the effect of a lower pressure of demand on production costs. There is evidence, reviewed in the following chapter, relating unemployment to the change in wages and prices and, generally, indicating a tendency for wages to rise faster the lower the level of unemployment. However, the relationship is not a particularly close one, and, more importantly, the evidence available to policy makers in the mid–sixties related to a period when unemployment was fluctuating and never stayed high for any length of time. The behaviour of institutions on both sides of the labour market could be expected to change for a shift to a permanently lower pressure of demand. For example, while trade unions may in the past have found it worthwhile not to press wage demands when unemployment was temporarily high, but to wait until their bargaining position was stronger, there is no reason to expect that they would behave in this way for a period of years. Indeed a recent piece of research by the Prices and Incomes Board suggests that there may have been some weakening in the explanatory power of the pressure of demand for labour variable and that autonomous cost-push forces have become more powerful.† Nevertheless, neglecting those considerations for the moment, on the basis of past relationships a fall of 1 % in unemployment added about 3 % to the rate of increase in wages and salaries per head (i.e., a 0·5 % change in wages for a 0·2 % change in unemployment).

A reduction of 0·5 % a year in the rise in wages is equal to a fall of 0·3 % a year in the rate of increase in the costs of goods produced for export (labour costs are equal to about two–thirds of total export costs excluding profits). This is not very significant in itself, but is equal to a

* This estimate is somewhat lower than that of Cooper who estimated the trade-off of imports for a 0·1 % change in unemployment at £29 million, at 1966 levels of trade. Over a period of three years the two estimates are roughly equal. (*Brookings Study*, page 162).

† Prices and Incomes Board, *3rd Annual General Report*, July 1968, Appendix A. Cmnd. 3715 H.M.S.O.

1 % gain over three years compared with what would otherwise have been the position if unemployment had stayed 0·2 % lower. With an assumed export price elasticity of demand of 2, a 1 % fall in export prices would raise the volume of exports by 2 % (in value by 1 %), equal to about £50 million a year after three years (in the first year perhaps by £15 million).

Adding together these estimates yields a net improvement in the current balance, as a result of lower pressure of demand, of around £115 million in year one declining to £80–90 million by year three (1965 prices and trade levels) for a shift to a permanently higher level of unemployment of 0·2 %. By how much, using these estimates, would unemployment have had to rise in order to eliminate the deficit, assuming that this was of the order of £250 million? If the starting unemployment position was 300 000 (1·3 % unemployment rate) then unemployment would have had to rise by 0·6 % points (to 450 000) in order to improve the balance of payments by £250 million. Starting at a higher unemployment level (500 000) then the increase in unemployment would have to be 0·9 % i.e., to about 750 000 or some 3 % unemployment.*

There may be other effects on the balance of payments of running the economy at a lower pressure of demand other than the above. It is held, though not very firmly by the authorities, that changes in the pressure for demand have two other effects. Firstly, by depriving manufacturers of home sales, firms are forced to seek export outlets which they previously did not do because of the differences in profitability of home export sales. Secondly, that reduction in the pressure of demand would reduce the length of order books thus reducing overlong delivery dates and so increasing demand for exports. There is some evidence for these pressure of demand effects but they may be entirely short-run phenomena. For example, a highly aggregated study by Ball, et al., found that in particular periods exports were lost because of the high pressure of demand in the U.K., for example in 1964. A further study of machine tool exports confirmed their conclusion, although they found that British exports of machine tools were most sensitive to the pressure of demand in Germany, her main competitor, than to the pressure of demand at home.† However, this evidence does

---

* This is quite different in scale from the statements made by the Prime Minister (Mr. Wilson) to the T.U.C. in 1966 that the only alternative to incomes freeze plus deflation was 'an international crisis with unemployment in the country reaching perhaps two million' (*Report of the 98th Annual Trades Union Congress*, London, 1966).

† See R. J. Ball, J. R. Eaton and M. D. Steuer, 'The Relationship between United Kingdom Export Performance in Manufactures and the Internal Pressure

not demonstrate the validity of the proposition that a reduced pressure of demand over a longer period would have solved the external payments problem. The effects in the longer-term of operating with a lower level of capacity utilisation may be quite different. Secondary effects on investment may occur, reducing the longer term trend of capacity, with unfavourable effects on innovation, and thus in the longer term having adverse effects on the composition and price of output.

COMMERCIAL POLICY

When the new Government attained office in October 1964 it found waiting for it an analysis by officials of the kinds of measures which were needed in order to meet the unprecedented payments deficit. Following this advice the Government imposed a surcharge of 15% on about £1500 million of manufactured imports. In February it was announced that the rate would be 10% from April 1965, and in May (1966) the Chancellor announced that it would be removed at the end of November. At the same time (October 1964) the Export Rebate was introduced equal to some 2%–2·5% of manufacturing costs.

These two measures together amounted to a selective, though temporary devaluation, which was bigger on the import side and aimed at that component of total imports which had grown most strongly in recent years. They constituted a distinct breach of faith with both the G.A.T.T. and E.F.T.A., and it was undoubtedly the furore within E.F.T.A. which led to the reduction of the surcharge to 10% in April. The Rebate also caused trouble within E.F.T.A. and finally the British Government agreed that exporters to E.F.T.A. could either claim the Rebate or E.F.T.A. treatment, but not both. Very little seems to be known about the effect of the Rebate on exports, which continued in operation until 31 March 1968, but from the evidence which is available it seems that it went to raise company profits and had no measurable impact on the level of exports.[*]

[*] The S.E.T. premium paid to British manufacturers from the autumn of 1966 until its partial removal at the time of devaluation was also intended to compensate manufacturers for the sharp increase in labour costs during 1965 and early 1966. It subsidised labour costs in export sectors by something like 0·5%.

---

of Demand', *Economic Journal*, **76**, 501–518 (Sept. 1966) and 'The Effect of Waiting Times on Foreign Orders for Machine Tools', *Economica*, **33**, 387–403 (Nov. 1966). Their results are partly confirmed by the National Institute who has estimated that of an average loss of share of manufactures equal to 0·6% (1955–1965) some 0·1% has been due to a lack of capacity *National Institute Economic Review*, Table 6, 16 (Feb. 1967).

The Temporary Import Charge was much more important, and at the time of its introduction Mr. Callaghan estimated the annual import savings at £200 million, subsequently raised to £300 million in his November 1964 Budget. It was expected to operate in the following way. Firstly, through a short-term effect on stocks as importers and businessmen drew down their stocks. They would behave in this way because they knew the charge was temporary and it had been announced by the Government that it would be reviewed in the spring of 1965. Such action would affect home output and imports while stocks were being drawn down, but stop as soon as the stocks reached a new level. It was also reversible. As soon as the charge was removed stocks would again be built up and imports be above trend. Secondly, some purchases, other than for stocks, might be delayed, but this again was reversible and thought likely to be small. Thirdly, there was a 'price-absorption effect'. As foreign exporters absorbed part or whole of the charge then this would reduce import prices and turn the terms of trade in Britain's favour. This was thought likely to be small, temporary and not reversible. Fourthly, the prices of those imports which continued to come in would rise (apart from those examples where the charge was fully absorbed by the overseas supplier) and this would affect domestic demand. However, the price effect would be mainly on personal consumption since neither Public Authorities consumption nor investment expenditure were considered price elastic, while exporters could claim for the import tax content of their exports. Finally there would be a 'substitution-effect' as the rise in import prices led to a substitution of domestic output for imports.

Many estimates have been made of the impact of the T.I.C. on imports—usually in a downward direction. The only official estimates were those given in 1964 (£200 million initially, raised to £300 million in November) and these were clearly excessively optimistic, although it is no simple matter to measure the effect of the surcharge. Both Johnston and Henderson and the National Institute have published studies using basically the same approach.* This amounted to constructing an import function in an attempt to explain as fully as possible, the behaviour of imports before the surcharge. This function was then used to forecast what imports would have been in the absence of the surcharge, and the effectiveness of the surcharge was analysed in terms of the residuals which appeared between forecast and actual

* J. Johnston and M. Henderson 'Assessing the Effects of the Import Surcharge', *Manchester School of Economic and Social Studies*, **35**, 89–110 (May 1967). For the Institute's initial analysis of the T.I.C. see the *National Institute Economic Review*, 9–11 and Table 3 (Nov. 1964), and 'Forecasting Imports: A Re-Examination', *National Institute Economic Review*, 52–57 (Nov. 1967).

imports. Johnston concluded that the import savings, goods and services, were equal to £156 million in the five quarters to the end of 1965, plus another £72 million in 1966, making a total surcharge effect of £228 million.*

The first estimate by the National Institute (November 1964) put the surcharge effect at £180 million in the first half of 1965, but by May 1966 had reduced this estimate to one of only £70 million for the whole of 1965. More recently (November 1967) using an equation including a special variable to denote the presence of the surcharge effect the Institute estimated that the T.I.C. reduced imports over the two years to mid-1967 by £350 million, although other equations yielded smaller effects. More recently still (February 1969) the Institute gave the results of yet a further re-assessment which suggested an import elasticity of demand for those goods affected by the T.I.C. of only −0·6 %. They gave no figures of the volume of imports saved, but assuming an 8 % rise in the price of imports as a result of surcharge then the reduction in the volume of imports was 4·8 % of £1500 million of surcharged imports, i.e., £70 million. The Johnston study also implied very low prices elasticity of demand of 0·8 % in 1965 and 0·5 % 1966.

Both the National Institute 1967 study and that of Johnston exhibited the same pattern of residuals.† There were large negative residuals in the first quarters of 1965 and in the final quarter of 1966. The first is mainly explicable in terms of a temporary rundown of stocks of surcharged goods (stockbuilding fell from £155 million in the last quarter of 1964 to only £68 million in the first quarter of 1965). Again both studies show a large positive residual in the third quarter of 1966, those imports which could not be delayed even though it was known that the surcharge would be removed at the end of November, and a substantial postponement of imports in the fourth quarter. Large positive residuals were, therefore, to be expected in the first half of 1967 (estimated by Johnston at £40–£50 million) and this is what both researchers found. These 'extra' imports in the first half of 1967 need to be deducted from the total T.I.C. effect in order to yield the net

---

* The results of equation 14 have been used here. This related imports to GDP at market prices with the stock component removed, retaining the latter as a separate explanatory variable. It should be noted that the estimate of £228 million given in the text is a gross figure and the net saving on imports was less than this.

† These were for Johnston and Henderson (equation 14):

£million (1958 prices)

1964 IV	1965 I	1965 II	1965 III	1965 IV	1966 I	1966 II	1966 III	1966 IV
−41	−79	−8	−4	−24	5	−32	26	−71

saving on imports in respect of the Johnston estimate given earlier, giving a final figure of £180 million for the two years to mid-1967.

Obviously great uncertainty surrounds these estimates but while the precise magnitude of the effect of the T.I.C. on imports is unknown all the estimates (apart from that of the Institute in November 1967) yield very low price elasticities of demand for imports. If the -0.6% estimate of February 1969 is adjusted upwards to eliminate the 'temporary' element in the surcharge, this gives an elasticity of around -0.8%. If all other non-surcharged imports are assumed to have a zero price elasticity then this yields an overall elasticity (all imports) of -0.45%. The question remains as to why the T.I.C. had such a small effect on imports, since manufactured goods are generally thought to be fairly sensitive to price changes.* One explanation which has been given, and for which there is a certain amount of evidence, is that overseas suppliers knew that the surcharge was temporary and seem to have been prepared to absorb 2–3 % of it on average. This still left a price rise of some 7–8 % but this seems to have been insufficient in itself to produce any large effect on the demand for imports given both the pace of internal inflation† and given the extent to which British output had already become uncompetitive.

The only other important innovation in commercial policy during the sixties was the Import Deposit Scheme, introduced on 22 November 1968 for one year as part of a package of measures including increases in taxation and credit restrictions.‡ Its introduction reflected the failure of the balance of payments to respond during 1968 to the devaluation strategy and was intended to buy more time for the export response to come through. The scheme required importers to deposit with the Government 50 % of the value of all imports covered (£2800 million, equal to two-fifths of total imports). In practice the import categories covered by the scheme were similar to those covered by the T.I.C. Deposits were paid at the time of arrival of the imports, were repaid 180 days later, and were expected to build up to a maximum of about £600 million at the end of six months. By the end of May 1969 import deposits were slightly below the forecast, at £540 million. Temporarily the deposits reduced the Government's borrowing requirement,

---

* Maurice F. G. Scott for example estimated the long-run elasticity of demand for imports of finished manufactures at 7. M. F. G. Scott. *A Study of United Kingdom Imports*, Cambridge (1963).

† The wholesale price of manufactures sold on the home market rose by 4·6% in 1965 and by a further 2·8 % in 1966, sufficient to erode a considerable part of the price advantage given to domestic import competing sectors by the T.I.C.

‡ The scheme was subsequently renewed in a slightly modified form for a second year.

but subsequently this effect was reversed as the deposits were repaid. In their instructions to the banking sector the Government emphasised that they should not provide credit to finance the import deposits, and in particular that they avoid finance for imports which added to stocks.*

In certain respects the scheme resembled the T.I.C. in that possibly a third of the net impact on imports was expected to be caused by its price effect, i.e., the increase in prices caused by interest payments on six-month loans used to finance the deposits. The other two-thirds of the impact on imports was accounted for by liquidity and availability effects (the company sector was at that stage already suffering pressure on its cash flow position as a result of Government fiscal and monetary policy). It was also anticipated that most of the impact would occur early on as stock levels of imported goods were drawn down, and that a short-run anticipatory reduction in purchases might also take place which would later reverse itself in the last quarter of 1969 and first quarter of 1970. At the time of its introduction the National Institute estimated that it would reduce imports in 1969, goods and services at 1958 prices, by £80 million, of which some £20 million would be due to the short-run anticipatory effect which would later be reversed leaving a net effect on imports of £60 million.†

The Treasury seems to have expected, at least initially, a substantially larger reduction in imports than £80 million due mainly to a large temporary fall in stocks of imported goods. It is also clear that they severely miscalculated the extent to which tight domestic credit controls would be offset by finance extended by overseas suppliers or their agents. In June 1969 the Treasury estimated that overseas finance accounted for about one-half of import deposits received during that quarter (£270 million), and that much of this credit was in the form of arrangements for delaying payment for imports, although some part of it may have been extended to allow importers to repay temporary loans from the banking system in respect of deposits paid in the fourth quarter of 1968.‡ Certainly the scheme reduced imports and therefore provided the authorities with a certain amount of welcome relief. But once again the out-turn seems to have been substantially different from official expectation.

---

* For further details of the scheme see the note on credit restriction in the *Quarterly Bank Bulletin*, **8** (Dec. 1968).

† *National Institute Economic Review*, 35 (Feb. 1969). They subsequently estimated the net direct effect of the scheme at £110 million excluding additional short-term capital inflows, *Review*, No. 50, 20 (Nov. 1969).

‡ 'U.K. Balance of Payments in the First Quarter of 1969'. *Economic Trends*, xiv–xv (June 1969).

THE BALANCE OF PAYMENTS COST OF MILITARY AND AID EXPENDITURES

MILITARY EXPENDITURE ABROAD

During the sixties important decisions were taken—always accompanied by bitter political dispute—about the role of Britain in International affairs. The decisions amounted if not to a reversal of her traditional role at least a substantial scaling-down in her international responsibilities. Acceptance of wide-ranging responsibilities round the world necessarily entailed substantial Government expenditure overseas and net Government expenditure abroad, which has not been less than a £100 million in any year since 1953, actually more than doubled between 1958-1969 (see *Table 8.1*). These expenditures are extremely diverse, including colonial grants, pensions, administrative and diplomatic costs, subscriptions and contributions to international organisations and a similarly miscellaneous group of receipts. But by far the most important are overseas military expenditures which increased four-fold between 1957 and 1969, from a net £61 million in 1957 to £268 million in 1969. As can be observed from *Table 8.5* most of this rapid increase occurred before 1964 and since then the Government has been successful in stabilising military expenditure abroad at about a net £270 million. Overseas grants is the other important category of Government overseas expenditure and this increased by some £100 million between 1957–1969, but since this is more akin to capital flow, analysis of this item is delayed until the following section.

While overseas military expenditure has risen rapidly during the past 10–15 years the actual size of Britain's military presence overseas has fallen—total military personnel outside Britain fell by almost a half between 1955 and 1967. This has produced a very sharply-rising balance of payments cost per man, from an estimated £410 in 1955 to £1405 in 1967,[*] due to rising local costs abroad, to increased Forces pay and to reductions in the contributions of other countries towards the upkeep of British Forces. Inevitably, therefore, by the early sixties the question was raised as to whether the benefits derived from maintaining an international military presence were large enough, given that the foreign exchange required to finance overseas military expenditure was a rival to the import needs of faster economic growth. By the end of the sixties the Government had decided that the balance lay in

[*] *Britain's Economic Prospects*, Brookings Institute: Allen and Unwin, Table 4-6, 169 (1968).

Table 8.5

U.K. MILITARY EXPENDITURE ABROAD

£ million

	Expenditures					
	Military Services	Military Grants	Military Subscriptions to International Organisations	Total	Receipts	Net Military Expenditures Abroad
1957	151	9	2	162	101	61
1958	173	6	2	181	55	126
1959	160	7	2	169	40	129
1960	203	7	3	213	41	172
1961	224	13	2	239	41	198
1962	243	12	2	257	33	224
1963	250	19	3	272	35	237
1964	270	30	6	306	38	268
1965	270	19	4	293	25	268
1966	283	19	5	307	25	282
1967	264	21	7	292	25	267
1968	274	12	7	293	28	265
1969	278	9	7	294	26	268

Sources: *U.K. Balance of Payments 1968* (C.S.O.), Table 9, and *Economic Trends*.

favour of a reduced military and political presence abroad, together with a reduction in the volume of national resources devoted to defence. Decisions taken between 1965–1968 implied a reduction in total defence expenditure to £1800 million by the mid-seventies (at constant 1964 prices) and cuts in military expenditure on Forces outside Europe from £175 million in 1967 to about £60 million in the mid-seventies.

This was a drastic re-appraisal of Britain's role in international affairs and was due in part to the continuous balance of payments difficulties of the sixties but also to a gradual awareness that Britain's future lay primarily with Europe. With this reconsideration of political, economic and military strategy has gone a determination to at least maintain Britain's military presence in Europe. The foreign exchange cost of maintaining forces in Germany is substantial and equal to £82 milllion in 1967, although this is partly offset by arrangements with Germany and the U.S.A. about defence procurement. Bargaining about offset has in recent years been continuous and tough although a substantial part of the direct military costs of British Forces in Germany are now offset.* If it is the case that none of the U.S. and German procurement expenditure would take place unless there were an offset agreement, then a reduction in military expenditure in Germany would not directly improve the balance of payments. This seems rather unlikely and some proportion of the goods bought under offset would almost certainly have been bought without the agreement. There would, in any case, be indirect gains to the balance of payments since cuts in military expenditure would release resources for other activities including commercial exports and import substitution.

Similar considerations apply to other military expenditures overseas. Clearly the expenditure figures do not measure the balance of payments cost of such activities—cost in the sense that they fall on the foreign exchanges reserves or increase the necessity to borrow abroad. Most of the countries outside Europe, where most of the military expenditure occurs, would use any foreign exchange received not for additions to reserves (except perhaps Singapore) but for increasing expenditure. Furthermore, they have a high propensity to import from Britain so that a high proportion of the local expenditure generated directly and indirectly by British military expenditure leads to a demand for British exports. It follows, therefore, that cuts in overseas military expenditure do not produce equivalent savings in foreign ex-

---

* Of the £82 million foreign exchange costs of British troops in Germany some £72 million was offset in 1967. Budget Statement, *Hansard*, 10 April 1967, col. 981. A subsequent agreement with Germany led to £146 million offset to foreign exchange costs of British troops, estimated over two years at £198 million.

change, so that, according to one estimate, the balance of payments savings would be equal to only 75 % of the reduction in military expenditures.*

If the Government is able to fully offset the foreign exchange cost of Forces kept in Germany and successfully cuts overseas military expenditure elsewhere to £60 million by the mid-seventies then the savings in foreign exchange will be at an annual rate of about £85 million. This is not very large in relation to the average annual growth in export earnings of more than £1000 million in recent years, and in the short run some of these gains will be offset by increased aid expenditures to soften the impact of the run down of British military expenditure (e.g., to Singapore, Aden and Malta). Whether the trade-off between less military expenditures abroad and a reduced political and military role in an unsettled world is in the long term beneficial or desirable is not a question which economists can answer.

OVERSEAS AID EXPENDITURE

Between 1957 and 1964 British economic aid to developing countries more than doubled from a net £84 million to £176 million.† Since 1964, however, Government policy has been to hold the net transfer of resources at its 1964 level, although as part of the July measures (1966) aid was actually cut by some £20 million, and, more recently in January 1968, aid was frozen for two years at its existing level. The result of these policies has been a fall in the real value of aid given to developing countries in recent years, and although Britain remains relatively generous about the terms on which aid is provided it is now very far from achieving the U.N.C.T.A.D. 1 % of GNP target. On the basis of present aid policies the underachievement of the U.N.C.T.A.D. target will continue until 1975.‡

The aid programme has included among its aims broad humanitarian considerations, a concern for economic development but also elements of political and economic self-interest.§ Increasingly also in

* *Britain's Economic Prospects*, Brookings Institute: Allen and Unwin, 171 (1968).

† The flow of net official financial resources to developing countries and multilateral agencies. Source: Development Assistance Committee, *Statistical Tables for 1969 Annual Aid Review*, Table 1, p. 10.

‡ While the grant element in British official aid was as high as 83 % in 1968 and the terms of the U.K. were within range of qualifying with the D.A.C. Terms of Aid Recommendation, the net flow of total official and private financial resources was equal to only 0·75 % of GNP.

§ See particularly 'Overseas Development: The Work in Hand' Cmd. 3180, H.M.S.O., and I. M. D. Little and J. M. Clifford, *International Aid*, Pt. IV, Allen & Unwin (1965).

recent years aid administrators have emphasised the need to reduce the cost of aid expenditure to the balance of payments and in so doing have demoted development objectives. The argument has been that the balance of payments would not permit any expansion in aid volume but also that a new mix of aid objectives was required which gave more emphasis to the purely economic interests of the donor. Furthermore, as the balance of payments constraint on aid expenditures becomes less pressing (in the early seventies) it is fairly clear that the Treasury will press alternative arguments of which the need for continued restraint in the growth of public expenditure will be the most significant. Be that as it may one result of the sixties was to freeze the net transfer of resources to developing countries during the second half of the decade. It also led to several estimates of the balance of payments cost of aid since it was clearly in the interests of the Overseas Development Ministry to demonstrate that this was significantly different from the expenditure figures.*

Table 8.6 presents the results of the most recent official study of the balance of payments cost of aid, for a marginal adjustment of aid volume in respect of the distributive pattern which existed during 1964–1966. A considerable proportion of the funds disbursed as aid either never leaves the U.K. at all, the aid being provided in the form of goods, or returns as payment for additional exports and in other ways. In the base period of £100 of bilateral aid £72·5 was aid tied to the purchase of British goods or in other ways led to direct expenditure on our goods and services. The rest (£27·5 per £100) includes untied aid, including budgetary assistance, which would not be identified as leading directly to expenditure in Britain, together with expenditures by technical assistance personnel in developing countries.

However, these *prima facie* returns are not the end of the analysis. Firstly, some aid is used to finance purchases from Britain which would have been made in any case using freely available foreign exchange, and thus does not lead to any additional exports. This is known as 'switching'. Secondly, aid which is spent within the recipient country on domestic output (equal to £21 per £100) or which frees foreign exchange (through 'switching') increases the foreign exchange at their disposal. Some of this foreign exchange is spent in the U.K. Finally, that part of additional foreign exchange spent in third countries will raise their export earnings and some part of the foreign exchange received will be spent in the U.K. There will be several rounds of such transactions which are technically known as 'reflection effects'.

* For the official figuring see Bryan Hopkin and Associates, 'Aid and the Balance of Payments', *Economic Journal*, **LXXH** (March 1970).

Table 8.6

ESTIMATED RETURN TO THE U.K. OF OFFICIAL BILATERAL AID 1964–1966
(£ million and %)

Type of Aid	Aid Disbursed Annual Average 1964/66	Prima-facie Return to U.K.	Amount Switched		Local Expenditure	Induced Imports	Reflection Effects on U.K. Exports	Total Return to U.K. Col. 2 less Col. 3, plus Cols. 4, 6, and 7	
			Total	Spent in U.K.	Total			Amount	% of col. 1
	1	2	3	4	5	6	7	8	9
CAPITAL AID									
Fully tied	67·06	67·06	41·51	9·00			2·75	37·30	55·6
Partially tied	34·15	20·49	2·17	0·44	13·66	2·66	1·48	22·90	67·1
Untied:									
Budgetary	25·03	0·88			17·53	2·92	3·37	7·17	28·6
Other	26·03	15·89			6·25	1·51	1·09	18·49	71·0
TOTAL	152·27	104·32	43·68	9·44	37·44	7·09	8·69	85·86	56·4
TECHNICAL ASSISTANCE									
Disbursed in U.K.	9·31	9·31						9·31	100
Disbursed Abroad	20·03	18·06			1·53	0·35	0·22	18·63	93·0
TOTAL	29·34	27·37			1·53	0·35	0·22	27·94	95·2
TOTAL BILATERAL AID	181·61	131·69	43·68	9·44	38·97	7·44	8·91	113·80	62·7

Source: Bryan Hopkin and Associates, 'Aid and the Balance of Payments', *Economic Journal*, LXXX, Table III (March 1970).

O.D.M. estimated 'switching' in the base period at £24 per £100 of total bilateral aid, and this has to be subtracted from the £72·5 per £100 of *prima facie* return noted above, bringing the return down to £48·5 per £100. Of the foreign exchange released by switching it was estimated that more than a quarter (£5·2) was spent in the U.K.; that aid spent within the recipient countries generated a further £4·1 of British exports and that the reflection effects gave rise to an additional £4·9 of British exports. These estimates add up to a net export of goods and services corresponding to a £100 of aid equal to £62·6.

All of these calculations refer to bilateral aid and assuming that marginal changes in this part of the aid programme will have no effect on other country's aid programmes. This does not hold true for subscriptions to multilateral aid agencies where an increase by the U.K. is matched by a much bigger combined increase. British exports benefit not only from the British contribution but also from those of other countries. In the past Britain has succeeded in winning orders equal to £116 per £100 of its multilateral aid (as high as £150/£100 for I.D.A. subscriptions).* Some £9 in every £100 of British aid was multilateral in 1964–1966, so that the return spending on British goods and services on bilateral and multilateral aid is raised from £62·6 to £67 per £100 of total aid.

However, aid financed exports may pre-empt productive capacity which would otherwise have produced commercial exports—the 'capacity effect'. If this happened to the extent of 20 % then it reduces the estimate of net additional spending on British exports from £67 per £100 to £58 per £100 (i.e., £53·5 per £100 for bilateral aid and £100 per £100 for multilateral). The balance of payments cost of overseas aid lies, therefore on the basis of the above considerations, in the range of 33 %–42 % with the exact position in the range depending on the size of the capacity effect. A larger capacity effect than 20 % would, of course, increase the balance of payments cost, but any figure for this effect is bound to be pure conjecture. Of this cost (33 %–42 %) by far the most significant element is that of switching, so that the cost could be reduced considerably by techniques for more effectively tying aid. Such a course would not be welcomed by recipients and it might in other ways reduce the value of development aid to them.

---

* This may not operate in the immediate future due to deferment of use of the U.S. contribution to the second replenishment of the I.D.A. In the short run this increases our effective share of contributions relative to procurement, with gains in the longer term as drawings are made on the deferred part of the U.S. contribution.

In the above calculations it was assumed that changes in British bilateral aid had no effect on other countries' bilateral aid and this seems perfectly reasonable for small changes. This would not be realistic for large changes or for the elimination of the total aid programme. In 1966 the bilateral aid programmes of the other donors, who are members of the Development Assistance Committee of the O.E.C.D., amounted in total to £330 million untied and £1500 million tied. The British share of the imports generated by the untied aid has been estimated by O.D.M. at 20%, i.e., £66 million. For tied aid there will of course be switching and this is estimated to benefit U.K. exports by £64 million. On the basis of these figures British exports are £130 million higher in total as a result of other donors' bilateral aid flows.

The above estimates are probably as good as any that could be produced, and although they contain a fairly substantial amount of guesswork are probably of the right magnitude. They suggest, firstly, that the balance of payments cost of aid is still fairly substantial (especially where the 'capacity effect' is operating), but quite different from the straight expenditure figures. Secondly, that different categories of bilateral aid have a significantly higher balance of payments cost than others, and that multilateral aid was less costly than bilateral aid. This may, however, no longer be the case (see footnote page 202). However, while the pattern of bilateral aid could be adjusted so as to minimise its balance of payments cost, this would hardly be consistent with the broad aims of the programme. It would be unfortunate if the purely development aims of the programme were to be sacrificed to what is essentially a short-run balance of payments problem.

CAPITAL EXPORT

During the 10 years prior to 1965 Britain earned an annual average surplus on current account of only £33 million and yet invested (net) abroad in all forms, official and private, an average of £160 million a year. In the 13 years between 1952 and 1964 the total flow of investment overseas in all forms, official and private, amounted to about £4000 million. By the end of 1964 the total stock of long-term assets abroad had risen to about £10000 million, some £9000 million of which were private assets. Of the £9000 million of private long-term assets about £5500 million were direct investments of all kinds. Over the same period the reserves hardly rose at all, while the short-term

Table 8.7
PRIVATE INVESTMENT
£ million

	Abroad (net of disinvestment)				In the U.K. (net of disinvestment)				Private Investment Net
	Direct	Portfolio	Oil & Other	Total	Direct	Portfolio	Oil & Other	Total	
1958	−144	−166 (brace)		−310	+87	+77 (brace)		+164	−146
1959	−196	−107 (brace)		−303	+146	+26 (brace)		+172	−131
1960	−250	+37	−109	−322	+135	+43	+55	+233	−89
1961	−226	+28	−115	−313	+236	+115	+75	+426	+113
1962	−209	+39	−72	−242	+130	+61	+57	+248	+6
1963	−236	−5	−79	−320	+160	+19	+97	+276	−44
1964	−263	−3	−133	−399	+162	−39	+38	+161	−238
1965	−308	+94	−140	−354	+197	−46	+91	+242	−112
1966	−276	+82	−110	−304	+195	−59	+140	+277	−27
1967	−281	−59	−123	−463	+170	+11	+200	+381	−82
1968	−410	−236	−89	−735	+283	+87	+245	+615	−120
1969	−508	+6	−91	−593	+254	+184	+236	+674	+81

Sources: U.K. Balance of Payments (C.S.O.), 1968, Table 20, and Economic Trends.

monetary position, excluding the change in the reserves, deteriorated by over £700 million.*

Table 8.7 provides data on capital flows since 1958. From this it can be seen that direct investment grew substantially, while there was a liquidation of overseas portfolio investments between 1960 and 1967 (subsequently largely offset by the large outflow of portfolio investment to Australia in 1968). Net private investment does not, however, exhibit any distinct upward trend over the whole period with a good deal of British capital outflow offset by inward investment, particularly direct investment in Britain by American companies.

Since the Second World War Britain has had direct controls over direct investment outside the sterling area, which technically also covered the rate of re-invested profits by foreign subsidiaries. This, the level of retained earnings, escaped control of any kind if it was within the sterling area, and was usually permitted within the non-sterling area countries provided the rate of repatriated earnings did not fall too far below their normal level. In July 1961, during the sterling crisis, the Government restricted direct investment in the non-sterling area countries to those cases, 'where it would produce clear and commensurate benefit to U.K. export earnings and thus to the balance of payments in the short-term'.† Firms were also asked to repatriate a larger part of their overseas earnings, but they proceeded during the next few years to actually repatriate less.‡ In May 1962 the regulations were relaxed and companies not satisfying the July 1961 criterion were permitted to invest abroad by purchasing dollars from the investment currency market, i.e., at a premium, or by borrowing abroad. Other controls existed in relationship to portfolio investment. Only sterling-area members were allowed to float bond issues on the London Money Market, and while British residents were freely permitted to purchase sterling-area securities, foreign securities could only be bought through the investment currency market.

Much has been written on the benefits and costs of overseas investment, and much of the discussion remained inconclusive until the

---

* Mr. Callaghan put the essential point very bluntly in his 1965 Budget. 'The tax system we have been operating is too favourable to investment abroad compared with investment at home. Partly, though of course by no means entirely, as a result of this, our long-term assets abroad have been built up over the years to a massive amount. But, at the same time, our vital gold and dollar reserves have remained stationary, and the short-term liabilities to which they constitute a backing have risen excessively. This is the problem, and the one which brings us to a halt every few years.' Budget Statement, *Hansard*, 6 April 1965, col. 265.

† *Economic Survey 1962*, 33, Cmnd. 1678 H.M.S.O. (April 1962).

‡ The percentage of overseas earnings repatriated fell from 51% in 1961 to 42% in 1964.

publication of the two reports on 'The Effects of U.K. Direct Investment Overseas' by W. B. Reddaway.* These reports deal with the effects of direct investment abroad by British manufacturing, mining and plantation companies on the U.K. balance of payments and the economy in general. Their conclusions were based on a sample of companies who accounted for some three-quarters of the investment in the specified categories, and yielded a set of estimates for the years 1955–1964. Broadly speaking, the Reddaway Reports supported the measures taken by the Government in the period since 1965 and are to a considerable extent a vindication of the rightness of these policies.

Clearly overseas investment entails a conflict between short-term and long-term advantages. These have been summarised by Reddaway as follows:†

1. An average act of overseas investment will strengthen the future balance of payments on current account—even after deducting the interest payable on overseas borrowing (or the equivalent) by which at least from the national point of view, such an act of investment is usually financed.

2. In consequence, a steady rate of direct investment overseas would, if maintained long enough, provide enough of an annual surplus on current account to finance the annual quota of direct investment.

3. Nevertheless, each single act of direct investment overseas has an immediate effect on the balance of payments (capital and current account together) which is far larger than any one year's 'continuing' benefit, so that a restriction of the outflow brings a 'cash' or 'financing' benefit for a substantial number of years.

Reddaway provided estimates of the effects on the balance of payments of adding a £100 to the net operating assets of overseas subsidiaries of manufacturing companies. In the year of the investment the current account of the balance of payments benefits by £11 of additional exports, and the capital account will be affected by an addition of £100 of net operating assets overseas, and of £89 to net external financial obligations. In subsequent years, on average, the £100 of net additional operating assets will earn profits of about £5·25 (after deduction of overseas taxes and after allowing for stock appreciation). From this has to be subtracted external obligations at 3 % per annum, i.e., £2·75. In addition there will be continuing effects on U.K. exports of goods and services, plus a reduction in U.K. imports since British

---

* W. B. Reddaway, *Effects of U.K. Direct Investment Overseas: An Interim Report*, March 1967; *Final Report*, July 1968, Cambridge University Press.

† W. B. Reddaway, *Effects of U.K. Direct Investment Overseas: Final Report*, Cambridge University Press 347 (1968).

production is lower, equal to about £1·15. The total effect is a continuing annual gain of £4 per £100 added to net operating assets, which would fall to only £2·5 if '90% substitution' is assumed.*

The reports permit a number of conclusions to be reached on the effects of overseas investment on the balance of payments, although Reddaway continuously emphasised the diversity of experience and, therefore, the misleading nature of some of the averages produced by the investigation. It is clear, nevertheless, that the initial effect on exports, i.e., in the year when the investment is done, is not very substantial, and that the continuing benefits to the balance of payments are relatively small. It follows, therefore, that even on the basis of quite different assumptions about the extent to which the overseas investment is financed by the U.K. or by substantial amounts supplied by overseas, a policy of restriction would considerably ease the country's external financing problem.† Furthermore, the 'national financing charge', i.e., the real interest payable on the additional external debt incurred as a result of the overseas investment, is an inadequate measure of the true cost to the nation, since the loss of reserves caused by the investment, at a time of crisis, leads to deflationary policies which reduces the national income. What is also very significant is that the profitability of overseas direct investment is as low as 5·25% after overseas tax (the relevant profit concept when measuring the return to the nation), which is considerably less than the pre-tax return on home investment. However, the Report did emphasise the great diversity of

---

* Reddaway assumed in his main calculations that if all of the production overseas undertaken by U.K. subsidiaries between 1955 and 1964 had not been undertaken, then it would have been replaced by an equal amount of production by non-U.K. enterprises in the same countries. If one alternatively assumed only 90% substitute production, then this would leave 10% of the market available to world exporters, including the U.K. On the assumption that the U.K. shared in this market in proportion to her average share in world trade (1955–1964), then U.K. exports would have been £150 million, which is more than the continuing effects on British exports as a whole. On the critical nature of this assumption for assessing the balance of payments return see *Effects of U.K. Direct Investment Overseas: Interim Report*, Cambridge University Press, 110–111 (1967).

† A restrictive policy, which reduced additions to net operating assets overseas by £100 million, would ease the U.K.'s external financing problem to the following extent, in £ million:

	With 100% U.K. Finance	With 40% Overseas Finance
1st year	89	49
2nd year	85	45
3rd year	81	41
4th year	76	36

Source: Reddaway, *Final Report*, pages 239–242, 347.

results (between investment in different countries and by different industrial sectors) so that selective controls make good sense.

The above considerations led the Government to changes in policy with respect to overseas investment in 1965, subsequently modified in later years. Policy aims were to be achieved in three ways—through changes in fiscal policy, via Exchange Control, and, after May 1966, through the Voluntary Programme. The company and profits tax system in operation before 1965 gave a special incentive to overseas portfolio investment to the extent that the U.K. shareholder in an overseas company secured a credit for all the other countries' tax on the underlying profits, whereas a U.K. shareholder in effect received credit for the income tax paid by the company but not for its profits tax. The new Corporation Tax is broadly neutral between home and overseas investment: the shareholder gets no credit for the underlying tax on the profits out of which the dividends are paid, whether his investment is in the U.K. or abroad. Similarly, overseas direct investment was encouraged by the tax system in that the overseas tax paid on the profits of overseas subsidiaries and branches could be used to frank the income tax liability of U.K. shareholders in the U.K. parent company, whereas, as noted above, the income tax liability of U.K. shareholders in a U.K. company with domestic investments could not be franked in respect of U.K. profits tax. The shift to a corporation tax was intended to remove this bias in the tax system.*

The broad effects of the Exchange Control rules are as follows. Portfolio investments by U.K. residents may take place only in quoted securities and may be financed only with investment currency. Prior to 1965 U.K. residents were allowed to sell as investment currency— that is at a premium—certain receipts of foreign currencies such as the proceeds of wills and gifts which accrued to them from abroad. Now all such accruals must be exchanged at the official rate and not at the premium rate, so that the foreign currency comes into the reserves and is no longer available for re-investment through the currency market. Similarly before 1965 any resident who acquired foreign currency by selling foreign securities abroad was allowed to re-invest the foreign currency in other foreign securities, or sell it at a premium in the investment currency market. After the 1965 Budget any resident

---

* 'Our present tax arrangements go well beyond what is justified in existing circumstances and mean that in a number of cases the U.K. investor incurs a lower tax burden by investing abroad than by investing at home. For example. . . . We treat a British investor in the United States better for our tax purposes than we treat a British investor in our own country and better than a U.S. investor is treated by his country for tax purposes if he invests either in the U.S. or in the United Kingdom.' Budget Statement, *Hansard*, 6 April 1965, cols. 264–265.

who sold foreign securities abroad was required to exchange into sterling at the official rate the equivalent in investment currency of 25% of the proceeds of the sale. This rule also applied to the sale of direct investments outside the sterling area. This measure was expected to reduce total private portfolio holdings (the capital value of which had grown substantially in recent years), but this was not considered undesirable in itself. The rate of return on portfolio investment has in any case been less than 4·5% per annum (1964–1967), and any loss of future earnings, below what they otherwise would have been, was believed to be substantially worthwhile in terms of the consequent strengthening of the reserves.

Oil investment is subject to Treasury scrutiny and an allocation of official exchange is allowed annually for the two major companies, Shell and B.P. For the rest of direct investment the normal methods of financing projects are the ploughing back of profits by existing enterprises (supervised by the Bank of England to ensure that retained profits are reasonable), or by borrowing abroad on appropriate terms—again scrutinised. For projects promising an early return to the U.K. balance of payments access to investment currency may be allowed, although this privilege was slight with premiums in excess of 40% at certain periods. Certain exceptionally favourable projects, promising a return to the balance of payments commensurate with the initial remittance within 18 months, are allowed limited access to official exchange under the super-criterion scheme. In 1968 this priviledge was extended to direct investment in the non-sterling area for projects directed to promoting immediate export sales.

In May 1966 the Voluntary Programme was introduced in order to slow down the flow of investment from U.K. to the developed sterling area countries (Australia, New Zealand, South Africa and the Irish Republic). Companies intending to invest in these countries were requested to submit their proposals to the Bank of England and these were permitted only whenever they were expected to produce a substantial and quick return to the balance of payments. For portfolio investment the aim was to ensure that there was 'no significant increase in total holdings of such securities by any given company or institutional investor over a period of time'[*] However, this restriction was relaxed in the 1969 Budget and thereafter institutions concerned with portfolio investment (investment trusts, pension funds, etc.) were permitted, within the normal rules of Exchange Control, to acquire foreign currency securities irrespective of the level of their holdings in May 1966. This relaxation entailed no net call on the reserves since such

[*] Budget Statement, *Hansard*, 2 May 1966, col. 1446.

investment was only permitted through the investment currency market or with special permission in cases of overseas borrowing.

Current policy on overseas investment contains therefore both temporary and permanent aspects. The shift to a corporation tax comprises the permanent fiscal aspect of policy, while the direct measures under Exchange Control and the Voluntary Programme are mainly designed to ensure that the high level of direct and portfolio investment which continues to take place, is financed so as to impose the minimum burden on the reserves and sterling liabilities. These measures, at least in their present severity, have been considered as temporary, to be relaxed when the nation's liquidity position has sufficiently improved.*

It is difficult to assess the effectiveness of these measures since, clearly the alternative position is not known. Nevertheless, there are various indicators of success. As can be seen from *Table 8.7* there were substantial net liquidations of privately owned foreign securities in both 1965 and 1966, and the Chancellor (Mr. Callaghan) estimated that the 25 % investment currency scheme benefited the reserves by £75 million in the first year of operation.† More recently the National Institute has estimated the balance of payments savings of the Voluntary Programme at about £40 million a year.‡ As for direct investment abroad the Treasury has made some interesting calculations for 1965 and 1966 of the extent to which direct investment abroad affected the U.K.'s reserves and sterling liabilities.§ On the basis of these estimates, taking 1965 and 1966 together, about one-tenth of gross investment in non-sterling area countries affected the reserves. Inter-company cash transactions accounted for about a third of gross investment but were largely offset by overseas borrowing by parent companies and the use of investment currency. In the overseas sterling area inter-company cash transactions also accounted for a third of gross investment.

In recent years Euro-dollar borrowing has also provided an important source of finance for U.K. outward investment. Investment financed in this way is in accordance with the Government's policy, operated through exchange control and the Voluntary Programme, in that it avoids a call on the reserves and is in effect self-financing. In 1968, for

---

* 'Whatever rate of return overseas investment may provide in the long-run, we cannot at present afford significant initial outflows of funds from our reserves to finance it. Our policies are not, and are not intended to be, totally restrictive of overseas investment. Their object is to avoid immediate burdens on the reserves.' Chancellor of the Exchequer (Mr. Jenkins), *Hansard*, 14 April 1969, col. 997.

† Budget Statement, *Hansard*, 3 May 1966, col. 1444.

‡ *National Institute Economic Review*, No. 45, 11 (Aug. 1968).

§ 'Direct Investment Abroad—Analysis of Cash Transactions', *U.K. Balance of Payments 1968* (C.S.O.). Annex 4.

example, net private investment was −£163 million, of which re-invested profits and trade credit between affiliates (net) was +£12 million, to which has to be added Euro-dollar borrowing to finance private investment abroad (+£155 million). The result, for 1968, is a net inflow of finance (+£4 million) in respect of private investment.* In the light of the 1968 results it is not surprising therefore, that the Chancellor in his 1969 Budget should have concluded that, 'It is . . . not the case, as is sometimes suggested that in the past year, or in the two or three years preceding it, the capital account has been responsible for a large part of our difficulties.'†

DEVALUATION

On 18 November 1967 sterling was devalued to a new parity of $2·40 after a final bout of speculation on a scale never previously experienced. Ever since May sterling had been under almost constant speculative attack and by the end of the year the reserves had suffered a very substantial underlying loss. This was partly caused by the deficit in the U.K. balance of payments but there was also a large net-with-drawal of short-term funds. Private sterling holdings in the non-sterling area fell by £119 million to a gross total at the end of 1967 which was well below its normal level. Sterling holdings by sterling-area countries was also reduced by £146 million, but there was little change over the year as a whole in net switching in or out of foreign currency deposits.

As can be seen from *Table 8.8* the current balance deteriorated from a substantial surplus in the second half of 1966 to a small deficit in the first half of 1967. This development was not entirely unforeseen, for the removal of the Temporary Import Charge in November had clearly led to a postponement of imports in the final quarter of 1966, and a restocking of imports in the first half of 1967 seemed highly probable. During the second half of 1967 the balance of payments worsened very sharply as a result of adverse developments. Exports fell continuously in volume, in each quarter from their high level at the turn of the year, in part reflecting the effects of exogenous factors (the closure of the Suez canal, the Arab boycott after the Middle-East War, and the sharp slowing down in the rate of growth of world trade), but also as a result of the dock strikes in London and Liverpool in September and October. However, even when all these special factors are taken into

---

* Source: *Economic Trends*. No. 194. Tables IV, xiv (Dec. 1969).
† Budget Statement, *Hansard*, 15 April 1969, col. 995.

Table 8.8

U.K. BALANCE OF PAYMENTS 1966–1969 (WITH SEASONAL ADJUSTMENTS)
£ million

	1966	1967	1968	1969	1967 I	1967 II	1968 I	1968 II	1969 I	1969 II
Exports (f.o.b.)	5 182	5 122	6 273	7 056	2 671	2 451	3 007	3 266	3 385	3 316
Imports (f.o.b.)	5 255	5 674	6 916	7 213	2 824	2 850	3 392	3 524	3 581	3 627
Visible balance	−73	−552	−643	−157	−153	−399	−385	−258	−196	+39
Government Services and transfers (net)	−470	−464	−462	−459	−235	−229	−235	−227	−231	−228
Other invisibles (net)	+583	+694	+808	+1031	+320	+374	+401	+407	+524	+507
Invisible balance	+113	+230	+346	+572	+85	+145	+166	+180	+293	+279
CURRENT BALANCE	+40	−322	−297	+415	−68	−254	+219	−78	+97	+318
Official long-term capital (net)	−80	−57	+21	−98	−23	−34	+17	−4	−71	−27
Private investment (net)	−27	−82	−120	+81	+13	−95	−171	+51	+8	+73
BALANCE OF LONG-TERM CAPITAL	−107	−139	−99	−17	−10	−129	−154	+55	−63	+46
BALANCE OF CURRENT AND LONG-TERM TRANSACTIONS (BASIC BALANCE)	−67	−461	−396	+398	−78	−383	−373	−23	+34	+364
Basic balance adjusted for Euro-$ borrowing	−55	−393	−220	+468						

Source: Economic Trends (C.S.O.), No. 200, June 1970.

consideration they only account for perhaps half of the identified deficit in 1967.* and an examination of data on export share suggests that there must have been a further underlying deterioration in the competitiveness of exports.

Apart from the weakening of exports, and the increased cost of imports associated with the closure of the Suez canal, the strength of domestic demand for imports contributed largely to the adverse balance of payments position. As noted above the level was inflated in the first half of the year as a response to the abolition of the T.I.C., but the outcome was more than simply this. In the second half of 1967 the volume of imports, goods and services, was 5·75 % higher than in the same period of the previous year while output was less than 1 % up over the same period. All the evidence points to a rise in the import propensity during the year.

In other words the proximate cause of the balance of payments crisis during the second half of 1967 were the special factors noted above. However, even when allowance is made for these special factors there is no sign of any improvement in either export or import propensities —indeed the evidence of 1967 points the other way. It follows, therefore, that even without the special factors, some set of measures, perhaps including devaluation, would have been necessary. Little respite could be hoped for in 1968, and it is evident, both from official statements and from Institute forecasts, that the outlook for 1968 was for a further, if reduced, external deficit.†

The failure to achieve a surplus on the balance of payments in 1967 represented for the Government a defeat for its economic strategy. Since 1964 it had gradually relinquished in the short-run a number of its longer-term aims. Restrictions had been placed both on current and capital transactions (in conflict with its liberalisation of trade objective): deflation had been tried in July 1966, and found wanting; and finally, the central pin of this strategy, the maintenance of a fixed exchange rate, had also been relinquished. Since 1964 external developments had led to large overseas debts, with due repayment dates in the late 1960s and early 1970s, which required, if they were to be met, substantial and sustained surpluses. By the end of 1967 it was evident that such surpluses could not be achieved with the existing parity. It had always been doubtful whether the strategy followed since 1964 would be successful, and its chances of success had always been founded on the

---

* *Economic Report on 1967*, H.M. Treasury, 8, H.M.S.O. (1968).

† 'The prospect, quite apart from the effects of devaluation, would have been for a considerable reduction from last year's rate of deficit, though the position would still have been unsatisfactory'. *Financial Statement 1968–1969*, para. 13, H.M.S.O. 19 March 1968).

ability of the Government, through incomes policy and in other ways, being able to bring about an increase in the competitiveness of exports and a reduction in the propensity to import. Developments in 1967 indicated the failure of these hopes, and, therefore, 'the inevitability of devaluation'.*

Mr. Callaghan, the Chancellor of the Exchequer at the time of devaluation, held later that devaluation had been planned for some time and that the authorities had not been pushed into a forced devaluation. If this was so then it is very odd that they should have waited so long—a delay so costly to the reserves—and Mr. Callaghan perhaps simply implied that contingency plans had already been prepared.† The Treasury is too fine a department not to have done this, and devaluation too complex a problem not to have invited detailed analysis. It is a relatively simple matter to superimpose on an existing short-term forecast the effects of a change in the exchange rate on the basis of different assumptions about the size of the devaluation, the consequent improvement in the balance of payments, and therefore, the real resource transfers which are necessary to permit the payments improvement to occur. The model is a relatively simple one—the assumptions on which it is based, e.g., about the size of the relevant demand elasticities and the timing of the effects of the devaluation on demand, are necessarily more heroic. No matter how good the preparatory work, the devaluation meant moving into entirely new territory, and inevitably this led to serious policy errors.‡

The first steps in the devaluation strategy were set out in a Letter of Intent sent by the Chancellor to the I.M.F. on the 23rd of November 1967.§ This provided a statement of the Government's balance of payments target—'an improvement of at least £500 million a year . . .

---

* Chancellor of the Exchequer (Mr. Jenkins), *Hansard*, 19 March 1968, col. 255. The Bank of England seems to have been in complete agreement on this point: 'In the end it [devaluation] became unavoidable because a real disequilibrium was demonstrably there . . .' Speech by the Governor of the Bank delivered to the Overseas Bankers Club, February 1968, reported in the *Quarterly Bank Bulletin*, **8**, No. 2, June 1968, p. 171.

† The Treasury estimated the loss due to the Exchange Equalisation Account's forward commitments entered into before devaluation at £105 million in 1967 and £251 million in 1968. These are very substantial losses and hardly support any claim for a planned devaluation. Source: *Economic Trends*, No. 194, Table 9 (Dec. 1969).

‡ For an example of this technique see the post devaluation forecasts of the National Institute in the *Reviews* for November 1967 and February 1968. Their forecasts of 1968 actually got worse between November and February and in neither case were they very successful. In November they forecast an identified deficit of £225 million and in February an identified surplus of £40 million, compared with an out-turn of an identified deficit of about £400 million.

§ See *House of Commons Debates*, **755** cols., 648–652.

Table 8.9

ECONOMIC POLICY AFTER DEVALUATION

MAJOR POLICY INITIATIVES: NOVEMBER 1967 – APRIL 1969

Date	Content of Measures
(1) 18 November 1967	In association with devaluation: Bank rate increased from 6·5% to 8%; corporation tax to be raised from 40% to 42·5% in the 1968 budget; the rebate of selective employment tax to manufacturers cancelled; export rebate cancelled. Hire-purchase terms for cars tightened and selective restrictions placed on bank lending. Reduction of £100 million to be made to the civil public expenditure programme for 1968–1969, and £100 million reductions in defence expenditure already planned to be brought forward.
(2) 18 December 1967– 16 January 1968	Premier announced wide-ranging review of Government spending on 18 December 1967; results, announced on 16 January 1968, provide for cuts of £325 million in 1968–1969 and £441 million in 1969–1970 over and above cuts to programmes made on 18 November 1967 (see above). Decisions include postponement of raising school-leaving age, cancellation of order for U.S. F-111 aircraft and accelerated withdrawal of forces East of Suez.
(3) 19 March 1968	Budget. Tax rate increases to raise £923 million in a full year; they include increases in corporation tax (see 1 above), a special charge on investment income, adjustments of income tax allowances and exemptions, and increases in motor vehicle duties, selective employment tax, purchase tax, and customs and excise duties. Estimated to reduce consumption spending by about 2%.
(4) 19 March 1968	Prices and incomes policy. New phase of policy announced in Budget speech; White Paper published 3 April. Nil norm, with 3·5% maximum for agreements satisfying criteria involving recognition that existing pay is 'too low to maintain a reasonable standard of living'. or is 'seriously out of line' with pay for similar work, or where a redistribution of manpower is necessary. Exceptionally, agreements involving a productivity bargain may exceed 3·5%. The maximum refers to an annual rate of increase since previous successful claim; the minimum period between settlements to be 12 months.

Date	Content of Measures
(5) 23 May 1968	Bank lending restrictions tightened. Banks are asked to contain total lending within a ceiling equal to 104% of the November 1967 level. The instruction roughly implies a limit at current levels to total private sector lending, and consequent cuts in non-priority loans to permit growth in priority categories.
(6) Spring– 9 September 1968	*Basle Agreement.* After consultations beginning in the spring, and a preliminary announcement in July, a White Paper was published covering the arrangements under which reduction in sterling area holdings of sterling could be funded for a ten-year debt to the participating countries. The scheme would be administered by the Bank for International Settlements.
(7) 1 November 1968	Hire-purchase terms tightened. Cars: minimum deposit raised from 33·33% to 40%, maximum repayment period reduced from 27 to 24 months; furniture and mattresses: minimum deposit raised from 15% to 20%, maximum repayment period reduced from 30 to 24 months. For all goods with 25% minimum deposit, and a 30 or 36 month repayment period, the tightening called for 33·33% deposit and 24 month repayment period; this covered *inter alia* radio and television, vacuum cleaners, refrigerators, and washing machines.
(8) 22 November 1968	'Regulator' power employed to raise indirect tax rates by 10%. Import deposit scheme announced: importers required to deposit 50% of value of goods for six months with H.M. Customs and Excise. Control of Bank lending tightened: a 2% reduction in non-exempt lending looked for by March. Estimated, with the measures summarised in (7), to reduce consumer spending by around 1% in the first half of 1969.
(9) 14 April 1969.	*Budget.* Tax rate increases to raise £272 million in 1969/1970; they include increases in corporation tax from 42·5% to 45%, adjustment of income tax allowances and exemptions, and increases in selective employment tax, purchase tax and Customs and Excise duties. Estimated to reduce consumption spending by 0·33% in 1969.

Source: *National Institute Economic Review*, No. 47, Table 1, p.5 (Feb. 1969); and No. 48 (May 1969).

[which] . . . on present prospects for world trade . . . should mean a surplus in the second half of 1968 at an annual rate of at least £200 million'. It noted, however, that 'calculations of the effect of a change in the parity of a currency, and still more of the timing of such effects, are necessarily extremely speculative', but the Government was prepared to take measures 'as and when required to free resources from domestic use on the scale necessary to secure the improvement referred to'. A number of measures had already been taken on 18 November (Table 8·9) The Letter then stated that 'the next review of the position and prospects of the U.K. economy and balance of payments will, in the normal course of business, be carried out in February 1968. At this time it should be possible to assess more accurately than can be done at present the effects of the decisions announced on 18 November 1967'.

The notion that further policy action could wait was soon dispelled. On 18 December the Prime Minister announced a wide ranging review of public expenditure to be undertaken immediately in order to cut future spending programmes (additional to those announced on 18 November). This review led to cuts in expenditure plans, including the £200 million announced on 18 November, of £500 million for 1968/1969 and with larger reductions in planned expenditures in later years. It seems likely that this review related to a reconsideration of the resource costs of existing programmes and not to any completely new factors entering the calculation. In any case it must have been perfectly clear, to the Government, as well as to others, that the deflationary package introduced at the time of devaluation was completely inadequate.* The cuts in public expenditure of £200 million were cuts from a steeply-rising trend, and given the large shortfalls of actual expenditures in existing programmes, would in part simply reduce shortfalls rather than actual expenditure. Most importantly, the reduction in demand flowing from the tax increases did not amount to very much, while the tightening of hire-purchase controls was confined to cars, and the restraint on bank lending involved no reduction in lending to the personal sector (in fact it permitted a substantial rise).

What was surprising about the package was its mildness. In order to produce a surplus on the balance of payments of £500 million in 1969 the resource transfer into the balance of payments (equal to the rise in the volume of exports less the rise in the volume of imports) had to be

---

* This was the view of the O.E.C.D. in its December 1967 issue of *Economic Outlook*, who forecast that the primary and secondary increases in demand flowing from the devaluation would raise output by 1·5 % in 1968, and this, on top of the demand pressures already present in the economy, would frustrate the transfer of resources into the balance of payments.

of the order of £1000 million.* For this transfer to resources to take place unemployment could not be permitted to fall significantly below 2% before the end of 1969, and this outcome would have occurred as a result of the initial and secondary effects on demand of the devaluation unless the measures taken to reduce absorption were on a sufficient scale. Devaluation provided the most favourable opportunity, in terms of national acceptability and in other ways, for a realistic package of measures. It is strange, in retrospect, that hire-purchase restrictions which have a substantial and immediate impact on demand, were not fully utilised, and that no changes in personal taxation were announced. Increases in the latter, effective from April 1968, could have been announced, as was earlier done in 1964, which would have permitted the tax changes to have become effective at an earlier point in the year.

It must have been immediately clear to the authorities that the scale of their action was inadequate, and the Treasury in its Economic Assessment for December noted 'that there can be little if any scope for an increase in personal consumption next year, given the need to shift resources into the balance of payments.'† Undoubtedly the failure of the Government to take sufficiently strong action in November, plus threats of a harsh Budget together with widespread expectations of rising prices, contributed to the personal consumption boom of the first quarter of 1968 and thus to a larger deterioration in the balance of payments than had been anticipated. The result of these developments was a very harsh Budget which reduced demand by an amount sufficient, on the face of it, to permit the transfer of resources into the balance of payments to take place.

The main criticism of post devaluation economic policy which can be made is with respect to the timing of the measures. In the *Economic Report for 1967*, released in mid-March, the Government stated that they 'recognised that further measures to release resources would be needed. But given the high level of unemployment, and the necessary uncertainty about the timing and magnitude of the response of exports and imports to devaluation, it did not wish to engineer this release before the additional demand for exports (and import substitutes) in-

* 'We need to put about a £1000 million in the balance of payments to get the turn around that we need.' Chancellor of the Exchequer (Mr. Jenkins). *House of Commons Debates*, **743**, col. 1788.

† *Economic Trends, ii* (Dec. 1967). This was released to the Press on 14 December and was probably drafted in late November or early December. Between the time of devaluation and the preparation of the assessment little could have happened to change the Treasury's view of the best post-devaluation strategy. There is a certain amount of evidence which suggests that neither the Treasury nor the Bank were satisfied with the November measures. On the Bank's views see *Quarterly Bank Bulletin*, **8**, No. 2, 174 (June 1968).

duced by devaluation had started to come through. It proposed there-fore to act during the course of the coming months, first on public consumption (since cutbacks in this field necessarily take time to become effective) and later on private consumption.'* The argument for delay is sophisticated but not very convincing.† Even the bringing of the Budget forward from its normal date in April to March had not prevented an anticipatory boom in consumer spending which had gathered momentum and thus led to a higher level of imports plus loss of confidence, both at home and abroad, in the ability of the Government to make devaluation work. An earlier Budget would have been better, and even more preferable would have been a more effective package at the time of devaluation. The advantages of waiting until the normal Budget were minimal, and the costs, as we can now with hindsight appreciate, were very considerable.

By the middle of the second half of the year it was clear that the devaluation strategy was not proceeding as expected. The balance of payments was improving, but very slowly, mainly because of the very high level of imports. Personal consumption had begun to rise again. The transfer of resources into the balance of payments (and into invest-ment) had clearly been delayed. These developments led the author-ities in November to take further deflationary action (*Table 8.9*) and to the introduction of the Import Deposit Scheme. The aim of the latter was clearly to strengthen the switch of resources initiated by the devaluation, but also to buy time for the full effects of the devaluation to come through.

By the end of 1968 most of the essential elements in the post-devalua-tion strategy had fallen into place. Deflationary measures had been introduced on a scale sufficient to allow the transfer of resources to take place and thus to permit the target external surplus to be achieved —but later than originally anticipated. Furthermore, action had been taken via the incomes and prices policy to preserve the competitive advantage produced by the devaluation. Unfortunately, the policies were not in themselves sufficient to achieve all their objectives for reasons which we turn to in the next section. However, by the end of 1968 it did make sense, in a way it had not done hitherto, to talk in

* *Economic Report on 1967*, H.M. Treasury 7, H.M.S.O. (1968).

† The National Institute rather cynically commented that the Government's explanation for postponing further deflation 'incorporate(s) a claim to a great deal of knowledge about the time pattern of response to economic change which it is doubtful anyone possesses'. and 'it would only require the time-lay of fiscal effects to be about one quarter longer than assumed (or for the response to devaluation to come in so much earlier), for the whole Government case for postponing the budget to become instead a credible case for deflation in December 1967'. *Review*, No. 47, p. 7 and note 2. (Feb. 1969).

terms of an economic strategy and one which had a good chance of success.

BALANCE OF PAYMENTS DEVELOPMENTS POST DEVALUATION

At the time of devaluation the Chancellor forecast a balance of payments surplus at an annual rate of £200 million in the second half of 1968. By the time of the March 1968 Budget the Treasury had become less explicit but still 'expected [the identified balance] to move from deficit into surplus during 1968 and a substantial surplus is forecast for the first half of 1969'.* This was to be achieved primarily through a big turn around in the balance of visible trade with the volume of exports rising sharply (in response to devaluation and growth in world trade) but with little change in the volume of imports.

The outcome in 1969 was quite different. As can be seen in *Table 8.8* the balance on identified current and long-term transactions showed a deficit for 1968 of £396 million—hardly any improvement on the 1967 record. If payments for American aircraft are excluded there was only a bare balance in the second half of the year, even though the authorities took a 'bisque' on the North American loan at the end of the year (a saving of some £40 million). But for the effects of the dock strikes in 1967, which pushed export deliveries into 1968, the deficit would have been substantially larger—perhaps by 50%. Furthermore the movements in long-term capital were exceptionally favourable in 1968, especially in the second half of the year when there was actually a surplus on official transactions. Finally, the growth in world trade was particularly fast, much faster than had originally been anticipated. Only on invisible account was there any clear net-gain as a result of devaluation, particularly on travel expenditure, but even here the outcome was not entirely favourable. Devaluation was expected to produce a virtually automatic increase in sterling terms in income from abroad, particularly interest profits and dividends, but there was actually a slight fall in net receipts of interest, profits and dividends partly due to a rise in the cost of servicing short-term debts, and in part a delayed response on the part of oil earnings to the Middle East crisis of 1967.

The outcome on visible trade was especially unfavourable. There was a substantial worsening on visible trade in spite of the devaluation and even taking advantage of the dock strike effects. The terms of trade worsened by some 3% as was to be expected as a consequence of

* *Financial Statement 1968–1969*, H.M.S.O., 37 (19 March 1968).

devaluation. A deterioration of this order was generally anticipated, although the Treasury clearly expected export prices in sterling terms to rise somewhat faster than they did, and thus for the terms of trade-effects to be weaker.* However, it had been expected that the adverse terms of trade effects would be more than balanced by a higher rate of growth in the volume of exports (assumed price elasticity of demand of −2) and a lower rate of growth in the volume of imports (price elasticity estimated at −0·5). In fact the volume of imports rose by more in relation to output, than would have been expected on the basis of past relationships even if devaluation had never taken place. Precisely what factors caused this exceptional rise in import volume is unclear, in part it reflected special factors, but even when allowance is made for these, there is still an apparent rise in the propensity to import.† One explanation is that U.K. competitiveness must have been deteriorating very sharply during 1967 and the early part of 1968, so that the price advantage given to domestic production by the devaluation was smaller than originally estimated.

Exports rose sharply in 1968 in both value and volume, even after taking account of the dock strike effects. Nevertheless, part of the explanation of the fast growth in exports lies in the exceptionally rapid increase in world trade. Even without devaluation, British exports would perhaps have increased by some 6·5 % in 1968. The actual rise in volume was about 9 %, which leaves a volume response for devaluation of only 2·5 % (and this includes dock strike effects). An analysis in this form led the National Institute to conclude 'that in the first twelve months the contribution of devaluation to the expansion of the volume of British exports must have been slight. Furthermore, since the rise in sterling prices has, so far been quite restrained, the performance in value terms is even less encouraging.'‡ The Chancellor put it more

* In the *Financial Statement 1968–1969* the Treasury avoided any forecast of export prices but the devaluation was expected to lead directly and indirectly to increases in costs which would raise sterling prices by 6% (para. 9). This yielded a competitive price advantage of almost 9% over those countries which had not devalued, but it was assumed that part of this would be used to increase profit margins and promotional expenditure (perhaps 2%). In addition there would be the normal upward drift in export prices of about 2% making a total sterling price rise of about 10%. Unit values of exports actually rose by about 7·5%. In assessing the volume response to these price changes it was obviously sensible to assume that higher profit margins would give some stimulus to exports, and to apply a performance elasticity to the net price advantage plus a proportion of the price rise caused by the increase in profit margins.

† This seems also to have been the official view as given in the *Financial Statement and Budget Report 1969–1970*, para. 14 (15 April, 1969).

‡ The explanation of the Institute was that the underlying competitive position must have been weaker than supposed and deteriorating sharply before devaluation. *Review*, No. 47, 13 (Feb. 1969).

graphically in his 1969 Budget speech. 'We were floated up more by the buoyancy of world trade than by our own efforts.'*

The balance of payments out-turn for 1968 could scarcely be called favourable. Neither exports nor imports had responded to devaluation as anticipated, and while devaluation had moved some of the speculative pressures on sterling it had certainly not eliminated them (see next section). In spite of the tough November 1968 measures, and the introduction of the Import Deposit Scheme, the balance of payments remained a serious problem in the first half of 1969. Even as late as June 1969 the external position was such that the Government was obliged to make a further drawing on the I.M.F. and to accept much more rigorous conditions with respect to its policy. One objective specified in the May Letter of Intent to the I.M.F. was a balance of payments target for the financial year 1969/1970 of £300 million on current and long-term transactions. As can be seen from *Table 8.8* this target was easily achieved (a basic surplus of £600 million), although at the time of the I.M.F. negotiations (early 1969) this seemed much more problematical.

In the first half of 1969 the balance of payments moved very strongly into surplus on current account, with a large improvement on visible trade and an even bigger surplus on invisibles. The result was an identified surplus in the first half of the year (excluding U.S. aircraft purchases) of £160 million at an annual rate. Exports rose rapidly as a result of fast growth in world trade, while imports increased at a much slower rate than during 1967. However, the high level of imports continued to cause concern, and even after adjusting the figures of imports for the effects of the Import Deposit Scheme and the presumed effects of devaluation, the level of imports still remained higher in relation to output than would have been expected on the basis of previous relationships. By the second half of 1969 the identified surplus had reached a substantial rate. In part this reflected changes in the presentation of the accounts (the adjustment for the under-recording of exports), but, there was, none the less, a substantial surplus on identified transactions for 1969.†

By the end of 1969 the target rate of a surplus of £500 million

---

* Budget Statement, *Hansard*, 15 April 1969, col. 998.

† The final row of *Table 8.9* adjusts the basic balance to take account of Euro-dollar borrowing to finance overseas investment. Borrowing for this purpose rose very rapidly in 1968 and 1969. In the standard form of the balance of payments the investment is recorded as a debit, while the Euro-dollar borrowing is recorded as a monetary inflow. When account is taken of Euro-dollar borrowing the basic balance improved substantially between 1968 and 1967, and was in surplus at an annual rate of £100 million in the second half of 1968.

(annual rate) had been achieved. However, this was the result not only of devaluation but of other factors as well. Firstly, the external position had benefited from the exceptionally fast rate of growth in world trade in the two years following devaluation. This had, in a sense, been a bonus. Secondly, a substantial part of the 1969 surplus was due to continuing restrictions on trade and payments. The Import Deposit Scheme perhaps reduced imports in 1969 by some £100 million, restrictions on travel expenditure may have saved another £40 million, while the Voluntary Programme perhaps reduced the capital outflow to the sterling area by another £40 million: a total saving of £180 million. Thirdly, the level of imports in 1969 reflected not only devaluation effects but also the behaviour of domestic demand. As a result of the November 1968 measures, plus another tough Budget in April 1969, together with a tightening of an already tough monetary policy, the growth in real output between the fourth quarter of 1969 and the fourth quarter of 1968 was reduced to only 1·5%. Real personal consumption increased by only 1% during the same period, while the trend in unemployment continued upwards.

The improvement in the balance of payments in 1969 had, therefore, been bought at the cost of very slow growth in output, at a rate well below productive capacity, plus continued restrictions on trade and payments. While the Government considered the position strong enough to remove the travel restrictions in October, it nevertheless thought it prudent to continue in a modified form the Import Deposit Scheme for a further year. A substantial rate of surplus had, however, been achieved and this became even larger in 1970. However, the constraint of the balance of payments has not been removed—it has only been reduced.* The unemployment situation remains unfavourable, and simply to prevent this from rising to very high levels there will have to be some reflation. While moderate reflation will reduce the size of the 1970 surplus it will still remain very substantial.

THE STERLING BALANCES

Sterling balances were originally held as working balances or as reserves of international currency by countries with close commercial or financial links with Britain. During the war they grew very rapidly

---

* The current account surplus in 1970 was £631 million, almost half as great again as the very substantial 1969 surplus.

as a result of the techniques used to finance military expenditure abroad, and in the process generated both increased domestic and international liquidity. At the outbreak of war net external liabilities in sterling were £517 million which was slightly more than covered by the gold and currency reserves (£545 million). By 1954 net external liabilities in sterling had increased to £3688 million while reserves had hardly risen at all, so that quick sterling liabilities exceeded reserves in the ratio of more than 5:1.* Since that time the level of net sterling liabilities has not varied very greatly until recent years, although there are years of very marked short-run fluctuations in their level. For most of the fifties and the sixties the U.K. balance of payments did not produce surpluses on a scale sufficient to permit any significant build up of reserves so that the ratio of liabilities to reserves continued unfavourable (during the fifties at 4:1 and between 1962 and 1969 at almost 5:1).†

Up to the mid-sixties the sterling area accounted for some 75%–80% of total net liabilities (*Table 8.10*), although by the end of the sixties their share had been substantially reduced. By 1968 the sterling area accounted for less than 60% of total sterling balances as a result of a sharp increase in official holdings of non-sterling area countries in 1967 and 1968, although they subsequently recovered to 70% by the end of 1969 as a result of the Basle Agreement. A further significant change during the sixties has been a marked shift in the proportions of the balances held officially and privately. This is important in so far as official holders can generally be assumed to be firmer holders of sterling and less likely to be affected by arbitrage or confidence factors. Recent experience has shown that this assumption may not always be realistic. Between 1962 and 1969 the proportion of total net liabilities (excluding international organisations) held officially by sterling area and non-sterling area countries rose from 69% to 106%, so that by the end of the sixties claims exceeded liabilities in respect of private holdings. Along with this shift in the proportion of official as against private balances has gone a radical change in the distribution of official balances between the sterling area and non-sterling area. While the private holdings of sterling balances in the sterling area countries showed almost no change between 1962-1968, those

---

* *Quarterly Bank Bulletin,* **8,** No. 4, Table 13, 389 (Dec. 1968).
† The ratios are not entirely comparable in that a new series of sterling claims and liabilities commenced in 1962. In that year the difference between the old overseas sterling holding series and the present series was some £170 million (total net liabilities excluding international organisations). On the differences in the two series see 'New Series of External Liabilities and Claims in Sterling'. *Quarterly Bank Bulletin,* **3** (June 1963).

Table 8.10

U.K. EXTERNAL NET LIABILITIES IN STERLING BY AREA AND TYPE OF HOLDER END OF PERIOD*

£ million

	Sterling Area Countries			Non-sterling Countries			All Countries		
	Total	Central Monetary Institutions	Other	Total	Central Monetary Institutions	Other	Total	Central Monetary Institutions	Other
1959	2 691			682			3 373		
1960	2 463			1 312			3 775		
1961	2 616			768			3 384		
1962	2 653			682			3 335		
1962	2 430	1 761	679	733	433	300	3 163	2 184	979
1963	2 592	1 888	704	670	409	261	3 262	2 297	965
1964	2 591	1 931	660	714	501	213	3 305	2 432	873
1965	2 594	1 880	714	781	605	176	3 375	2 485	890
1966	2 599	1 834	765	895	914	−19	3 494	2 748	746
1967	2 453	1 707	746	1 353	1 491	−138	3 806	3 198	608
1968	2 311	1 627	684	1 649	2 153	−504	3 960	3 780	118
1969	2 444	1 964	480	1 062	1 758	−696	3 506	3 722	−216

Sources: *U.K. Balance of Payments 1968* (C.S.O.), Table 28; *Economic Trends* (C.S.O.), p. XXVIII (Dec. 1969).

Minus sign indicates that claims exceed liabilities.

* 1969 third quarter.

of the non-sterling area have been continuously declining since 1962.*

Within the sterling area there have been significant changes in the distribution of balances between different countries, not only during the fifties when India and Egypt ran down their large balances, but also more recently. Middle East holdings were substantially increased during the fifties, largely as a result of oil earnings, although since 1967 their holdings have been deliberately run down as a means of bringing political pressure on the British Government. By the end of the sixties the biggest single holdings were those of the Far Eastern countries who accounted for almost 30% of O.S.A. balances.† As can be seen from (*Table 8.11*) the development sterling area countries as a matter of policy ran down their sterling balances between 1967 and 1968. In the non-sterling area the biggest single holder is now the United States and with Canada they accounted for 27% of total sterling liabilities at the end of 1969.

For the whole of the post-war period, therefore, Britain has been faced with the continuous problem of managing the sterling balances, in a situation where the gold and foreign exchange reserves were clearly inadequate relative to quick liabilities. The relationship between the sterling balances and the reserves is, however, highly complex. The normal situation, as described by Radcliffe, is one where the overseas sterling area is in overall balance: in deficit with the U.K., but in surplus with the rest of the world. In this case the U.K. receives the gold and foreign exchange earned by the O.S.A. surplus and sets it against sterling due to it. There is no change in sterling liabilities and the U.K. can use the gold and foreign exchange to finance its own deficits with third countries. Alternatively, deficits in the overall balance of payments of O.S.A. (unless it is concentrated on the U.K.) will lead them to run down their sterling balances and so put pressure on the reserves. Fluctuations, therefore, in the official sterling area balance will, in general, be due to changes in their overall balance of payments position. Examples of this are 1949, 1957 and 1965, all years when

---

* By the end of the third quarter of 1969 the U.K. liabilities to private holders in non-sterling area countries were substantially exceeded by corresponding claims of the U.K. (£488 million of liabilities against £1184 million of U.K. claims). The claims are largely in the form of commercial credit and the liabilities in the form of deposits with the U.K. banks.

† The sterling holdings of O.S.A. countries fell by £112 million in the second quarter of 1967 as Middle Eastern countries either sold sterling or transferred it from London banks to banks in non-sterling countries. At other times the sterling balances have been used as political weapons, for example, by Malaysia during the Indonesian confrontation, and by Zambia (on the Rhodesian issue).

Table 8.11

U.K. STERLING NET LIABILITIES
BY GROUPS OF COUNTRIES
END OF PERIOD
£ million and %

		Overseas Sterling Countries						
	Total	Australia, New Zealand and South Africa	India, Pakistan and Ceylon	Caribbean Area	East, Central & West Africa	Middle East	Far East	Other
1962	2 338	421	131	127	323	418	616	302
	(100)	(18)	(6)	(5)	(14)	(18)	(26)	(13)
1965	2 594	408	145	169	278	528	693	373
	(100)	(16)	(6)	(7)	(11)	(20)	(27)	(14)
1968	2 305	303	145	233	200	379	656	389
	(100)	(13)	(6)	(10)	(9)	(16)	(28)	(17)

		Non-Sterling Countries			
	Total	North America	EFTA	EEC	Other
1962	733	82	186	171	294
	(100)	(11)	(25)	(23)	(41)
1965	781	330	290	197	−36
	(100)	(42)	(37)	(25)	(−4)
1968	1 649	1 200	731	148	−430
	(100)	(73)	(44)	(9)	(−26)

Source: Bank of England Quarterly Bulletin, statistical annex, various issues.
Minus sign indicates that claims exceed liabilities.

O.S.A. deficits led to reductions in sterling balances and thus to reserve losses.

Apart from balance of payments deficits in the O.S.A. other factors have led to large short-term fluctuations in the sterling balances. Most important of these have been confidence effects, which have often led to speculative withdrawals of privately held sterling balances outside the sterling area. For example, during the sterling crisis of the fourth quarter of 1964 private balances fell by £55 million: they fell by £141 million in the third quarter of 1966, and were reduced continuously from the third quarter of 1967. Private sterling balances, particularly those held outside the sterling area, have been very volatile and caused substantial reserve losses during periods when pressure on the reserves was already considerable as a result of deficits in the U.K balance of payments.

On the other hand official holdings in the non-sterling area countries have generally been firm. This was also generally true of official holdings in the sterling area, that is until recent years. O.S.A. official balances were reduced by £127 million in 1967, and by a further £224 million in the first three quarters of 1968, with most of the fall occurring in the second quarter of the year (£284 million). These reductions cannot be attributed to balance of payments deficits in O.S.A. countries but represent a deliberate policy of diversification of reserves.

In recent years the balance of payments of the O.S.A. as a whole has shown a surplus on current and long-term capital transactions, except for a deficit of £252 million in 1965. The balance of payments moved into surplus in 1966 and 1967, with surpluses of £74 million and £122 million, and into very large surplus in 1968 (£512 million). Between 1963 and 1968 the current account was in persistent deficit but this was more than offset by inflows of long-term capital, mainly private investment. Usually, in recent years, the O.S.A. has been in deficit with the sterling area countries (i.e. essentially with the U.K.), but in surplus with the non-sterling area. However, the overall balance of payments surpluses of the O.S.A. have been mainly used to raise the gold and foreign exchange reserves of O.S.A. countries, and these rose by £372 million in 1966, by £278 million in 1967 and by £751 million in 1968. In other words over the whole period 1962-1968, O.S.A. countries ran down official sterling balances by £130 million, and increased their holdings of gold and foreign currencies by £1580 million.

Diversification of resources on this scale was hardly in accordance with the 'rules' of the sterling area, and the reduction of official balances clearly exaggerated the already severe reserve losses of 1967/1968. To reduce their balances before devaluation was merely rational behaviour, to do so after devaluation was wholly irrational, if understandable.* However, reduction of the sterling balances of the scale of 1967 and

* In contrast with 1949, when almost all the currencies of the sterling area followed sterling in devaluing against the U.S. dollar, in 1967 the great majority of the sterling area countries made no change of parity. Devaluation entailed for them a loss of dollar purchasing power, plus for most of them, a loss in terms of their own currencies also. As a result of devaluation there was a marked increase in the diversification of reserves on the part of sterling area countries, particularly in the second quarter of 1968. On the other hand the additional interest earned on official sterling balances placed in London, in the 10 years prior to devaluation, over and above the interest earned on comparable liquid assets in other countries, more than compensated for the devaluation of 14·3%.

1968 could clearly not be borne by the reserves and the British authorities were thus forced to seek a means of preventing any further reserve losses.

The result was the Basle Agreement of September 1968. This was not the first attempt to help the U.K offset the effects on her reserves of fluctuations in the sterling balances. In June 1966 central banks made available funds which were intended to relieve the stresses on the U.K.'s reserves which arose from her position as an international currency. It was specified at the time that the facility must not be used to finance deficits in the U.K.'s balance of payments. Swap arrangements were made available to the Bank of England which could only be drawn when the sterling balances fell below a particular level. The facility was not large, and was not intended to produce any permanent reduction in the sterling balances, but only to offset fluctuations. The facility was renewed in 1967 and 1968.[*]

Under the new arrangements concluded in September 1968 the U.K. is permitted to draw U.S. dollars or other foreign currencies from the Bank for International Settlements as and to the extent that the sterling balances of the overseas sterling area fall below a given starting level. It can be used to meet both official and private balances, but unlike the June 1966 facility does not cover N.S.A. balances. Once again it is not available to finance U.K. deficits. It has a 10 year life: drawings can only be made in the first three years, which must be repaid between the sixth and tenth years, and the total facility is for $2000 million.

As part of the arrangements the U.K. Government entered into agreements with individual O.S.A. countries. The U.K. guaranteed to maintain the dollar value of eligible official sterling reserves of sterling area countries provided they maintained not less than an agreed proportion of their total reserves in sterling, during the period of the agreements. The guarantee applies to that part of each country's official sterling reserves which exceeds 10% of its total reserves. Thus, taking account of their existing gold and non-sterling currency reserves, plus guaranteed sterling, 90% of each country's reserves is protected against any further loss as a result of a devaluation of the pound against the dollar.[†]

In the first year after completion of the agreements official balances rose by £475 million giving some indication of the success of the

[*] See: *Quarterly Bank Bulletin*, **VI**, No. 3, 29 (Sept. 1966).

[†] The texts of the agreements are set out in the Command Papers 3834, and 3835, while Cmnd. 3787 provides a general introduction to the agreements. Initially the agreements are for three years with the possibility of renewal for a further two years (with a number of exceptions).

scheme in reversing the movement towards reserve diversification. From the viewpoint of the sterling area countries the scheme is highly desirable, They continue to earn high interest on balances held in London, with no exchange risk at all in relation to the guaranteed portion of their holdings. At the same time they have maintained their privileged access to the London capital market, and have built into the agreements the obligation that the U.K. consult with the developed sterling area countries before any extension of the Voluntary Programme is introduced.

Even before the end of the sixties the fabric of the sterling area had worn decidedly thin, and a good deal of the rationale for its existence no longer very convincing. Initially, the sterling area was supposed to convey two distinct varieties of advantage upon its members. In the first place the pooling of reserves permitted 'a great economy of gold and other international currency'.* This only held true as long as the pattern of surpluses/deficits of the O.S.A. and the U.K. were complementary, but there is some evidence that this complementarity has been reduced during the sixties.† As long as it lasted, however, the saving of reserves did permit a higher level of capital formation within O.S.A. This weakening of the complementarity of O.S.A. and U.K. net payments is mainly due to a reduction in the importance of trade between the two areas so that both O.S.A. and U.K. external balances are more powerfully affected by general world demand developments. Furthermore, in certain areas of production O.S.A. countries and U.K. are now direct competitors, reflecting the increasing industrialisation of the O.S.A., and this development has reduced both the complementarity of payments and also adversely affected the coincidence of economic interests.

The second main advantage held out for the sterling area related to its effect on the volume of multilateral trade. Since gold and foreign exchange were only necessary to meet deficits of the area as a whole with the rest of the world, then, provided the sterling area remained in balance with the rest of the world, restrictions on payments within the area could be reduced to a minimum. This encouraged the growth of multilateral trade which can be considered highly beneficial. However, persistent deficit countries within the sterling area create problems for other sterling countries in so far as they resort to retrictions on trade

* Radcliffe: Report, para. 649.

† For example, Britain drew 40% of its imports from the O.S.A. in 1950 but only 28% in 1968. As a market for British exports O.S.A. has similarly declined in importance; in 1950 the O.S.A. purchased 51% of U.K. exports, but this had fallen to less than a third by 1968. Implicit in the decisions not to devalue along with the U.K. in 1967 was a recognition of the weakening of trading links since 1949.

and payments to alleviate their payments problems. During the fifties and sixties many sterling area countries have introduced restrictions, sometimes temporary, which have weakened the multilateral argument.* More significantly, perhaps the gains through multilateralism are now substantially less on account of the much greater freedom of world trade and payments in the sixties.

The conclusion one draws from the above is that the sterling area while it once yielded significant gains to its members, including the U.K., perhaps no longer yields much benefit. From the viewpoint of the U.K it may indeed entail net disadvantages. In recent years the behaviour of official holders of sterling balances in the sterling area has undoubtedly intensified the pressure on the U.K. reserves and so made the task of economic management more difficult. The existence of the balances has also enabled certain countries to 'blackmail' the U.K. into following policies which might otherwise not have been acceptable. Furthermore, the actual size of the net sterling liabilities has undoubtedly contributed to the scale of speculative attacks on sterling during periods of payments weakness—manifesting itself in 'leads and lags' but also in massive withdrawal of funds. On the other hand it is probably not true that capital flows to the O.S.A. have been at the expenses of home investment.† and it would probably be wrong to attribute the 'stop-go' cycle in U.K. to the sterling balances. The kind of fluctuations which the U.K. has experienced have their origin elsewhere, although clearly the balances have exerted some effect on the timing of economic policy.

Undoubtedly, in one important respect, the balances have affected economic policy and economic development in general. In order to prevent the withdrawal of balances the authorities have persistently followed policies aimed at maintaining U.K. interest rates, adjusted for forward cover, at a higher level than elsewhere, in order to retain short-term funds in the U.K. The effects of this have been to worsen the U.K. balance of payments by increasing interest payments made abroad.‡

---

* This is particularly true of the developing countries, but not confined to them. Clearly the Voluntary Programme has had some effect on capital flows to the developed sterling area countries (see page 210) and some part of these countries' exports to the U.K. have been adversely affected by the T.I.C. and Import Deposit Scheme.

† This was the general conclusion of Reddaway on the question of whether overseas investment was at the expense of home investment. See W. B. Reddaway, *Effects of U.K. Direct Investment Overseas, Interim Report*, Cambridge University Press 93–95 (1967).

‡ Radcliffe estimated the cost to the balance of payments of an increase of Bank Rate by 1% at the rate of £15 million a year provided other short-term rates also rose by 1%. *Report*, para. 438.

More importantly, the high level of domestic rates must have had some effect on the level of capital investment in the U.K., and thus on the rate of growth. In this respect it has weakened other Government policies, e.g., investment allowances, aimed at raising the propensity to invest.

Unfortunately, by the end of the sixties the situation was if anything perhaps worse than it was at the beginning of the decade. Net sterling liabilities ended the decade substantially higher. This perhaps contained an advantage in so far as a higher proportion were now in official hands, and, therefore, more firmly held. However, the greater firmness of the official O.S.A. holdings has been bought at a substantial cost. In effect they have been given a gold guarantee for most of their sterling reserves, so that holding sterling balances entails no risks, and yet ensures them of a high rate of return. For the U.K., the main problem remains. Events during the sixties have surely emphasised the need for a partial funding of the sterling balance, something which will not be achieved by the Basle Agreement.

APPENDIX: U.K. OFFICIAL SHORT- AND MEDIUM-TERM DEBT

Appendix: Table 1

U.K. OFFICIAL SHORT- AND MEDIUM-TERM BORROWING FROM ABROAD*
(£ million)

	Total	Borrowing with a sterling counterpart					Foreign Currency Deposits
		Total	I.M.F.†	Swiss loan‡	F.R.B. swap arrangement	Other	
1959	116	116	—	—	—	—	—
1960	—	—	—	—	—	—	—
1961	370	370	370	—	—	—	—
1962	—	—	—	—	—	—	—
1963	—	—	—	—	—	—	—
1964	573	501	357	28	71	45	72
1965	1 172	1 172	846	42	169	115	—
1966	1 481	1 467	861	42	125	439	14
1967	2 067	1 874	628	17	438	791	193
1968	3 363	3 152	1 134	11	480	1 527	211
1969	2 664	2 514	1 104	—	271	1 139	150
1970	1 369	1 369	970	—	—	399	—

* Drawings outstanding at end of period. The sterling value has been calculated at $2.80 — £1 to end of September 1967; and $2.40 — £1 thereafter.

† Drawings from the I.M.F., net of repayments by the U.K. and drawings of sterling from I.M.F. by other countries; excludes interest and charges in sterling.

‡ Borrowing from Switzerland in parallel with drawings from I.M.F. under G.A.B.

Sources: *Bank of England Statistical Abstract*, No. 1, Table 26 (1970), and *Bank of England Quarterly Bulletin*, **II**, No. 1 (March 1971), Statistical Annex Table 25.

The above table provides data on U.K. short- and medium-term borrowing outstanding in the period 1959–1970. The build-up of debt began in the second half of 1964 and reached its peak in the final quarter of 1968. By that stage the level of debt outstanding was very substantial; including very large loans from the I.M.F., and extensive borrowing from other overseas monetary authorities (including central bank swaps). It was generally anticipated that repayment of the debt in the Seventies would face the authorities with a very severe problem, and require policies on their part which generated large and continuing surpluses on external payments. Everyone expected that the authorities would at some stage have to re-schedule some of the debt—particularly that owed to the I.M.F.

As can be seen from the *Table 1* and *Chart 1* this has not proved necessary, and debt outstanding was reduced to a relatively low figure by the end of 1970. The early months of 1971 saw further repayments, including the complete repayment of debt to other central monetary institutions, and the advanced repayment in one lump-sum (£285 million) of the £551 million outstanding on the 1968 I.M.F. loan. This left a total debt outstanding by April 1971 of only £683 million—still considerable, but £2680 million below the peak 1968 level. Action on this scale was made possible only by the very substantial gearing effect of the reduction in the cumulated deficit on current account since the middle

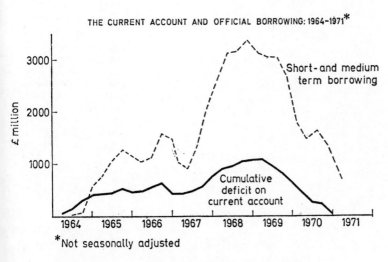

THE CURRENT ACCOUNT AND OFFICIAL BORROWING: 1964–1971*

*Not seasonally adjusted

Appendix: Chart 1

of 1969, the unwinding of leads and lags in payments and the extra-ordinary return of confidence in sterling. The inflows of foreign currency towards the end of 1970 and during the first quarter of 1971 were huge and so permitted repayment of overseas debt whilst maintaining a fairly constant level in the reserves.

9

INCOMES POLICY

Incomes policy, in varying forms, was experimented with almost continuously during the sixties. It varied not only with respect to its main aims and the machinery for implementation but also in terms of the commitment of labour market organisations and Government. Prior to 1964 the T.U.C. and the trade unions generally refused to co-operate with the Government either in the formulation of an incomes policy or in its implementation, although after 1964 (at least for a few years) they exhibited a greater willingness to co-operate in the 'planned growth in incomes'. At the beginning of the decade much was hoped for from incomes policy, as an additional instrument of economic policy, but experience during the sixties led to disillusionment with it both as a short-term measure and as a means of influencing long-term pay and price developments.

One of the most significant features of incomes policy development during the period 1961–1969 was the degree to which it varied between tightness and looseness. In general the periods of tightness (1961 and 1966/1967) centred on a wage freeze which aimed essentially at holding an inflationary wage round at a time of severe external difficulties. In time the freeze was eroded as a result of changes in demand, changes in profits and prices, increases in import costs, the rate and incidence of wage drift, etc., which led to modifications of the incomes policy machinery and the criteria whereby it was conducted. This kind of pattern of developments has led one informed writer to the conclusion that this is inevitable, and that policy makers should 'work on the basis of forecasting the rate of breakdown and attempt to contain it within bounds'. In other words the criteria for success do not lie in the 'impossible task of constant and perfect control' but in aligning the incomes trend with the productivity trend over a period of years.★

Obviously the basic and essential assumption of any incomes policy is that labour market organisations and Government are able to influence the course of wages and prices. There would clearly be no case, at least in the short run, for incomes policy if wages and prices were entirely the outcome of market forces. If this were so, then the appropriate policies would be those (fiscal and monetary) which aimed at controlling the level of demand for output, and thus the demand for factors, and/or policies concerned with the supply side of the system, e.g., labour market policies to raise labour mobility. Since the late 1950s economists have been extensively engaged on research into the factors determining wage and price developments (see *The Determinants of Incomes and Prices*), and although questions have recently been raised about the validity of the models which have been tested and the usefulness of their results, these do suggest that price and wage developments can be explained largely by economic variables such as unemployment, recent price experience, etc. However, it is clearly not the case that pay and prices are entirely explicable in terms of economic forces, and it follows, therefore, that policies aimed at changing the attitudes and practices of labour market institutions can affect price and pay developments.†

The main advantage of incomes policy, at least in the British context, is seen to lie in reducing the social costs of counteracting inflationary pressures compared with the use of other economic policy instruments. This attitude was expressed most clearly in the first general report of the Prices and Incomes Board where it was observed 'that the country has a choice: to pitch demand so much below the limits of capacity that the uncertainties attendant on its fine regulation are diminished and the power of managements and unions to contribute to inflationary pressures is reduced; or to secure appropriate behaviour by managements and unions with regard to prices and incomes so that demand can be pitched nearer the limits of capacity and a higher rate of growth achieved'.‡ Implicit in this argument is the belief that traditional

★ John Corina, 'Can an Incomes Policy Be Administered', *British Journal of Industrial Relations*, **V**, No. 3, 287–310 (Nov. 1967).

† This was the conclusion also of a valuable study by the Economic Commission for Europe, *Incomes in Postwar Europe: A Study of Policies, Growth and Distribution*, Geneva, 1967. It found that 'in no Western European country has the rate of changes in wages—whether conventional rates or earnings—been so immutably determined by external forces that any effort on the part of those concerned to change the response would have been futile' (chapter 3, p. 18).

‡ National Board for Prices and Incomes, *General Report, April 1965 to July 1966*, H.M.S.O., Cmnd. 3087, para. 20 (Aug. 1966).

demand management policy entails short-run costs in so far as it has its effects by holding demand below productive potential, and may in the longer run entail a slower growth in capacity through adverse effects on private investment expenditures. The advantage of incomes policy, therefore, lies in its ability, when harmonised with other instruments of short-term economic management, of allowing the economy to operate at a rather higher level of output and employment than would otherwise be required in order to achieve or maintain internal and external equilibrium.

However, the phase of the cycle during which incomes policy is most desirable is when the pressure of demand for labour is high. Unfortunately, this is precisely the time when it is likely to be relatively ineffective. During periods of high pressure of demand union leaders will be pressed by their members to take advantage of the economic situation and demand large increases in pay. Simultaneously managements will be faced by demand conditions in product markets which will make it relatively easy for them to pass on increases in costs arising from increases in labour charges. High current profits encourage firms to expand output and in conditions of tight labour markets they are prepared to bid up the price of labour.* The probabilities of success of an incomes policy are, therefore, inversely related to the state of demand in product and labour markets. It follows that an incomes policy is not likely to be successful in dealing with inflationary conditions unless its foundations, criteria and machinery were constructed during a period of slightly greater slack in the economic system.

Although British incomes policy has been fairly comprehensive in its coverage, it has nevertheless basically ignored distributional questions. But any incomes policy which has as its main aim the stability of the general price level has to operate through policies aimed at modifying specific prices, or incomes of certain groups, and thus have effects on the distribution of income. Nevertheless, incomes policy as operated in the U.K. has neither been based on any broad principles relating to factor shares nor has it included detailed and explicit aims in respect of the pay structure. No Government has been prepared to suggest

---

* The role of both labour market and product market variables was tested in a very interesting and realistic model by Eckstein and Wilson for the United States. They found that manufacturing money wage rates between 1948–1960 could be significantly explained by institutional factors, such as that wages are determined in bargains between unions and employers, wages are determined in wage rounds, and that there exists a key group. In this model wages of the key group are determined by profit rates and unemployment rates in the group, and these largely set the rate for other industries. See O. Eckstein and T. A. Wilson, 'The Determination of Money Wages in American Industry', *Quarterly Journal of Economics*, **76** (1962).

that redistribution of national product in favour of employment incomes is desirable (at least as an objective of incomes policy) and the nearest Government has come in recent years in this respect is the regulation of divided payments. These have been considered as analogous to wage incomes, and although they have been subject to various 'norms' since 1965 this does not appear to have led to any shift in the income distribution. Again, for the purposes of incomes policy, the authorities have accepted the existing pay structure. The only exception to this was the introduction of the low wage case in 1965, a relatively uncontroversial element in the incomes policy likely in any event to be largely offset by wage drift. Instead the Government have broadly taken the structure of pay as exogenously determined—the result of strong economic and social factors which cannot easily be modified by an incomes policy.

Basic to all experiments with incomes policy has been the setting of norms (see *The Development of Incomes Policy Criteria*), the purpose of which has been to preserve balance in the economy between factor incomes and resources. In order, so it has been argued, to achieve stability of the general price level the increase in average money incomes must not be faster than the average increase in output per head. Setting a zero norm for the general price level does, however, raise a number of problems. In the first place the economic system is a lagged system within which increases in prices lead to increases in pay claims to preserve real income, to increases in pay and thus to price changes. The most an incomes policy can hope for is to gradually stabilise prices as the lagged effects wear off, and it is obviously both impracticable and impossible to cut off these lagged responses via an incomes policy at any particular point in time. Secondly, for overall price stability it follows that some prices must actually fall, but no incomes policy is likely to be able to enforce price declines. Finally, there is the question of price increases originating outside the domestic economy—as a result of inflationary trends in other countries or through increases in the prices of primary products. The more open the economy the more powerful will be these factors in effecting the price level leading to subsequent rounds of pay increases.

But setting a zero norm for the general level of prices raises the more fundamental question of whether absolute price stability is really desirable. There has been no general agreement among economists on this point, and many Governments throughout the world seem now to be reconciled to 'creeping' inflation as an inevitable result of operating fully- or almost fully-employed economies. Those economists who oppose complete price stability emphasise the benefits to be derived from high levels of private investment (induced by rising prices) and the higher level of real output associated with operating the system at or near full employment. Others have emphasised the social injustices and inequities caused by inflation, the high rates of interest (with its effects on investment) and the implications for external balance. British Governments have, while paying lip-service to the disadvantages of inflation, not seriously concerned themselves with price stability as an aim in itself. Instead inflation has been condemned because of its external effects, and a more precise aim has been to maintain a situation where prices did not rise faster than those in competitor countries, rather than absolute price stability. The achievement of the latter would undoubtedly have required, in the post-war period, a substantial gap between demand and potential capacity. Even in the post-devaluation period the aim of incomes policy was not to maintain absolute price stability (impossible anyway in the immediate aftermath of devaluation since the latter could only achieve its objectives through changing relative prices), but to preserve the competitive advantage given by devaluation. How fast prices could be allowed to rise in Britain became, therefore, partly a function of the rate of inflation in other industrialised countries.

Incomes policy was, however, not merely concerned with negative questions (restraint of incomes and prices) but also aimed at raising productivity. This particular aim figured prominently in the activities of the National Board for Prices and Incomes (N.B.P.I.) set up in 1965, and many of its reports contained recommendations on positive action for inducing change in the economy. In its reports it identified the need in many sectors (both private and public) for improved investment criteria, for faster diffusion of new technology together with a removal of restrictive practices in industry, and for radical change in the structure of earnings so as to reduce resistance to change. Undoubtedly this aspect of incomes policy was desirable, and the N.B.P.I. filled a very valuable role as a catalyst as well as fulfilling its narrow review functions.[*]

THE DETERMINANTS OF INCOMES AND PRICES

Table 9.1 and *Chart 9.1* provide data on incomes, output and prices, 1959–1969. These data are presented in a form which has now become

[*] The best source of information on the activities of the N.B.P.I. are its Annual Reports, of which four were issued between 1966 and 1969, Cmnd. 3087 (1966), Cmnd. 3394 (1967), Cmnd. 3715 (1968) and Cmnd. 4130 (1969). Of the general references to the Board the two most important were *Payment by Results Systems*, Cmnd. 3627 (1968) and *Productivity Agreements*, Cmnd. 3311 (1967).

Table 9·1
INCOMES, OUTPUT AND PRICES, 1959–1969 (INDEX NUMBERS 1959 = 100)

	Gross domestic product*	Output per person†	Income from employment	Income from rent and self-employment	Gross trading profits of companies	Retail prices
1959	100·0	100·0	100·0	100·0	100·0	100·0
1960	105·7	102·9	107·6	107·1	112·6	101·0
1961	108·4	103·8	116·3	113·5	109·8	104·4
1962	109·7	104·8	122·7	118·6	108·4	108·9
1963	114·0	108·1	129·0	124·3	123·8	111·0
1964	119·3	113·1	139·7	132·8	138·7	114·7
1965	123·8	115·0	150·7	144·3	144·0	120·1
1966	125·8	116·8	161·2	154·0	134·3	124·9
1967	127·5	120·3	167·4	162·8	139·8	128·0
1968	131·8	125·8	179·1	170·9	154·3	134·0
1969	133·7	128·8	192·7	184·4	149·2	141·1

* Compromise estimate of GDP at constant 1963 prices.
† Output per person employed in producing GDP.
Source: *National Institute Economic Review* Statistical Appendix (Feb. 1970); *Economic Trends* (Oct. 1970).

fairly general and is intended to identify the difference between the rate of growth of money incomes and the rate of growth of real output. During the sixties the problem of inflation was analysed mainly in these terms—a continuous upward drift in prices caused by a faster growth in money incomes than of output. While dispute has continued as to the relative importance of cost-push or demand-pull factors,

INCOMES, OUTPUT AND PRICES

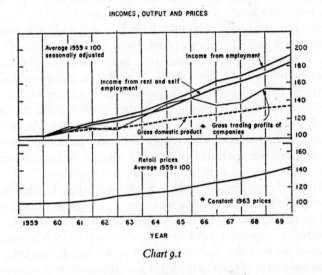

Chart 9.1

at least one point is certain, i.e. that the money supply was continuously increased and so permitted the inflation to continue.*

Over the decade 1959–1969 retail prices increased by rather over a third, with an acceleration of inflation in the second half of the decade. This more rapid increase in prices during the second half of the sixties at a time of reduced pressure of demand (in terms of the average unemployment percentage) seems to have had a number of causes. It was partly the result of the devaluation which substantially raised import prices which led to subsequent adjustment of wages and thus again

---

* Cost-push factors have been identified as important in explaining inflation in Britain. However, for these factors to lead to continued inflation there has to be adjustment of the money supply in that there are limits to the extent to which cash balances can be economised. For example, an increase in wage costs which led to a rise in the general price level will require a higher level of transactions balances. If the money supply did not rise, or not rise fast enough, then there would occur an increase in interest rates which would reduce aggregate demand. As Hicks has noted, 'The world we live in is one in which the monetary system has become relatively elastic, so that it can accommodate itself to changes in wages, rather than the other way about'. J. R. Hicks, 'Economic Foundations of Wage Policy', *Economic Journal*, **65**, 391 (Sept. 1955).

of prices. In part the more rapid rate of inflation was due to the more extensive use of indirect taxes. Between 1966 and 1969 the consumer price index increased by some 18% and more than a quarter of this (5%) was accounted for in increases in indirect taxation.* Finally, during the second half of the decade both hourly wage rates and hourly earnings (see *Table 9.2*) rose at a faster rate, and since this was not matched by any acceleration in the rate of increase of output per head, there occurred a faster increase in unit labour costs.

During the last two decades there have been a considerable number of statistical studies of the factors determining wages and prices. In part these investigations were intended to throw further light on the process of inflation and, in particular, to resolve the controversy about the relative importance of cost-push and demand-pull factors. But they have also had additional aims, including the identification of the effects of policy and the derivation of short-term forecasting relationships. In practice the results of such studies have not silenced controversy since the models tested can often be used with only slight modifications of the techniques or data to support alternative hypotheses.

Of the earlier studies, by far the best known are those by Phillips and Lipsey.† Phillips related the annual rate of change of average wage rates to the % rate of unemployment (lagged seven months), and calculated a regression equation for 1861–1913 which adequately explained not only the experience of that period but also the inter-war period and post-war years to 1957. The fit of the equation was improved by using changes in the rate of unemployment as an additional variable. In the study the main emphasis was on the role of demand, although allowance was made in certain years for exceptional increases in the cost of living. Lipsey introduced the cost of living as an explanatory variable, as well as unemployment, and found that the cost of living was a more important factor in explaining changes in money wage rates in the period after World War I than in the preceding years (the coefficient of price changes rising from 0·4 to 0·7). Both these studies related to historically long periods and emphasised the importance of demand pressures in determining changes in money wage rates. More importantly, they appeared to indicate over many years relative

* These were July 1966 (regulator) +0·7%; September 1966 (S.E.T.) +0·6%; March 1968 (Budget and S.E.T.) +1·7%; November 1968 (regulator) +0·8%; and April 1969 (Budget and S.E.T.) +1·1%.

† A. W. Phillips, 'The Relationship between Unemployment and the Rate of Change of Money Wage Rates in the United Kingdom, 1861–1957', *Economica*, **25**, 283–299 (1958) and R. G. Lipsey, 'The Relationship between Unemployment and the Rate of Change of Money Wage Rates in the United Kingdom, 1861–1957: A Further Analysis', *Economica*, **27**, 1–31 (1960).

stability of the relationship between changes in money wage rates and unemployment.

Dicks-Mireaux and Dow,[*] in a study of the years 1946–1956, gave most weight to the influence of the demand for labour, although they also introduced two cost-push variables (retail prices and trade union pushfulness). The response of wages to a 1% change in prices was put at 0·5%, and the response of wages to a 1% change in unemployment was estimated at 3·5%. As for trade union pushfulness (subjectively assessed), they estimated that a difference between 'marked restraint' and 'marked pushfulness' might affect the rate of change of wages by up to almost 5%. Their equation included a time trend which implied that with stable prices, zero excess demand for labour, and average trade union pushfulness, that wages would still rise by 2%–2·5% a year (explicable perhaps by productivity growth of this order[†]).

One problem present in these statistical investigations is the interaction between wages and prices (wages push up prices, prices push up wages within a year) which may bias the coefficients. In order to eliminate this bias Dicks-Mireaux attempted to estimate a simultaneous wage and price model.[‡] In this model average wages and salaries (on a national accounts basis) were expressed as a function of the simultaneous, $P_{(t)}$ and the one year lagged, $P_{(t-1)}$ increases in the prices of total final expenditure at factor cost, together with an index measuring the pressure of demand for labour lagged one quarter, $D_{(t-0·25)}$. In the second equation, the percentage increase in prices, $P_{(t)}$ was estimated as a function of the simultaneous average wage income, $W_{(t)}$, modified by the annual growth in output per man, $X_{(t)}$ and the rise in import prices lagged one quarter, $I_{(t-0·25)}$. Using the method of two-stage least squares the model was fitted to the years 1946–1959 and yielded the following results.:

(1) $W_{(t)} = 3·90 + 0·30\,P_{(t)} + 0·16\,P_{(t-1)} + 2·78\,D_{(t-0·25)} \ldots$

(2) $P_{(t)} = 2·47 + 0·27\,W_{(t)} + 0·21\,I_{(t-0·25)} - 0·54\,X_{(t)} \ldots$

Equation (1) implies that a 1% rise in the general price level induced a 0·3% simultaneous rise in average wages and salaries, other things

[*] L. A. Dicks-Mireaux and J. C. R. Dow, 'The Determinants of Wage Inflation: United Kingdom, 1946–1956', *Journal of the Royal Statistical Society*, Series A, **122**, 145–184 (1959).

[†] This was one of the explanations later put forward by Dow in *The Management of the British Economy 1945–1960*, Cambridge University Press, 360–363 (1965).

[‡] L. A. Dicks-Mireaux, 'The Interrelationship between Cost and Price Changes, 1946–1959: A study of Inflation in Post-war Britain', *Oxford Economic Papers*, **13**, 267–292 (1961).

being equal, and contributed 0·16 % to the increase of wages and salaries in the following year. These figures (as in the earlier Dicks-Mireaux and Dow study) imply a less than full compensation for price increases but needs to be considered alongside a constant term which suggests that wages and salaries would have risen by almost 4 % a year even if prices had been stable, provided there was no excess demand for labour. The study confirms earlier studies of the importance of the demand for labour indicating that a fall of 1 % in the index of demand for labour added almost 3 % to the rate of increase of wages and salaries per head, other things being equal.

This model, excluding the $P_{(t-1)}$ variable, has subsequently been applied to the longer period 1946–1966.* Some changes in the co-efficients were to be expected given that the later years of the period included the years when incomes policy was being developed. The coefficients of the price determination equation showed little change from the Dicks-Mireaux results. On the other hand, the pressure of demand variable in the employment income equation declined in importance to a figure of only about a half of that found by Dicks-Mireaux. These results led the N.B.P.I. to fit the employment income equation separately to the two decades covered by their study (1946–1966), with significant results. They found that the value of the price coefficient had fallen substantially as well as that for the pressure of demand for labour so that 'these two variables provide for the second decade [1956–1966] a much less satisfactory "explanation" of changes in average employment incomes'. Alongside the decline in importance of these two variables had gone an increase in the size of the constant term (from 4·25 % to almost 6 %) which they considered explicable in terms of 'an increase in autonomous cost-push, or the original variables appearing now with more complicated leads and lags'.†

Almost all of the relationships discussed above have been recently re-investigated by Colin Gillion of the National Institute in an attempt to find usable forecasting relationships for wage rates and average earnings.‡ He retained the basic proposition that the rate of change of wages is a function of unemployment but also experimented with an

* National Board for Prices and Incomes, *Third General Report, August 1967–July 1968*, H.M.S.O. Cmnd. 3517, Appendix A (July 1968).

† The simple least-squares regression equations for the two decades were, respectively:

$$W_{(t)} = 4·29 + 0·40 \, P_{(t)} + 2·12 \, D_{(t-0·25)}$$
$$R^2 = 0·77;$$
$$W_{(t)} = 5·97 - 0·07 \, P_{(t)} + 1·60 \, D_{(t-0·25)}$$
$$R^2 = 0·37.$$

‡ C. Gillion, 'Wage Rates, Earnings and Wage Drift', *National Institute Economic Review*, No. 46 (Nov. 1968).

index of capacity utilisation as a direct measure of the pressure of demand for labour. Regressions were also tried which included the rate of change of unemployment (following Phillips and Lipsey), a price variable, and a real wage adjustment process, i.e., that money wages always adjust by the full amount of any price change but do so only with a time-lag.

Gillion found, as in earlier studies, that, during the years 1950–1956, the level of unemployment had a 'strong influence'—a 1% change in the unemployment rate was associated with a change of 3% in the level of wage rates—but that the rate of change of unemployment had no significant effect. The substitution of a capacity output index for unemployment gave only a slightly better fit. In most equations tested the direct price effect was small and generally insignificant, However, the equations using a real wage adjustment did better than those using a direct price effect, and implied that equilibrium real wages (in terms of the retail prices index) increase at about 2% a year as a consequence of productivity changes and are increased by 5·5% for every 1% change in the unemployment rate. Actual wage rates adjust to this equilibrium by 25% of the gap between actual and equilibrium wage rates each quarter, so that in the long run the wage rate fully compensates for the rise in the cost of living. This seems on a priori grounds reasonable, and almost certainly helps to explain the behaviour of wages during the post-devaluation period (1968–1969).

These then are some of the explanations which have been put forward to explain wage and price developments. There have been other proposals. For example, Kaldor* suggested that profits rather than unemployment is the main determinant of wages changes. This hypothesis was tested by Lipsey and Steuer but did not yield significant results for the post-war years.† An alternative explanation, emphasising cost-push factors, was put forward by Hines, who explained wage rate changes by retail prices and the annual change in the % of workers unionised. On his data unemployment is a weaker explanatory variable than the measure of trade union strength.‡

Two important features of the British wages system are often mentioned in the context of discussions on inflation and incomes policy. Firstly, basic wage rates are primarily set as the result of a lengthy process of centralised collective bargaining which takes place at infrequent intervals. This practice has led to the familiar wage round, and

---

* N. Kaldor, 'Economic Growth and the Problem of Inflation', *Economica*, **29** (1959).

† R. G. Lipsey and M. D. Steuer, 'The Relation between Profits and Wage Rates', *Economica*, **28** (1961).

‡ A. G. Hines, 'Trade Unions and Wage Inflation in the United Kingdom: 1893–1961', *Review of Economic Studies* (Oct. 1964).

although it has not proved possible to identify key bargains (as in the U.S.A.) it is still the case that changes in rates in any one year tend to cluster around a particular figure. One result of this has been a remarkable rigidity of the pay structure, which cannot be attributed to purely economic factors, but is in part the product of history, social institutions and deep-seated beliefs in 'justice' and 'fairness' as principles which ought to determine relative pay. Incomes policy will, therefore, not find it easy to alter the structure of relative pay, nor can the authorities hope to be able to influence certain key bargains as a way of determining the size of the wage round in any particular year.

Secondly, there is the problem of wage drift, i.e., the excess of earnings over negotiated rates. This is not a problem peculiar to Britain, but appears to be typical of those countries with highly centralised collective bargaining structures who are also operating their economies at or close to full-employment. As can be seen from *Table 9.2* there has been a drift of wage earnings over wage rates for many years. Between 1959–1969 average hourly earnings increased by 90% and average hourly wage rates by 67%. However, the process of drift has not taken place at a continuous rate, and the gap between earnings/wages widened sharply in 1959–1960 and 1964–1965. These were both periods when unemployment was falling, which suggests that drift is associated with the rate of change of unemployment. This hypothesis was tested by Gillion, who found that a fall of unemployment of 1 % added 2·5 % to the change in hourly earnings, but that neither the level of unemployment nor the movement of prices were significant as explanatory variables. He also found that, although there is a short lag (six weeks) between a change in wage rates and a change in earnings, a 1 % increase in hourly wage rates leads to a 0·6 % increase in total average earnings (wages and salaries per employee).* This conclusion is important, from the point of view of the possible success of income policy, in that it suggests that on the basis of past relationships a policy which is successful in reducing the rate of increase in wage rates will also reduce the rate of increase in earnings, although not in the same proportion.†

As well as the pressure of demand for labour a further factor which has been emphasised by many researchers is the influence on earnings of

---

* C. Gillion, 'Wage Rates, Earnings and Wage Drift', *National Institute Economic Review*, No. 46, p. 66 (Nov. 1968), K. Lomax found that about 80 % of wage drift was explained by the rate of change of industrial production in the period 1950–1964 (reported in E.C.E., *Incomes in Post-war Europe*, chapter 3, page 22).

† This was also the conclusion of L. A. Dicks-Mireaux and J. R. Shepherd, 'The Wages Structure and Some Implications for Incomes Policy', *National Institute Economic Review*, No. 22 (Nov. 1962).

Table 9.2
EARNINGS, BASIC RATES OF WAGES AND WAGE COSTS PER UNIT OF OUTPUT
(Index numbers, 1959 = 100)

	Weekly wage rates	Hourly wage rates	Weekly earnings	Hourly earnings	Unit wage costs*
			in all industries		
1959	100·0	100·0	100·0	100·0	100·0
1960	102·5	104·0	106·7	107·5	102·2
1961	106·8	110·7	113·2	114·9	108·7
1962	110·7	115·7	117·2	120·0	109·8
1963	114·7	120·0	122·0	124·8	108·7
1964	120·1	126·3	130·6	134·5	109·8
1965	125·2	134·1	140·4	147·1	115·2
1966	131·2	143·2	149·4	158·8	120·7
1967	135·9	148·9	154·4	164·3	122·8
1968	144·8	158·9	166·8	177·0	121·7
1969	152·4	167·3	179·6	189·4	128·3

* Manufacturing

Source: *National Institute Economic Review*, Statistical Appendix (Feb. 1970 and Aug. 1970).

payments by results systems. This factor has indeed been singled out for special criticism by the N.B.P.I. in its report on P.B.R. It found that in the mid/late sixties about 50% of the annual increase in average hourly earnings of manual workers was attributable to wage drift and concluded 'that conventional P.B.R. had contributed to drift both directly and by disturbing wage differentials within the enterprise in a way which led to pressures for further wage increases. . . .'* This distinction, between primary and secondary drift, has been emphasised by many writers, and is valuable as an indication of the way in which a spiral might be perpetuated.†

As well as the above econometric studies there has also been a certain amount of research into the pricing behaviour of industrial companies.‡ What these studies tend to confirm is the hypothesis that 'businessmen generally set prices by assessing their costs when operating at some "normal" or "full" working capacity, and adding some conventional margin to them'. According to this theory businessmen do not raise prices when demand suddenly rises, nor do they reduce them when unit costs begin to fall as output increases on the upswing of the cycle. Godley and Rowe found that the movement of most retail prices between 1955–1963 could be excellently explained by changes in 'normal' labour costs (actual hourly earnings corrected for cyclical fluctuations in overtime divided by a smooth productivity trend), import prices and indirect tax rates. In a later study the Institute disproved the conventional view that prices in manufacturing industry never fall, and found many examples of price reductions as a consequence of cost declines— a result favourable to incomes policy.

What in general these studies of pricing behaviour deny is the possibility of general inflation being the result of the pricing practices of companies. Such an hypothesis has been advanced to explain U.S. inflation, but receives no support from the British evidence. However, the research does not rule out a role for companies in the inflationary process. It has long been recognised that oligopolies, for example, might take a weak stance in the face of inflationary wage

---

* The Economic Commission for Europe estimated that in 1959 average wage earnings in manufacturing were 36% above standard wage rates (compared with 25% in 1948). See N.B.P.I., *Payments by Results Systems*, H.M.S.O., Cmnd. 3627 (May 1968), and *Third General Report*, H.M.S.O., Cmnd. 3715 (July 1968).

† For a valuable assessment of the research on this problem see E. H. Phelps-Brown, 'Wage Drift', *Economica*, **29**, 339–356 (1962).

‡ R. R. Neild, *Pricing and Employment in the Trade Cycle*, N.I.E.S.R.: Cambridge University Press (1963); W. A. H. Godley and D. A. Rowe, 'Retail and Consumer Prices, 1955–1963', N.I.E.R., No. 30 (Nov. 1964); and W. A. H. Godley and C. Gillion, 'Pricing Behaviour in Manufacturing Industry', N.I.E.R., No. 33 (Aug. 1965).

demands knowing that these would be generalised between competitors, and, through administered pricing, could be passed on to consumers.

A number of conclusions can be drawn from the above studies. Firstly, almost all of the research seems to confirm the importance of the pressure of demand for labour as a significant variable in determining wage changes. Secondly, in many studies historical price experience was found to exert a direct influence on wages, although the size of this coefficient varied. The first conclusion emphasises the role of the demand factors in the process of pay determination, while the second suggests that unions are capable of raising the level of pay as a response to previous price increases and is consistent with a cost-push view of inflation. However, most of the studies contain a wage/price relationship which is less than one, suggesting that wage increases do not fully compensate for price increases, and that conditions do not exist for a continuous inflationary spiral. Exceptions to this view were the studies by Gillion and Sargan who found, using a real wage adjustment model, that wages did fully adjust (but with a lag) to price increases. None of the models tested contains price expectations as an explanatory variable, and the influence of this factor has not been determined.

A third important conclusion, noted in the N.B.P.I. study, is the increase in the size of the constant term in its employment income equation. This could represent an increase of cost-push factors in the sixties compared with the fifties, but however explained it does amount to an increase in the pressure of autonomous forces in determining the level of pay. With this development has gone a reduction in the significance of the pressure of demand for labour as an explanatory variable. This development is extremely important in its implications for policy The earlier Phillips and Lipsey studies, in particular, suggested the existence of a trade-off between increases in general prices and unemployment, with unemployment determining the rate of change of money wages and the rates of change of wages determining the change in prices (given the level of import prices and the rate of growth of productivity). Since the level of unemployment (and to some extent the rate of change of unemployment) is an instrumental variable, determined by the level of demand for output which is determined by demand management policies, there exists a trade-off between the level of unemployment and the rate of inflation. In this view the authorities can choose the pressure of demand at which they prefer the economy to operate, and thus the rate of price inflation. Even if a trade-off does exist in the short run (its existence has been

R

denied in the long-run*) there is considerable evidence that this relationship weakened during the sixties.

THE DEVELOPMENT OF INCOMES POLICY CRITERIA

The 1948–1951 experiment was essentially a short-run response to external problems at a time of excess demand, and relied extensively upon the co-operation of union leaders in moderating demands for wage increases. It also owed a great deal to the moral force of Chancellor Cripps who managed simultaneously to persuade companies not to increase dividends. As for prices, these were restrained by the use of surviving war-time powers. The criteria for wages, announced in 1948, was straightforward: 'In present conditions, and until more goods and services are available for the home market, there is no justification for any general increase in individual money incomes.'† Only one exception was permitted; wages could be increased only where it was necessary to attract labour to a sector suffering from labour shortage. Up to 1964 this was the only example of wage restraint which the unions accepted, and amounted to the voluntary introduction of lags into the process of employment income determination (through delay in wage claims and settlements). It began to disintegrate towards the end of 1950 under the impact of union revolt caused by the widespread increases associated with devaluation and the Korean War, plus a resurgence of the traditional aim of preserving wage relativities (which had been upset by wage drift during the period of restraint).

There were two further attempts by the Government, in 1956 and 1961, to get agreement with the unions on a temporary pause on increases in pay and prices. On both occasions the unions refused to co-operate. The earlier attempt in 1956–1957 seems to have been due, in part, to a gradual acceptance by the Conservative Government of cost-push explanations of inflation which led them to turn to incomes policy. Their aims at this stage were imprecise and amounted to vague attempts to establish a price plateau by encouraging employer resistance to wage demands in the private sector. It was associated with the establishment in 1957 of the Council on Prices, Productivity and Incomes which issued reports in 1958 (2), 1959 and 1960. In its first report the Council placed the blame for inflation on excess demand, and rejected any norms for average increases in incomes. By its final report (1961), it

---

* The existence of a long-run trade-off between unemployment and inflation has been strongly denied by Friedman and Phelps, see below page 261.

† *Statement on Personal Incomes, Costs and Prices*, H.M.S.O., Cmd. 7321 (1948).

had changed its views; strongly espoused cost-push explanations of inflation and pointed to the desirability of some form of incomes policy.

In the summer of 1961 a pay pause was announced to halt increases in wages, salaries and dividends until the spring of 1962. Once again the freeze was a short-run response to balance of payments problems (proximately the crisis of July 1961). Once again the unions refused to support the pay pause, which operated through a standstill on pay in the public sector with special arrangements for controlling the size and timing of arbitration awards. On this occasion the lags were mainly imposed by the Government and the private sector was encouraged to follow the public sector's example. In February 1962 the Government issued a White Paper, the main aim of which seems to have been to convert the freeze into a more permanent incomes policy.*

The criteria for incomes contained in the 1962 White Paper are interesting partly because they foreshadowed the criteria adopted in later Government statements. It set a guiding light of 2%–2·5% for average increases in incomes—some incomes to rise faster than this, some less—which was based on past trends in productivity. In assessing particular wage and salary proposals various criteria were suggested. Firstly, that productivity should be an element in determining wages only where 'those concerned made a direct contribution, by accepting more exacting work, or more onerous conditions, or by a renunciation of restrictive practices'. Secondly, demand and supply arguments were acceptable only where it was absolutely necessary to retain or attract labour. Thirdly, that comparability arguments were to have less weight than hitherto, although these were not entirely excluded. The guiding light of 2%–2·5% gave way in 1963, in the announcements of the National Incomes Commission, to one of 3%–3·5%, a change which was related to the N.E.D.C. *Plan to 1966* which forecast a trend growth of productivity per head of this magnitude.†

Mr. Wilson's Government took office in October 1964 against a background of huge external deficit and during a period of rising pressure on domestic resources. One of the immediate actions of the Government was to set in motion negotiations for setting up new

* *Incomes Policy: The Next Step*, H.M. Treasury: H.M.S.O., Cmnd. 1626 (1962).

† The National Income Commission (1962–1964) was a review body set up by the Government. It issued four reports, on specific wage agreements referred to it by the Government, and came under severe attack from the T.U.C. and unions. One of the main criticisms of the N.I.C. was that its powers did not extend to prices, and that it was entirely concerned with limiting wage incomes.

R*

machinery for an incomes policy which was to accompany a new experiment with national planning. These negotiations led, at the end of 1964, to a 'declaration of intent' wherein unions, management and Government expressed a willingness to co-operate in setting voluntary norms for judging prices and incomes changes, and in operating machinery for reviewing such changes. They set a norm for future increases in earnings per head of 3 %–3·5 %, based on the estimated trend in productivity growth. Since this norm made no allowance for past or inevitable future increases in prices, which had been rising during 1964 at 4·5 % per annum, it implied a fall in real wages for these groups whose last increase had been a year ago or longer. The incomes policy was to be based on voluntarism and the Government stated that it 'would resort to other methods only if they were convinced that the voluntary method had failed.'*

The next important statement of official criteria came in the April 1965 White Paper.† This established a norm for the average annual rate of increase in money incomes, consistent with price stability, of 3 %– 3·5 %. This was based on a projection of output per head in the National Plan. But not all incomes were to rise at the same rate; 'It is necessary not only to create the conditions in which essential structural readjustments can be carried out smoothly but also to promote social justice.'‡ It declared four criteria to justify wage and salary increases in excess of the norm. These included three of the exceptions included in the 1962 White Paper (contributions to productivity, manpower shortages, and pay differences in comparable occupations), but also additionally introduced the low pay case, i.e., 'where there is general recognition that existing wage and salary levels are too low to maintain a reasonable standard of living'.§

The other main departure from the 1962 criteria was the inclusion of specific criteria on prices, and this represented a major shift of emphasis of incomes policy. Enterprises were not expected to raise their prices except in the following cases:‖

1. If output per employee cannot be increased sufficiently to allow wages and salaries to increase at a rate consistent with the criteria for incomes . . . without some increase in prices, and no offsetting reductions can be made in non-labour costs per unit of output or in the return sought on investment.

2. If there are unavoidable increases in non-labour costs, such as

---

* *Machinery of Prices and Incomes Policy*, H.M.S.O., Cmnd. 2577 (1965).
† *Prices and Incomes Policy*, H.M.S.O., Cmnd. 2639 (1965).
‡ *Prices and Incomes Policy*, H.M.S.O., Cmnd. 2639, para. 17 (1965).
§ *Prices and Incomes Policy*, H.M.S.O., Cmnd. 2639, para. 15 (1965).
‖ *Prices and Incomes Policy*, H.M.S.O., Cmnd. 2639, para. 9 (1965).

materials, fuels, services or marketing costs per unit of output which cannot be offset.

3. If there are unavoidable increases in capital costs per unit of output which cannot be offset.

4. If after every effort has been made to reduce costs, the enterprise is unable to secure the capital required to meet home and overseas demand.

Apart from the resemblance of the above criteria to those of 1962 there is also a marked resemblance to the guideposts announced in the U.S.A. by the Council of Economic Advisers in 1962. In both countries the norm for increases in average money incomes was related to a trend in output per head, with the difference that after 1963 the norm for the U.K. was based on forecasts of productivity trends rather than on past performance. Both countries included the same exceptions, although the 1965 White Paper added the low wage case. In both cases increases and decreases in prices were to be based on the same criteria.*

The 1965 criteria remained operative until the sterling crisis of 1966 July when the Government strengthened the machinery for incomes policy, and called for an emergency standstill on pay and price increases and reductions in working hours. During the preceding fifteen months the 3·5% norm had become a minimum on which almost any group improved. The freeze imposed statutory lags over everyone in both the private and public sectors. Until the end of 1966 effectively no increases in pay or prices were permitted, and this was followed by a further six months of severe restraint. During the period of the freeze price increases were allowed only where these arose from rises in import costs or taxes which could not be absorbed. Pay increases were permitted only where they resulted from increases in output (e.g., payment for necessary overtime), from promotions or from incremental scales. Pay increases already arranged and due for payment after July 1966 were postponed for six months. Wage negotiations were permitted to continue, but increases could not be paid before 1967, and negotiations were to be based on a zero norm. Decisions by arbitration and Wages Councils were also postponed. Company dividends and distributions were also subject to the standstill.

A second White Paper, of November 1966, set out stringent criteria for the first six months of 1967, and established once again a zero norm. During this period the four grounds for exceptions specified in the 1965 White Paper were permitted to lead to some adjustment of pay, but the exceptions were interpreted more stringently.

* See D. J. Robertson, 'Guideposts and Norms: Contrasts in U.S. and U.K. Wage Policy', *Three Banks Review* (Dec. 1966).

More stringent considerations were also applied to proposed price increases.*

Most of the 1965 criteria again became operative after June 1967, with a number of important modifications.† Of these perhaps the most important was the decision to abandon any norm related to a trend in national productivity. Between mid-1967 and mid-1968, no increase in employment incomes was to be automatic, because of the precarious nature of the economic situation and because the previous 3·5% norm had become the minimum rather than the average. This was a belated recognition of the obvious fact that no union leader could afford to accept the norm, i.e., the norm provided a floor to expectations on which subsequent negotiations were based.‡ During this period the four exceptions to the norm (1965 criteria) became the criteria by which all increases in money incomes were to be judged. Other important changes included an attempt to set a minimum period of twelve months for wage and hours negotiations, to 'stagger' incomes increases where these were substantial, and to try to prevent any attempt on the part of groups to adjust for income increases foregone before the freeze.

In the March 1968 Budget the Chancellor announced the criteria which applied during 1968 and 1969. The criteria continued to be operative within a ceiling on incomes (including dividends) of 3·5% with the exception that incomes could rise by more than 3·5% as the result of genuine productivity agreements. One useful and seemingly valuable extension on the price side was the increase in the powers of the N.B.P.I. which could henceforth require price reductions.§

Thus it did not prove possible during the sixties to construct and maintain any fixed set of criteria by which to judge incomes and prices. As noted earlier, each of the experiments with incomes policy in the post-war period were centred on a wage freeze which aimed essentially at holding an inflationary wage round at a time of severe external difficulties. In time the freeze was eroded and this led to modifications of the incomes policy machinery and the criteria by which it was

---

* The details are set out in *Prices and Incomes Standstill*, H.M.S.O., Cmnd. 3074 (July 1966), and *Prices and Incomes Standstill: Period of Severe Restraint*, H.M.S.O., Cmnd. 3150 (Nov. 1966).

† *Prices and Incomes Policy After 30th June, 1967*, H.M.S.O., Cmnd. 3235 (1967).

‡ What policy makers are attempting to establish by operating a 'wages norm' is the substitution of a constant for the relationships in the wages equation. It has been suggested by some writers, e.g., by Lipsey and Parkin, that this leads some industries to regard this norm not only as a maximum but also as a minimum. Other sectors then feel constrained to give larger increases than they otherwise would have done in order to maintain customary differentials. In this model the setting of a 'wages norm' has some impact, but is far from perfectly effective.

§ *Productivity, Prices and Incomes in 1968 and 1969*, H.M.S.O., Cmnd. 3590 (1968).

conducted. One of the interesting features of these criteria, particularly after 1964, was their comprehensiveness; dealing with all aspects of employment incomes (earnings, overtime, hours reductions, etc.) as well as taking account of factors determining price and output trends in different sectors of the economy.

What was lacking in the incomes policy were any clearly defined distributional objectives. It is true that after 1965 one of the exceptions to the norm was the low pay case, and the identification of groups of workers who fitted this category became an important (and difficult) task for the N.B.P.I. However, the main focus of incomes policy from the Government's point of view was on its ability to reduce the rate of increase in money incomes, and the unions were only persuaded to co-operate (at least between 1964–1966) because of their fear of external constraint rather than because of the real wage gains which an incomes policy might yield. They were prepared to accept the extension of legal powers in 1966 because of the state of the economic situation and loyalty to the Government, but not thereafter.

One of the main problems related to the setting of a norm for increases in money incomes which was consistent with increases in output per head. For a while the authorities based the norm on past productivity trends, although they subsequently shifted to forecasts of productivity growth. However, the attempt to set norms for incomes, which defined the average increase with specified exceptions, clearly proved a failure. The norm simply became the minimum, rather than the average, so that from 1966 the exceptions criteria became the criteria by which all wage increases were judged. The zero norm of 1966–1967 subsequently gave way to a ceiling of 3·5 % for pay increases which satisfied the exceptions criteria, but in effect this ceiling simply became once again the minimum for wage increases.

By the end of the sixties of the exceptions criteria those relating to productivity and low wages had become the most important in the work of the N.B.P.I. However, simply to take productivity as the only criterion did not make sense and clearly conflicted with other views of what was a socially desirable distribution of income. Nevertheless, as interpreted by the N.B.P.I. this criterion became useful in that it permitted the Board to make recommendations in its reports on conditions affecting productivity growth. Similarly with price criteria: no simple set of criteria proved possible in respect of prices, and the criteria operative from 1965–1969 were not rigidly interpreted.

THE EFFECTIVENESS OF INCOMES POLICY

It is not easy to assess the effectiveness of incomes policy and simply to compare out-turn for wages and prices with policy aims in these directions is not sufficient. The fact that actual wages and prices rose faster than incomes policy targets is not proof that incomes policy was totally ineffective, since without the policy wage and price changes might have been even larger. Similarly, even where wages and prices increased in line with incomes policy aims, this is not in itself evidence of the effectiveness of the policy in that these movements may have been due to other factors operating simultaneously. Perhaps the simplest way of assessing the impact of incomes policy is to compare the actual movement of wages and prices during the period when incomes policy is in effect with the predicted movement determined by relationships based on periods when there was no incomes policy. Alternatively, and this is the procedure followed in a number of studies referred to below, researchers have included in their wage and price equations dummy variables to denote the presence of incomes policy. Whatever the technique, and whatever the exact form of the relationships tested, there must remain considerable doubt about the preciseness of the results.* One value of such investigations is that they throw some light on ancillary questions relating to the effectiveness of incomes policy. Such as, for example, whether the effectiveness of the policy has varied with its form, whether prices have been less amenable to control than wages, whether negotiated wage rates have been more easily influenced than wage earnings, and so on.

Most researchers seem to have been fairly unanimous in attributing success to the Stafford Cripps experiment with wage restraint at the end of the forties. Phillips, in his pioneering study, found that the rapid rise in prices 1947–1948 did tend to stimulate wage demands in 1948 but 'that the tendency was offset by the policy of wage restraint introduced . . . in the spring of 1948; that wage increases during 1949 were exceptionally low as a result of the policy of wage restraint'.† Lipsey in

---

* A dummy variable might not catch effects which might change the value of an independent variable or the coefficient attached to that variable. For example, a successful incomes policy might reduce union aggressiveness, and thus reduce the value of this term in the wage equation. Or it might make unions more aggressive in other directions, so changing the coefficient attached to this term. More importantly, wages policy might change both the slope and the intercept of the Phillips Curve relation between unemployment and the rate of change of wages, so that neither a slope nor a shift dummy variable alone would capture the change.

† A. W. Phillips, 'The Relationship between Unemployment and the Rate of Change of Money Wage Rates in the United Kingdom, 1861–1957', *Economica*, **25** (1958).

his follow-up study found that the actual increase in money wages in 1949–1950 were some 1·5% points below what would have been expected on the basis of past relationships, and attributed the difference to wage policy.* A later study by the Economic Commission for Europe† concluded that the 1948 experiment 'had some success' in checking negotiated wage increases although wage drift continued. This was also the view of Corina, who found that the policy 'made a discernible impact upon the short-run rate of income increase'.§

Several studies, growing in number in recent years, have attempted specifically to examine the impact of incomes policy during the post-war years. Brechling§ investigated the period 1948–1965 (using dummy variables) and concluded that incomes policy may have reduced the annual rate of increase of weekly wage rates by about 2·25% points 1948–1950, by 1% point 1961–1962, and by about 2% points from the fourth quarter of 1964 to the fourth quarter of 1965. None of his tests found any significant effects of incomes policy on prices. Bodkin et al.,‖ also using dummy variables, combined the two experiments with incomes policy in the first half of the sixties (1961–1962 and 1964–1965) and found that the annual rate of increase of weekly wages averaged about 1% point lower during periods when incomes policy was operating compared with other periods. They again identified no statistically significant effects on prices—either directly or indirectly (through slower growth in labour costs as a result of the slowing down of wage increases by incomes policy).¶

Smith, in the Brookings Study, using relationships similar to those developed by Dicks-Mireaux, examined four series relating to wages and earnings for the period 1948–1967, and three different series for prices. His conclusions varied depending upon the series used and indicated a differential impact on rates and earnings. The 1948–1950

* R. G. Lipsey, 'The Relation between Unemployment and the Rate of Change of Money Wage Rates in the United Kingdom, 1861–1957: A Further Analysis', *Economica*, **27** (1960).

† *Incomes in Postwar Europe*, United Nations Economic Commission for Europe, Geneva, ch. 4, 15 (1967).

‡ J. G. Corina, 'Can an Incomes Policy Be Administered', *British Journal of Industrial Relations*, **V**, 305 (Nov. 1967).

§ F. Brechling, 'Some Empirical Evidence on the Effectiveness of Price and Incomes Policies', quoted by D. C. Smith in *Britain's Economic Prospects*, Brookings Institute: Allen and Unwin, 131 (1968).

‖ R. G. Bodkin et al., *Price Stability and High Employment: The Options for Canadian Economic Policy, An Econometric Study* (Ottawa, Queens Printer, 1967).

¶ A further finding of Bodkin et al., was that 'there seems to be no rate of unemployment in Britain within the realm of recent experience or slightly beyond, which might be expected to achieve complete stability of the price level'. In their findings a 2·5% unemployment is associated with a 2·5% annual price rise.

wage pause reduced the annual rate of increase of weekly wage rates by about 2 % points, with a smaller impact than this on hourly earnings. No effect was discernible on either wages or earnings for the 1956 experiment. The 1961–1962 pause reduced the annual rate of increase of weekly wage rates by about 1·5 % points, and may also have reduced hourly wage rates and earnings. Between 1962–1964 no discernible impact for income policy was discovered on any of the wages or earnings series. The experiment with a voluntary policy (first quarter of 1965 to second quarter of 1966) may have slowed down the annual rate of increase of weekly wage rates by about 1 % point, although hourly earnings were *above* the predicted level. This was a period of movement to a shorter working week, and the statistical significance of these results must therefore be in doubt. During the 1966–1967 standstill and period of severe restraint the tests indicated a lowering of the annual rate of increase of weekly wage rates of about 1·25 % to 1·5 % points, with other wages and earnings affected in the same direction. During each of the three periods of incomes policy 1961–1966 the tests did not point to any significant reduction in the rate of increase of prices although the freeze and standstill (1966–1967) was found to have led to a significant impact. However, Smith concluded his analysis with the warning that 'the complexity of economic factors affecting incomes and prices calls for more complete models of economic relationships. The effects of incomes policies may appear to be weaker in these tests because the policies were introduced during periods when special factors, not considered in the tests, were increasing wages, earnings, and prices more quickly'*

In July 1968 the Prices and Incomes Board made its own attempt to measure the impact of incomes policy, although it stressed the preliminary nature of the results.† The model used was similar to that of Smith, a modified Dicks-Mireaux model with different dummy variables representing incomes policy when policy was essentially voluntary (1948–1950 and 1965) and years of tighter control (1961–1962 and 1966). It found that the annual increase in wages and salaries had on average been reduced by rather less than 1 % during years when incomes policy had been operating, but that, surprisingly, the size of the impact did not vary with the form of the policy (voluntary or involuntary). The price equation, however, produced price coefficients which were perverse in sign indicating a tendency for prices to rise

---

* D. C. Smith, 'Incomes Policy' in *Britain's Economic Prospects*, Brookings Institute: Allen and Unwin, 135 (1968).

† National Board for Prices and Incomes, *Third General Report*, Cmnd. 3715, Appendix A (July 1968).

faster, rather than slower, when incomes policies were operating. However, the N.B.P.I. study only attempted to measure the direct effects of policy on prices, and some indirect effect on prices was thought likely.

Two other studies are perhaps worth noting, relating to particular years. In their review of the years 1964–1965, the E.C.E. concluded that 'if policy exercised a moderating influence, that influence cannot be observed statistically or in overall terms'.* In 1964 and 1965 hourly earnings rose by about 8·5 %, which was some 1·5 %–2 % more a year than would have been expected on the basis of the relationships used by the E.C.E. Part of this excess was believed to be due to the extensive reductions in working hours during the period. In 1966 on the basis of previous relationships the calculated increase in hourly earnings was 7·5 % the actual increase was about this size but had shown no signs of slowing down before July.

A review of incomes policy made by the National Institute in February 1968 concluded that 'the experience of incomes policy over the last three years . . . cannot be regarded as encouraging . . . not all incomes policy must necessarily be a failure; it is rather that the institutional framework of incomes policy in this country has not been strong enough to stand the burden imposed on it'.† Over the period October 1964 to July 1966 average earnings of all employees increased at a rate of 7·5 % a year. Using an earnings equation the National Institute would have expected a rise of about 7 % per annum; there was no evidence of abnormal drift and indeed the increase in wage rates was above expectations. In their view, therefore, the voluntary incomes policy was too weak to have any restraining effect on incomes, given the high pressure of demand for labour prevailing.

As for the period of the freeze (July 1966 to December 1966) they had 'no doubt there was an effect' with both the wage rates index and the average earnings index levelling off for about six months. However, in the view of the Institute this was not a permanent gain—but simply a postponement. Comparing similar periods of low economic activity (October 1957 to April 1959, April 1961 to October 1962) the increase in earnings was actually fractionally higher between April 1966 and October 1967, and this was not due to excessive wage drift. Indeed the increase in the wage rates index was considerably higher in the 1966/1967 period.‡

* *Incomes in Postwar Europe, Economic Commission for Europe*, Geneva, ch. 4, 19 (1967).
† *National Institute Economic Review*, No. 43, 27 (Feb. 1968).
‡ *National Institute Economic Review*, No. 43, Table 10, 27 (Feb. 1968).

What of experience with incomes policy in 1968 and 1969? This could scarcely be called favourable: in these years the increases in average hourly wage earnings were 7·75 % and 7 % respectively, with increases in average hourly rates of 7 % and 5 %, indicating substantial drift in 1969. Pay increases of this magnitude have to be considered in relation to an incomes ceiling of 3·5 % between mid-1968 and the end of 1969, and were certainly excessive in terms of productivity growth during this period. As a result, therefore, there occurred an increase in the rate of inflation. While actual price and pay developments cannot be taken as evidence that incomes policy had no effect during 1968-1969, they do, nevertheless, demonstrate the failure of the authorities to restrain inflationary wage demands.

One unusual feature of pay developments during 1968-1969 was that the large increases in wages occurred at a time of high unemployment by past British standards. Indeed, Phillips had concluded that 'assuming an increase in productivity of 2 % a year . . . that if aggregate demand were kept at a value which would maintain a stable level of product prices the associated level of unemployment would be a little under 2·5 %'.* With a more usual assumption of a trend increase in productivity of 3 % the critical level of unemployment falls to 2 %. However, with an unemployment rate of almost 2·5 % in 1968 and 1969 both prices and wages rose by very substantial amounts.

Several explanations are possible of these unusual developments. One explanation is in terms of changes in the value of the unemployment index as an indicator of pressure in the labour market. It has been suggested, and there is undoubtedly some truth in this, that the unemployment percentage during 1968-1969 exaggerated the extent of the slack in labour markets compared with earlier years.† This is not in itself a sufficient explanation. In part, at least the wage increases of 1968-1969 are explicable in terms of union attempts to recoup the cut in real wages caused by the devaluation of 1967, and indeed Phillips in formulating his rule for stable prices, specifically abstracted it from a situation where import prices were rising sharply, Undoubt-

---

* 'The relationship between Unemployment and the Rate of Change of Money Wage Rates in the United Kingdom, 1861-1957', by A. W. Phillips, page 297, reprinted in *Inflation*, edited by R. J. Ball and Peter Doyle (Penguin, 1969).

† For an analysis of some of the factors determining the high level of unemployment relative to output between 1967 and 1970, compared with earlier years, see *National Institute Economic Review*, No. 51, 34–39 (Feb. 1970). No evidence was found that supported the thesis that the high unemployment relative to output was due to an increased propensity to register as unemployed, and the *Review* concluded that the explanation lay in factors affecting employment, e.g., introduction of S.E.T. in 1966, the introduction of earnings related unemployment benefits, and structural changes in the economy, etc.

edly, also, union 'pushfulness' increased during this period relative to the state of the labour market. Whereas in earlier years unions seem to have preferred not to press wage claims during periods of high or rising unemployment, but to wait until unemployment began to fall and their bargaining position improved. By the late sixties the shift to a higher unemployment target by the authorities had reduced substantially the value of this strategy.

However, as both Friedman and Phelps have noted, the Phillips Curve, stated in terms of the rate of change of nominal wages, can only be expected to 'be reasonably stable and well defined for any period for which the *average* rate of change of prices, and hence the anticipated rate, has been relatively stable'.* To express this view differently, there is an indefinitely large number of Phillips Curves and not a single unique and stable one. The Phillips Curve will shift upwards or downwards in response to any steady inflation rate, so that given any particular (higher) expected inflation rate there will now be a higher rate of change of money wages at any level of unemployment. That such a shift occurred in the Phillips Curve is a probable, and highly persuasive, explanation of pay developments in the immediate post-devaluation years. The empirical evidence which is available confirms that there is both a short- and long-run trade-off between employment and inflation. Both Solow and Parkin have found coefficients for expected price inflation which are less than unity.†

CONCLUSIONS

It is possible to draw a number of tentative conclusions from the above analysis of the effectiveness of incomes policy.

1. All of the published studies indicate that incomes policies do have some impact on the rate of increase of weekly wage rates. That they have similar effects on other series is more doubtful. Such policies appear to have been more effective in the periods 1948–1950, 1961–1962, and 1966–1967 than in other incomes policy periods—1956,

* Milton Friedman, 'The Role of Monetary Policy' *American Economic Review*, **LVIII**, p. 9, note 5 (March 1968). For a more extended discussion of this approach see E. S. Phelps, 'Money Wage Dynamics and Labour Market Equilibrium', *The Journal of Political Economy*, **76**, No. 4 (July/August 1968), and 'Wage-Price Dynamics, Inflation and Unemployment' (several papers) *American Economic Review* (May 1969).

† R. M. Solow, 'Price Expectations and the Behaviour of the Price Level', Manchester University Press (1969), and M. Parkin, 'Incomes Policy: Some Further Results on the Determination of the Rate of Change of Money Wages', *Economica* (Nov. 1970).

1962–1964, 1965–1966. Studies available on the effectiveness of incomes policy during the post-devaluation period (1968–1969), also indicate that such policies failed to achieve their stated objectives.

2. It follows, therefore, that incomes policies do have some disinflationary effects but only for short periods during times of severe restraint and statutory freeze requiring a good deal of union co-operation, usually during deflationary periods. While such freezes inevitably disintegrate in the long term, during their period of 'on' they do impose a lag on a competitive wage round, and can be a useful policy instrument, particularly at a time of exchange weakness.

3. There must remain, nevertheless, a certain amount of scepticism about the results of the various econometric studies. Any such study to have any validity must identify periods of 'strong' incomes policy from periods when the policy operated in a 'loose' form. A further weakness of some studies is that they primarily test for the effectiveness of incomes policy on weekly wage rates, do not test for effects on hourly wage rates and actual earnings, nor do they take account of changes in direct taxation. Furthermore, the method of using dummy variables contains serious weaknesses as a technique for identifying the impact of incomes policy.

4. Finally, incomes policies have had not only short-term objectives but also long-term aims. These longer-term effects have probably been quantitatively important, but are probably also unmeasurable. It seems probable that incomes policies have achieved some success in affecting the rate of growth in productivity (along with other policies), through identifying deficiencies in the use of resources and through stressing the need for structural change. They have had one additional desirable result. While not having clearly defined distributional objectives, they have nevertheless focused public attention on deficiencies in the income structure as an area for policy action.

10

CONCLUSIONS: STRATEGY FOR ECONOMIC POLICY

A substantial proportion of the above analysis has been highly critical of short-term economic policy during the sixties. Even the Bank and Treasury have recently admitted that 'economic policy may be said quite simply to have failed, in that none of the major economic problems facing the U.K. in 1959 can be said to have been solved and some of the most important of them have become more severe'.* Policy has, if anything, been de-stabilising and thus falsified the hopes widely held at the opening of the decade that the growth of the economy would be steadier than in the fifties. Nor was any success achieved in the acceleration of the rate of growth compared with previous historical experience, and Britain's comparative performance in terms of output remained unsatisfactory. Indeed, in the five years from the end of 1964 to the final quarter of 1969, real GDP grew by under 12 %, (i.e.) at an average annual compound rate of only 2·3 %. In other respects the decade closed with a distinct worsening of possibilities. Unemployment had remained relatively high for a number of years and yet this was associated with an acceleration in the rate of increase in prices. Only in relation to the balance of payments had there been partial success, and even there a substantial price was exacted for the surplus which finally emerged during 1969.

* 'The Operation of Monetary Policy since the Radcliffe Report', a paper prepared by the Bank of England in consultation with the Treasury, *Bank of England Quarterly Bulletin*, 458 (Dec. 1969).

ECONOMIC GROWTH

Government objectives in relation to economic growth can be distinguished as both short-term and long-term. In the short-term the overriding objective of policy has been to match demand to potential capacity, i.e., to regulate demand so as to achieve an even pressure of demand for labour. In this objective it has clearly failed, and Britain experienced during the past decade considerable variation in the pressure of demand, in part at least directly as a result of policy action. The longer-term objective was to raise the potential capacity growth rate, or, what is the same concept, the underlying rate of growth of which the economy is capable.

Changes in productive potential are due to changes in labour supply and trends in productivity, so that policies aimed at raising the productive potential must either increase the labour inputs available and/or achieve a higher rate of growth of productivity. Regional policy, with the objectives of reducing the incidence of regional unemployment and raising participation rates, has been used as one way of raising the effective supply of labour, but more generally policy has concentrated on the myriad of factors which determine productivity growth. Some earlier research did indicate a shift in the long-term trend of productivity* and Shepherd subsequently estimated an increase in the potential annual rate of growth from 2·9% (1955–1960) to 3·3% (1960–1966).† There has been no evidence of any further acceleration since the period 1960–1966, and indeed it is now thought that the potential capacity growth rate for the economy is about 2·9%.‡

In the early years of the sixties it was generally assumed that Britain's growth performance could relatively easily be improved, and a great deal of energy was devoted to the identification of the factors which are important in the process of economic growth, and to the establishment of institutions and policies which would remove obstacles to faster growth. In this respect both the Conservative and Labour administrations had similar objectives and they both experimented with some form of indicative planning—the N.E.D.C. Growth

---

* W. A. H. Godley and J. R. Shepherd, 'Long-term Growth and Short-term Policy', *National Institute Economic Review*, No. 29, Table 2 (Aug. 1964).

† J. R. Shepherd, 'Productive Potential and the Demand for Labour', *Economic Trends*, No. 178, XXVI (Aug. 1968).

‡ This was the figure chosen by the Green Paper 'The Task Ahead' which looked at the prospects for the economy up to 1972. R. J. Ball and T. Burns have relatively recently argued for a target growth rate for the seventies of 3·5% per annum ('The Prospects for Faster Growth in Britain', *National Westminster Bank Review*, Nov. 1968).

of the U.K. Economy to 1966, and the National Plan.* Both plans contained 'check lists for action' and both identified as central to the problem of growth the need for greater investment.†

Neither of these experiments were successful. Developments in the economy quickly diverged from the N.E.D.C. Plan and it was subsequently abandoned by the Labour Government in 1964. The new National Plan—which was less a plan than a set of targets—was also quickly overtaken by events. It was not internally consistent (the infamous manpower gap), contained obvious signs of being a rush-job and, more importantly, was critically unrealistic in its assessment of the feasibility of the targets set in the light of projected short-term developments.

Unfortunately these experiments with planning produced a widespread disillusionment which was not wholly justified. In itself the National Plan represented the first really coherent attempt to plan for long-term growth; to attempt to identify potential resources and to rationally allocate these to end-uses. In some form or other such a plan is essential to the achievement of long-term objectives—in the planning of public expenditure in particular—and is entirely necessary for the conduct of any long-term economic strategy. After the abolition of the D.E.A. (its separate existence never made economic sense after its abandonment of the National Plan) most of its personnel dealing with medium and long-term planning were transferred to the Treasury where they have continued to research into these problems. It is clearly preferable to have this type of work more closely integrated with short term policy, particularly in a situation where the imperatives of the short-term are weaker. However, it should still remain an objective of policy to try to involve as many representative groups as possible in the planning of the economy, and it is to be hoped that future Governments will once again experiment in this direction.

At least one dissenting voice was raised against the conventional wisdom of the early sixties. After an investigation of Britain's growth performance Knapp and Lomax concluded that economic growth by the U.K. in the post-war period was good by historical standards; that it was difficult to tell whether it was good or bad compared to other countries; that it was about as good as it could have been, and 'that the ill effects of short-term mismanagement may well have been much

---

* *Growth of the United Kingdom Economy to 1966*, N.E.D.C.: H.M.S.O. (1963) and *The National Plan*, H.M.S.O., (1965).

† For example, the National Plan states, 'Investment lies at the heart of the plan'.

exaggerated . . .'* In their views on short-term mismanagement and the effects of this on the rate of economic growth they were supported by both Dow and Day.† On the other hand Angus Maddison in his influential *Economic Growth in the West* clearly thought differently: 'The maintenance of high and steady levels of demand has therefore been a major condition for the vastly improved performance of the European economies as compared with the past. . . . The fact that in the U.K. demand has continually had to be interrupted by deflationary measures to right the balance of payments is one of the major reasons why that country has grown more slowly than the rest of Europe.‡

The main point at issue is whether greater stability would raise the rate of growth, and it is not a question of filling in the troughs of the stop-go cycle. Instability causes losses, so it is argued, through the loss of output during the stop phase of the cycle which would have raised future levels of efficiency. Furthermore, instability has effects on confidence, liquidity and innovation and thus reduces the level of investment. In addition, instability is supposed to encourage attitudes and behaviour on the part of labour and management which is not conducive to the efficient use of resources.

If anything the evidence does not support the view that instability, particularly instability of investment, has been especially unfortunate to growth in Britain. Many other industrial countries have also experienced instability of GDP, plus sometimes much greater instability of investment, together with, and sometimes the result of, stop-go policies. They have still, nevertheless, managed to grow at a much faster rate. It would be wrong, therefore, to attribute too much of Britain's poor growth performance to the instability of the economy in the sixties, although it is perfectly possible that the fluctuations which occurred further reduced the already slow rate of growth.§ It should, nevertheless, be an important objective to try to achieve a smoother pattern of economic growth, which requires in the seventies a much improved

---

* John Knapp and Kenneth Lomax, 'Britain's Growth Performance: The Enigma of the 1950's, *Lloyds Bank Review* (Oct. 1964).

† 'The reasons for the slow growth of the British economy seem then deep-seated, and not due chiefly to Government policy', J. C. R. Dow, *The Management of the British Economy 1945–1960* (Cambridge University Press), p. 398. Alan Day, 'The Myth of Four Per Cent Growth', *Westminster Bank Review*, p. 3 (Nov. 1964), is quite certain of the rightness of his view—'our repeated balance of payments crises (which have, indeed been stupidly unnecessary, but which cannot be demonstrated to have had more than a minor effect in slowing down the country's underlying rate of growth)'.

‡ Angus Maddison, *Economic Growth in the West*, Allen and Unwin, 49 (1964), and 'How Fast Can Britain Grow?' *Lloyds Bank Review* (July 1966).

§ For a comparative analysis see T. Wilson, 'Instability and the Rate of Growth', *Lloyds Bank Review* (July 1966).

performance on the part of the authorities compared with the sixties.

The sixties was not lacking in many further explanations of Britain's poor growth record. Of these the most interesting, and most comprehensive, was that by Edward Denison.* His study is a pathbreaking piece of research which attempted to quantify the sources of growth and thus shifted the discussion of comparative performance on to a completely new plane. He identified as most important the factor of difference in labour supply as a variable explaining variation in growth rates, and was led to conclude that 'To a considerable extent, conditions beyond the control of the U.K. were responsible for higher growth rates in other countries. The most general cause concerns gains from reducing waste in the use of resources in agriculture and self-employment.' But only to 'a considerable extent' was labour supply an explanation: 'The low growth rate of the U.K. cannot be ascribed entirely to built-in handicaps.'†

The average rate of economic growth has remained low during the sixties, and the economy has continued to be subject to instability in part caused directly by defective policy. Such instability seems, through its effects on investment, to have contributed to the slow rate of economic growth. One lesson of the sixties is that a faster rate of economic growth is not so easily attainable as was initially thought. Planning has been discredited as a technique for achieving better performance, and the evidence is lacking which would support the thesis that positive government (1964–1969) has successfully restructured the economy. If the activities of Ministry of Technology, N.B.P.I., I.R.C., the merger boom of the sixties, and the structural shifts caused by devaluation, have raised productive potential, then this is not yet apparent. For the moment it seems realistic to assume an annual average growth rate during the seventies, consistent with balance of payments and price objectives, of no more than 3·5 % Even this modest target represents an improvement on past achievement, but still places the U.K. among the countries experiencing slow growth. That there exists scope for raising efficiency has been amply demonstrated, but recent history hardly suggests that the opportunities will be grasped.

* E. F. Denison *Why Growth Rates Differ: Post-war Experience in Nine Western Countries*, Brookings Institute: Allen and Unwin (1967), and chapter VI *Britain's Economic Prospects* (ed.) R. E. Caves, Allen and Unwin (1968).

† E. F. Denison in *Britain's Economic Prospects*, edited by R. E. Caves, Allen and Unwin, 243 and 246 (1968).

THE BALANCE OF PAYMENTS AND THE STERLING BALANCES

One of the most important conclusions to be drawn from British experience during the sixties is the need for a radical reappraisal of policy with respect to the exchange rate. It is now generally agreed that a change in the exchange rate is a powerful way of altering a country's balance of payments, and that a change of parity is the right way to correct a position of fundamental disequilibrium, although it will need to be accompanied by an appropriate policy package (except in the case of an economy which is already suffering from deflation). However, there still remain wide differences of view about both the timing and the size of the effects of parity changes, and also about the nature of external disequilibrium.

There is some evidence that in the short-run relative changes in international prices are swamped by demand effects, although in the long-run the correlation between foreign trade performance and relative prices is much closer. In the short-run, therefore, depreciation of a country's exchange rate may lead to a worsening of its current account position through a deterioration in its terms of trade. Furthermore, it is evident that other factors apart from prices are significant in explaining balance of payments disequilibrium, and that to some extent there are dynamic forces present which are de-stabilising. Such theories of disequilibrium emphasise the relationships between good export performance, high investment in export sectors, rapid productivity growth, improved competitiveness and further balance of payments gains.* If such 'virtuous and vicious circles' do exist then it follows that 'the longer underlying disequilibrium persists, the larger will be the change in relative costs and profitability needed to remedy the situation over a reasonable period of time. If, on the other hand, exchange rates were adjusted sooner, these dynamic factors making for disequilibrium would have less time to gather momentum, and might not emerge at all.'†

Analysis has suggested that Britain was in fundamental disequilibrium at least from the early years of the sixties, and perhaps from an

---

* The development of this thesis owes a great deal to the writings of Wilfred Beckerman. See Chapter II of *The British Economy in 1975* (Cambridge University Press, 1965) and more recently P. D. Henderson, *Economic Growth in Britain*, Weidenfeld & Nicolson ch. 3 (1966).

† Stephen Marris, 'The Bürgenstock Communiqué: A Critical Examination of the Case for Limited Flexibility of Exchange Rates', *Princeton University Essays in International Finance*, No. 80, 9 (May 1970).

even earlier date.* Failure, therefore, to adjust the sterling parity before the end of 1967 added to the cumulative forces at work, and the authorities can be rightly criticised for maintaining an overvalued currency. However, under the system of fixed exchange rates established at Bretton Woods this type of behaviour on the part of national governments is to be expected, and is not itself evidence of political and economic culpability. In part at least the failure of the British authorities is a reflection of the inadequacies of the international monetary arrangements of the sixties.

The Bretton Woods system permits a country suffering from fundamental disequilibrium to adjust its exchange rate, but it can be argued that this provision, together with the system of international co-operation which developed in the post-war period, did not provide for sufficient flexibility in exchange rate policy. Infrequent adjustment of the exchange rate by even 10%–15%, which is small in comparison with the large changes which took place in the 1930s, does lead to serious problems for national authorities. In the case of the U.K. the devaluation entailed a substantial increase in demand requiring a switch of resources into the balance of payments of about £1000 million. This is equivalent to an increase in total demand over a period of one to two years of about 3% of GNP, which is very large in relation to the normal annual growth in output. To be successful there must occur a shift in the distribution of income (favourable to profits) which is not subsequently nullified by full adjustment of wage incomes to the price-raising effects of devaluation. However, the ability of the authorities to hold the explosion of wage incomes is limited, and they proved largely incapable of doing so in the years following devaluation.

Infrequent changes of the parity by between 10%–15% which overnight leads to adjustment in the prices of transactions accounting for about 25% of GNP, severely limits the political and technical freedom of the authorities. At the technical level the adjustment to domestic demand which is required to permit the easy transfer of resources into the balance of payments is well beyond the scope of the normal policy package. It entails cuts in public expenditure, with the real economic and social costs which this causes; sharp increases in personal and indirect taxation are required, and monetary policy has to shift into an even higher gear. From experience in 1967 and 1968 it is clear that the authorities found it almost beyond their capacity to design and implement such a massive policy package.

There are other constraints on effective and timely policy on the

* See chapter VIII and 'Towards a Rational Exchange Policy: Some Reflections on British Experience', *Bulletin of the Reserve Bank of St. Louis* (April 1969).

exchange rate. In the first place the need to secrecy in the planning of a devaluation inevitably excludes from the processes of discussion groups and individuals, even within the machinery of government, so that the policy package may itself be inadequate for this reason. In addition, the decision to devalue may be (and was) too long delayed because of the essentially short–run considerations, such as the extent of Central Bank forward commitments, and the desire to prevent speculators from reaping their profits. Much more important, however, has been the association of political failure with a devaluation; the presumption that such a policy entails substantial and significant damage to national prestige, and that it represents clear and unequivocal failure of economic policy. That there should be powerful political feed-back from a devaluation of 15 % is not surprising. As indicated above it requires restrictive policies of draconian severity, has substantial income redistributive effects and is thus bound to be unpopular with the electorate. Undoubtedly, political factors played an important role in the timing of the 1967 devaluation, but even given a stronger and more viable Wilson administration in October 1964, it is clear that they would have preferred not to devalue and, in so acting, confound those critics who associate devaluation with a Labour Government.

Strangely enough it appears that the expansion of the international network for consultation and examination of economic policy (O.E.C.D., E.E.C., Group of Ten, I.M.F., etc) has contributed little to more rational discussion of exchange rate policy. Before 1968 it seems that discussion of individual country's exchange rates received scant attention in the various fora, and instead discussion and criticism focused on general monetary and fiscal policy, the appropriateness of specific adjustment measures and the extension of international central bank co-operation (including swaps, new and extended credit lines, and actual central bank assistance). Such discussions where related to the balance of payments, concentrated on all aspects of adjustment other than exchange rates, so that when the re-appraisal of parities took place in the late sixties (Britain in November 1967, France in August 1969, Germany in October 1969) there was too little international discussion and analysis.

What the above analysis suggests is that the Bretton Woods system contains basic deficiencies, and that if anything it has tended to impede rational decision making. It follows, therefore, that some of the severe disadvantages, both technical and political, can be avoided through an acceptence of the need for more flexibility in exchange rates.* Where

* No attempt is made here to assess the many proposals for increasing exchange rate flexibility. For readers who are interested two papers by James Meade set out

adjustment of the parity takes place more frequently there will be clearly defined benefits. Firstly, small adjustments of the exchange rate will not require massive demand management measures but simply perhaps a package which is more typical of normal conjuncture policy. Secondly, since both the policy package and the parity is smaller there will be fewer income redistribution effects, and thus less public opposition. Thirdly, there will be less need for secrecy, with all of the advantages which go with wider participation in decisions. Fourthly, a movement towards more flexible rates will alter the political climate, and, hopefully, political attitudes. While alteration of the parity will retain some of its importance it will, when it becomes a question of adjustment of 1% or so, be more akin to ordinary decisions on conjuncture policy. With this will be a new realism which no longer identifies a particular exchange rate with nationalism, but instead views exchange rate adjustments in the same light, with similar income, price and demand effects, as other intruments of economic policy. Finally, more realism about exchange rates will put decisions on parities firmly on the agendas of international fora, so that discussions there are less concentrated on every other form of balance of payments adjustment.*

Clearly any proposal for greater flexibility of exchange rates has important implications for the use of sterling as an international currency. The Government has often been urged to permit the pound to float as a solution to the sterling problem on the grounds that if the exchange rate was entirely variable that the problem of external balance would theoretically disappear. International reserves, so it is argued, would no longer be necessary, and in this ideal world the balance of payments would no longer impose any constraint on the achievement of domestic policy objectives. There are formidable reasons against accepting fully flexible rates, there is no reason to argue these here, and indeed they have received little support in official circles. One fairly certain result, nevertheless, of full flexibility would be the elimination of sterling as an international currency, as holders of sterling balances switched into more stable asset-reserve media.

* This analysis draws heavily on the incisive short discussion by Stephen Marris, 'The Bürgenstock Communiqué: A Critical Examination of the Case for Limited Flexibility of Exchange Rates', *Princeton University Essays in International Finance*, No. 80 (May 1970).

more fully the arguments for greater flexibility of parities, both of them in the *Three Banks Review*: 'The Case For Variable Exchange Rates', No. 27 (Sept. 1955) and 'Exchange Rate Flexibility', No. 70 (June 1966). On the semantics of the problem a short note by Fritz Machlup is well worth consulting: 'On Terms, Concepts, Theories and Strategies in the Discussion of Greater Flexibility of Exchange Rates', *Banca Nazionale Del Lavoro Quarterly Review*, No. 92, 3–22 (March 1970).

However, even in the case of fully flexible rates, not all of the costs of the liquidation of the sterling balances would fall on the holders (through a lower exchange rate being received). This is so because today the largest part of the sterling balances are now covered by exchange guarantees. I.M.F. drawings have always had the usual fund gold-value guarantee, and liabilities incurred through central bank swaps are now also guaranteed. Furthermore, since the Basle Agreement of 1968, most liabilities to official sterling area holders are guaranteed, so that only privately owned sterling balances—23 % of the total outstanding at the end of 1969—are still without a guarantee. In reality, therefore, more than three-quarters of the sterling balances would have to be paid-off at their gold or dollar value, which would require a massive long-term loan from abroad, with the assumption by the U.K. of yet further substantial fixed-term debt. Funding of the sterling balances on this basis—the substitution of fixed-term debt for liquid liabilities of undetermined maturity—would not make economic sense.* While some of the economic disadvantages of freely fluctuating rates could be reduced by adopting one of the alternatives ('wider-bands' and/or 'creeping pegs') this would still leave the problem of the sterling balances.

There is obviously no case for trying to revive the reserve role of sterling outside the sterling area either from the point of view of Britain or of the members of the non-sterling area. Similarly, within the sterling area diversification of reserves has been fairly general in recent years and this trend is unlikely to be reversed. Nor would it be in Britain's interest to attempt to reverse this trend towards diversification, but rather to try to achieve a gradual reduction in the use of sterling within the area for the purposes of settling official transactions. It has been convincingly argued that the complete domestication of sterling—by funding or in other ways—is impracticable and would entail costs which are greater than those imposed by the existing role of sterling. Instead the aim of the authorities ought to be to partially fund the sterling balances on the basis of the Basle Agreement, which it is generally agreed has worked remarkably well.† It is highly desirable, therefore, that the various agreements negotiated in 1968 be

---

* This is amply demonstrated at Appendix B of 'The Reform of Sterling by Benjamin J. Cohen, *Princeton Essays in International Finance,* No. 77 (Dec. 1969). To attempt to fund all sterling liabilities, even on the basis of a nominal rate of interest of 2½% per annum amortised over 100 years, would still entail annual instalments of some £77 million a year.

† By the end of 1969 U.K. liabilities in sterling to sterling area countries was actually higher than it had been in September 1967.

extended, with suitable modifications, when they expire in 1971, so as to make them a permanent feature of the sterling system.

As was noted in Chapter 8 in *The Sterling Balances*, the Basle Agreement did not eliminate the role of sterling as an international currency and, indeed, there is some suggestion that this was never its intention.[*] However, what the Basle Agreement and the associated agreements with individual countries did incorporate were three principles which can become the base for a reform of sterling.

In 1968 for the first time the British Government accepted the principle of an exchange guarantee as part of the reform of sterling. Such guarantees as were given in 1968 were undoubtedly excessively generous, but rather than relinquish the principle of exchange guarantees the authorities in the re-negotiations after 1971 should force concessions from sterling area countries. The second principle related to the rate of withdrawal of the balances, with the introduction of the 'minimum sterling proportion', which set a limit on the rate of diversification of the reserves of sterling area countries. This provision entails no great cost to these countries, and has the benefit from the British viewpoint of reducing the threat of unforeseen withdrawals. Finally, it established the principle of partial funding of the balances. Sterling area countries were offered the exchange guarantee as an inducement not to run-down their sterling balances, although they have retained the right to do so. It was precisely to meet any calls on the British reserves which such a run-down might cause that the $2 billion Basle facility was made available. In effect it established the principle of funding which was partial and self-regulating.

It follows from the foregoing analysis that Britain should adopt a much more flexible attitude towards the exchange rate, and that to do so would significantly improve the balance of payments adjustment process. Britain ought also to re-negotiate the Basle facility and associated agreements of 1968 with the aim of partial funding of the sterling balances. Furthermore, given the open nature of the British economy it is in Britain's interest to press for further increases in world liquidity at regular intervals during the seventies. The S.D.R. allocation of 1970 was particularly welcome to the U.K., although it is unfortunate that Britain did not drive a harder bargain over allocations. While

---

[*] There is some doubt about the precise attitude of the authorities towards sterling at the time of Basle, although many commentators wrongly concluded that it heralded the end of sterling's international role. As the Treasury's own White Paper put it, 'In proportion to world reserves and world trade it [sterling] has indeed contracted, and in 1968 it has contracted in absolute terms also. But it will continue in the future as a major part of the international monetary system' (Cmnd. 3787, para. 23).

devaluation substantially improved Britain's current account position the balance of payments constraint has not been removed. For the near future substantial surpluses will have to continue to be earned, and these will be easier to achieve in a world characterised by an expanding volume of trade. Increasing world liquidity, and an expansion of international trade through dismantlement of tariff and non-tariff barriers, should be major objectives of policy.

WHAT MIX OF POLICIES?

The history of short-term economic policy during the sixties is basically one of failure. But it need not inevitably have been so, and there are some seasons for believing that some of the lessons of the decade have been learnt by the authorities. In part the failure of policy stemmed from imperfect understanding of the functioning of the economic system, from poor short-term forecasts which on occasion misled policy, from excessive optimism about the efficiency of fiscal instruments and to downright bad policy decisions. Even the authorities admit to the failure of their policies, and indeed the whole concept of fine-tuning (and, therefore, discretionary fiscal and monetary policy) has come under attack. There seems little reason to redefine the mix of policy aims which the authorities have set themselves. An acceleration of the rate of growth, full employment (not quite so full) and reasonable stability of the general price level should continue to be the main domestic policy aims. But we now know from experience that the simultaneous achievement of these objectives is extremely difficult, and it would be unrealistic to believe that either Governments or economists are any nearer success in solving these problems.

Because of the open nature of the British economy it is inevitable that fluctuations in export demand will lead to instability in the economy, and, similarly, fluctuations in investment expenditure will also continue to cause fluctuations in output and employment. Given the policy aim of maintaining a constant pressure of demand (the employment objective) the authorities will necessarily have to take contra-cyclical policy action when faced by fluctuations in export and investment expenditures. No Government can afford in such circumstances to stand idly by, and if the timing of policy is to be appropriate then the authorities require reliable short-term forecasts. Within this framework good short-term forecasts become a pre-requisite for adequate and timely economic policy. Instability will continue, therefore, to be a problem for the authorities, but it is to be hoped that policy will no longer (as in the sixties) be a contributory factor to the instability of the economy.

With much more flexibility in policy relating to the exchange rate it is to be expected that the problems of external balance will be less pressing. The seventies have opened with the balance of payments in substantial surplus so that this particular constraint is no longer so powerful. Nevertheless, as noted above, fluctuations in the external balance, due to fluctuations in the demand for exports or to excessive growth in imports caused by domestic inflation, will still face the authorities with short-term problems. In so far as the fluctuations in the balance of payments are due to exogenous factors then there is little the authorities can do except to try to offset the impact on domestic employment and to finance the deficit. Where the deficit is due to excessive demand, probably accompanied by inflation, then the solution is to remove the excess demand through fiscal and monetary policies. Subsequently, any erosion of the competitive position of the economy ought to be corrected by a small adjustment to the exchange rate. One lesson to be learnt from the sixties is that various restrictions on current trade and payments (the import surcharge and import deposit scheme) brought much less relief to the balance of payments than was originally anticipated, and should be resorted to very infrequently in the future.

Whereas the problem of maintaining external balance ought to be much less of a headache for the authorities during the first half of the seventies, the problem of internal balance looks like being as severe as ever. Governments, and economists, have patently not found a solution to the problem of price stability and full employment. The high hopes held for incomes policy have largely been confounded, and yet it is perfectly clear that traditional fiscal and monetary policies by themselves cannot achieve price stability and simultaneously maintain reasonably full employment. But perhaps we expected too much of incomes policy in the face of severe strains imposed by statutory freeze and the income redistributing impact of the devaluation. In the post-devaluation phase incomes policy was bound to be relatively ineffective (to enter a 'loose' phase), and the lesson to be learned is not that incomes policy is useless. The evidence of the sixties does not support this proposition, but the evidence does support the view that incomes policy needs to be primarily a voluntary matter with periods of 'looseness' and 'tightness'.

While incomes policy may be imperfect as an instrument of policy it is nevertheless the only means open to a democratic society of keeping increases in money incomes in a reasonably close relationship with the growth in productivity. It is obvious nonsense, therefore, for any Government to proclaim itself opposed to an incomes policy. In a sense they have no options, in that a Government at the minimum must have some policy in relation to employees in the public sector, which must entail some policy on pay and prices in the private sector. Everyone agrees that instruments of economic policy are always imperfect, but it is foolish on the part of any Government to rule-out a wage-price policy as a useful part of its policy armoury.

One aspect of the debate on economic policy in both Britain and the U.S.A. has been the conflict between the monetarists and what Heller has called the 'economic activists'.* Now no one would deny that the Friedmanians have not made valid points about the inadequacies of fiscal policy as conducted during the sixties, or that traditional monetary policy has achieved all of its objectives. As was shown in Chapters 6–7 monetary policy has its disadvantages when used as a short-term regulator of demand. It is extremely difficult to estimate its effects on expenditure and the time-lags may be quite long. Furthermore, as Friedman has noted, at a time of inflation rising nominal interest rates (perhaps falling real rates) may not be a good indicator of the severity of monetary policy. It may indeed be preferable in such a situation for the rate of growth in the money supply to be taken as a more reliable indicator of the thrust of monetary policy. However, it is a far cry from having admitted this, to accepting the view that policy ought to be based only on this indicator, and that rules should be substituted for discretionary policy.

This is an unacceptable proposition; to follow the tenets of the Chicago School would be to introduce new and damaging rigidities in the conduct of short-term economic policy. Although it is admittedly true that policy has in the past been severely inadequate, it does not follow that we must give up the attempt to operate an effective set of discretionary policies. Rather, history suggests that we should try to improve the conduct of policy, and through a better mix of monetary, fiscal and wage-price policies strive to achieve our wider economic and social policy objectives. It will not be easy.

* In a very interesting confrontation of views which took place in New York between Walter Heller and Milton Friedman, reprinted as *Monetary vs. Fiscal Policy* (W. W. Norton & Co., New York, 1969). For a recent summary of the empirical evidence relating to the controversy see, 'The Importance of Money', *Bank of England Quarterly Bulletin* (June 1970).

INDEX